Made in Chinatown

China and the West in the Modern World

William Christie, Series Editor

China and the West in the Modern World publishes original, peer-reviewed research on relations between China and the West from the accession of the Manchu Qing dynasty in 1644 to the present. The series brings into play different national and disciplinary perspectives to achieve a more thorough and cross-culturally nuanced understanding of the political, economic, and cultural background to the negotiations and realignments currently underway between China and Western nations.

The Poison of Polygamy
Wong Shee Ping, translated by Ely Finch

South Flows the Pearl: Chinese Australian Voices
Mavis Gock Yen, edited by Siaoman Yen and Richard Horsburgh

Tribute and Trade: China and Global Modernity, 1784–1935
Edited by William Christie, Angela Dunstan and Q.S. Tong

Made in Chinatown: Chinese Australian Furniture Factories, 1880–1930
Peter Charles Gibson

Made in Chinatown

Peter Charles Gibson

SYDNEY UNIVERSITY PRESS

First published by Sydney University Press
© Peter Charles Gibson 2022
© Sydney University Press 2022

Reproduction and communication for other purposes
Except as permitted under the Act, no part of this edition may be reproduced, stored in a retrieval system, or communicated in any form or by any means without prior written permission. All requests for reproduction or communication should be made to Sydney University Press at the address below:

Sydney University Press
Fisher Library F03
University of Sydney NSW 2006
Australia
sup.info@sydney.edu.au
sydneyuniversitypress.com.au

 A catalogue record for this book is available from the National Library of Australia.

ISBN 9781743327852 paperback
ISBN 9781743328453 epub
ISBN 9781743328491 pdf

Contents

List of Figures vii

Acknowledgements ix

Chinese Language xi

Introduction xiii

1 Industry Beginnings 1

2 Setting Up Shop 29

3 Workers 67

4 In the Marketplace 99

5 Restriction and Resistance 129

Conclusion 165

Bibliography 174

Index 195

List of Figures

Figure 1.1 Map of Pearl River Delta, Guangdong, China. 16

Figure 2.1 Chung Lee's Factory, Crown Street, Sydney, 1901. 45

Figure 2.2 Furniture Makers, *Australasian Sketcher*, 24 April 1880. 54

Figure 2.3 Machine horsepower per Sydney furniture factory. 58

Figure 4.1 Wing Lee Brothers Dressing Table, Melbourne, c. 1900s. 107

Figure 4.2 Gangton Brothers, *Evening News*, 17 April 1922. 108

Figure 4.3 Simpson's, *Tung Wah Times*, 12 April 1919. 120

Figure 4.4 War Sing and Co., Sydney, c. 1902. 122

Figure 5.1 'Chinese labour' stamp, Melbourne, early 20th century. 130

Acknowledgements

I would first like to thank the people whose stories appear in this book. I have only known them through glimpses into their lives, yet they have given me so much.

I am equally grateful to Julia Martínez, Jane Carey and Claire Lowrie, supervisors of my doctoral dissertation at the University of Wollongong, the basis for this book, as well as Mae Ngai and Keir Reeves, my examiners. I am also indebted to Simon Ville, Frank Huang and many others at the University of Wollongong and elsewhere for help in the thesis-writing process.

For research materials, I thank New South Wales State Records, the Public Record Office of Victoria, the National Archives of Australia, New South Wales State Library, Victoria State Library, City of Sydney Archives, Sydney Living Museums, Melbourne's Chinese Museum and Bendigo's Golden Dragon Museum.

I am particularly grateful, too, for aid with Chinese-language sources from Zhuqin Feng, Qinqing Xu, Jolin Sweet, Cathy Wang, Kai Huang, Mengyun You, Mango He, Jessica Tian and Sunchao Huang.

As for turning the dissertation into a book, I thank the team at Sydney University Press, especially Denise O'Dea, Susan Murray,

Nathan Grice and Agata Mrva-Montoya, and the anonymous reviewers for their rigour and professionalism.

For the time and support to finalise the book, I thank my employer, the School of History at Nanjing University, Nanjing, China. Many thanks, too, to Qin, Feng Shushu and Nie Ayi for help in this regard.

Finally, I would like to acknowledge my dad Wally, my mum Jackie and my siblings Karen and David for their support and encouragement in everything over the years.

Chinese Language

For historical individual and business names, I have used romanisation from their era, and, where possible, traditional Chinese characters and Hanyu Pinyin (e.g., Sun Yat-sen [孫逸仙 Sun Yixian]).

I have provided translations, characters and Pinyin for excerpts from Chinese text (e.g., 'to play with an axe at Lu Ban's door' [班門弄斧 ban men nong fu]).

Even though the Chinese migrants and their descendants discussed in this book spoke various dialects of Cantonese, I have used Pinyin for Mandarin rather than Jyutping or Yale for Cantonese, since I am most competent with Pinyin.

I have not used Chinese characters in footnotes or in the bibliography, only Pinyin (apart from authors' names where cited).

My approach to Chinese language conforms closely to the approach used by English-language scholarly journals such as the *Journal of Asian Studies* and *Twentieth-Century China*.

Unless I have specified otherwise, all the translations and transliterations are my own. I accept full responsibility for any errors.

Introduction

In the early twentieth century, Ah Wong (王金鐘 Wang Jinzhong) had a furniture factory in Surry Hills, Sydney. The operation spanned several buildings, all close to each other on the same street, Exeter Place.[1] The main premises, pictured on the cover of this book, housed a coal-fired boiler used to run steam-powered circular saws and lathes. Willie Wing, one of forty-five men who worked there, looked after the boiler and the saws. As he described his responsibilities, he needed to 'put coal on and keep steam up', as well as 'saw wood'.[2] Attached to the main building was the shed where timber and articles of furniture were stored. Timber can be seen stacked on the shed's roof, and completed furniture and furniture components – washstands, hallstands, tables and doors (perhaps for chiffoniers) – can be seen in the shed and on the street. A man of modest stature can also be seen looking out from inside the shed, next to the fence. This could have been the factory

---

1   Edgar Cutler Testimony, 6 March 1906, Furniture Trade Union v. Ah Wong, New South Wales Court of Arbitration, New South Wales State Records 5340–2/74–18, 4.
2   Willie Wing Testimony, 9 March 1906, Furniture Trade Union v. Ah Wong, 167.

manager, Ah Fat (亞發Ya Fa), a short man by certain accounts, whose responsibility was to purchase the timber and, as he described it, 'go 'round and sell furniture'.[3] Ah Wong was not personally involved in running the factory, having had 'other business to look after', as he said, 'in the vegetable markets at Belmore'.[4] Luckily for him, he had another business, since the factory was demolished in a government 'slum clearance' program in 1908.[5]

Furniture factories such as Ah Wong's were once among the most important Chinese commercial operations in Australia. Established by migrants from Guangdong's Pearl River Delta and their families, mainly after the gold rushes of the 1850s and 1860s, there were close to 200 factories and 2000 workers in Australia at their peak in 1912. These were concentrated almost entirely in the two largest cities of Sydney and Melbourne.[6] Only market gardening, with around 7000 Chinese participants at this time, attracted more Chinese involvement.[7] Chinese Australian furniture establishments were also distinctive, there being no evidence of furniture production like this by Chinese migrants in similar Pacific Rim migration destinations such as California.[8]

As well as being vital to Chinese communities, Chinese furniture factories constituted a substantial part of Australia's furniture industry between 1880 and 1930. In Sydney, they dominated for most of this period, surpassing their non-Chinese counterparts until 1909. From

3   'Not a Chinese Giant', *Evening News*, 7 March 1906; Ah Fat Testimony, 9 March 1906, Furniture Trade Union v. Ah Wong, 152.
4   Ah Wong Testimony, 9 March 1906, Furniture Trade Union v. Ah Wong, 140.
5   'New Sydney', *Sydney Morning Herald*, 30 October 1908.
6   *Report on the Working of the Factories and Shops Act during the year (NSW FSA Report) 1912*, 47; *Report of the Chief Inspector of Factories, Workrooms, and Shops (VIC FSA Report) 1912*, 10. The Chinese sectors in Perth and Brisbane each peaked at around 150 workers, and there were a few factories in other cities and towns, but they are not examined in this book.
7   *Census of the Commonwealth of Australia 1911*, 1026.
8   See, for instance, Ta Chen, *Chinese Migrations, with Special Reference to Labor Conditions* (Washington: Government Printing Office, 1923).

Introduction

1912, however, Chinese furniture production began a gradual decline. Table 0.1, a table of industry size according to worker ethnicity, originally recorded as 'Chinese' or 'European' (primarily British and British-descended), shows the relative composition over time of the furniture industry in Sydney and Melbourne, where the greater majority of Australian furniture manufacturing took place.[9]

The Australian labour movement and Australian governments sought to restrict Chinese furniture factories. They saw them as a serious danger, in line with what Mae Ngai has called a 'forcefully masculinist and racialist' ideological formation, that is, 'White Australia' – the broad principle that Australia should be a place for the 'white man'.[10] As such, Chinese furniture establishments became focal points for anti-Chinese campaigning and were made subject to racialised industrial law, especially the *Factories and Shops Acts* in Victoria from 1887 and in New South Wales from 1896.[11] These pieces of legislation gave Chinese factories an unfair burden in terms of their operating hours, employees' pay, and sanitation and safety standards,

---

9 On 'Chinese', 'Chinese overseas' and 'Chinese Australian', see Wang Gungwu, 'Greater China and the Chinese Overseas', *China Quarterly*, 136 (1993), 939; Jen Tsen Kwok, 'Postscript: Beyond "Two Worlds"', in Sophie Couchman and Kate Bagnall, eds., *Chinese Australians: Politics, Engagement and Resistance* (Leiden: Brill, 2015), 290–307. On 'European', 'British' and 'white', refer to Marilyn Lake and Henry Reynolds, *Drawing the Global Colour Line: White Men's Countries and the Question of Racial Equality* (Melbourne: Melbourne University Press, 2008), 75–94; Ann Curthoys, 'White, British and European: historicising identity in settler societies', in Jane Carey and Claire McLisky, eds., *Creating White Australia* (Sydney: Sydney University Press, 2009), 3–24. Table 0.1 was created using data from 'Chinese Increase', *Newcastle Morning Herald and Miners' Advocate*, 18 November 1878; 'The Furniture Trade', *Sydney Morning Herald*, 30 October 1886; *NSW FSA Report 1897–1931*; *VIC FSA Report 1885–1931*.
10 Mae M. Ngai, 'Chinese Gold Miners and the "Chinese Question" in Nineteenth-Century California and Victoria', *Journal of American History*, 101:4 (2015), 1103.
11 Yong Ching Fatt, *The New Gold Mountain: The Chinese in Australia, 1901–21* (Richmond: Raphael Arts, 1977), 63–70.

	Sydney		Melbourne	
	Chinese	European	Chinese	European
1881	≈ 350	< 350	≈ 150	≈ 650
1891	≈ 500	≈ 350	428	1340
1901	621	510	574	1238
1911	841	1080	790	1793
1912	862	1338	818	2108
1921	281	2393	338	2202
1931	21	1280	22	1200

Table 0.1 Furniture workers by ethnicity, 1881–1931.

and required furniture to be stamped with the particulars of its makers. Vivid reminders of this discrimination today can be seen in the stamps found on antique Australian-made furniture, declaring 'Chinese labour' or 'European labour only'.[12] During the same period, racist lobbying in the furniture industry contributed to racialised restrictions on Chinese migration to Australia from 1881.[13]

This book is the first dedicated history of Chinese furniture factories in Australia. With a focus on Sydney and Melbourne and an emphasis on manufacturers' and workers' descriptions and records of their experiences, we will explore here how Chinese furniture makers negotiated the obstacles laid before them by anti-Chinese campaigners

---

12 Susan Maushart, 'Pine and Prejudice', PocketDocs, ABC Radio National, http://www.abc.net.au/radionational/programs/pocketdocs/pine-and-prejudice/7275008.
13 Joseph Lee, 'Anti-Chinese Legislation in Australasia', *Quarterly Journal of Economics*, 3:2 (1889), 219–222.

Introduction

and legislators. We will see that Chinese furniture factory operators and their employees worked in ways suited to the Australian industrial milieu, thereby undermining the political and legislative impediments they faced. They did this with the tacit approval and active support of numerous non-Chinese Australians, who ignored or even defied anti-Chinese measures. Indeed, Chinese furniture manufacturers and workers were adaptable: 'White Australia' could not control their destinies.

Previous histories

Although this is the first book on Chinese furniture factories in Australia, it is scarcely the first history of Chinese Australian economic activity, which was already being studied by historians in the early twentieth century under the trope of 'cheap labour'. Historians such as Myra Willard wrote in firm support of the 'White Australia' principle, describing the 'threat' presented by Chinese labour.[14] William Pember Reeves even touched on the furniture industry specifically, adamant that the Victorian *Factories and Shops Act* of 1896 was necessary to guard against Chinese workers in Melbourne 'degrading' industry working conditions.[15] Similar studies were written in North America about Chinese migrants involved in clothing, footwear and cigar making, and in canning, none of which attracted much Chinese interest in Australia.[16] This book revisits the persistent idea of 'cheap Chinese

---

14   Myra Willard, *History of the White Australia Policy to 1920* (Melbourne: Melbourne University Press, 1923), 51–58, 195–201.
15   William Pember Reeves, *State Experiments in Australia & New Zealand*, V2 (New York: E. P. Dutton & Co., 1903), 9–12, 43–44, 61–62. See also Edward Shann, *An Economic History of Australia* (Cambridge: Cambridge University Press, 1930), 374.
16   Examples are Mary Coolidge, *Chinese Immigration* (New York: H. Holt and Co., 1909), 344–345, 363–364 and Elmer Sandemeyer, *The Anti-Chinese*

labour', which most early historians based uncritically on descriptions by non-Chinese observers. It brings new evidence to bear, especially the views of Chinese manufacturers and workers, onto the image of 'cheap labour'. There was so much more to the operation of Chinese furniture factories than 'cheap' workforces, and Chinese workers understood their own work in more complex ways.

This book also follows on from histories authored during the 1960s and 1970s, which re-examined Chinese economic pursuits in terms of how they were met by racism. Mostly in order to shine a light on the injustice of 'White Australia', historians including Choi Chingyan and Yong Ching Fatt explored Chinese enterprise and work in more detail than earlier researchers, and scrutinised the associated racist campaigning and legislation.[17] Chinese furniture factories featured in these studies. Yong stressed that they were no threat to 'white industry', that the measures instituted against them were grounded in racist ideology.[18] Andrew Markus similarly argued that Chinese furniture workers in Melbourne were victims of 'virulent racial antipathy'.[19] Histories exploring Chinese business and work across the Pacific were written in the same tone around this time, with an emphasis on discrimination and victimisation.[20] Drawing on new evidence, this

---

Movement in California (Chicago: University of Illinois, 1939), 15, 29–33, 65, 85, 98.

17 Choi Chingyan, *Chinese Migration and Settlement in Australia* (Sydney: Sydney University Press, 1975), xi, 3–54, 78–94, 105–112; Yong, *The New Gold Mountain*, 35–112. See also Alexander Yarwood, *Asian Migration to Australia* (Melbourne: Melbourne University Press, 1964), 104–123.

18 Yong, *The New Gold Mountain*, 41–45, 63–70. See further Yarwood, *Asian Migration to Australia*, 118–119.

19 Andrew Markus, 'Divided We Fall: The Chinese and the Melbourne Furniture Trade Union, 1870–1900', *Labour History*, 26 (1974), 4–6, 10.

20 Landmark comparative studies include Charles Price, *The Great White Walls Are Built: Restrictive Immigration to North America and Australasia, 1836–1888* (Canberra: Australian National University Press, 1974) and Andrew Markus, *Fear and Hatred: Purifying Australia and California, 1850–1901* (Sydney: Hale & Iremonger, 1979). Refer also to Gunther Barth,

Introduction

book returns to the question of racism raised in the 1960s and 1970s. Racist activism and legislation, along with Chinese experiences of racism, varied markedly in the furniture industry. Chinese manufacturers competed energetically with their rivals in the Australian marketplace, and, while Chinese workers may have sympathised with their non-Chinese equivalents, they also had their own, separate agendas.

The book is a continuation too, of late twentieth century efforts by historians to study Chinese Australian enterprise and labour more directly and less in terms of discrimination. Informed by Australia's reinvention as a 'multicultural' country – as well as by historian Jennifer Cushman's criticism of what she deemed an inordinate emphasis on racism in Chinese Australian history – researchers during this period moved to look more closely at Chinese entrepreneurs and their employees.[21] This included those in the furniture industry. Eric Rolls and Shirley Fitzgerald, in their broad histories of Chinese Australian communities, credited 'specialisation' and high-density worker dormitories respectively for the success of Chinese furniture manufacturers.[22] Bon-Wai Chou described failures as a consequence of the Chinese 'sojourning attitude' (that is, failing to invest long-term

---

Bitter Strength: A History of the Chinese in the United States, 1850–1870 (Massachusetts: Harvard University Press, 1964); Alexander Saxton, *The Indispensable Enemy: Labor and the Anti-Chinese Movement in California* (Berkeley: University of California Press, 1975).

21 Gavin Jones, 'White Australia, National Identity and Population Change', in Laksiri Jayasuriya, David Walker and Jan Gothard, eds., *Legacies of White Australia: Race, Culture and Nation* (Crawley: University of Western Australia Press, 2003), 110–128; Jennifer Cushman, 'A "colonial casualty": the Chinese community in Australian historiography', *Asian Studies Association of Australia Review*, 7:3 (1984), 100–113.

22 Eric Rolls, *Citizens: Continuing the Epic Story of China's Centuries-Old Relationship with Australia* (St. Lucia: University of Queensland Press, 1996), 111–114; Shirley Fitzgerald, *Red Tape Gold Scissors: The Story of Sydney's Chinese* (Sydney: Halstead, 2008), 100–103, 106.

in their migration destination), not simply as the product of racialised legislation.[23] Studies centring Chinese migrants in North America and South-East Asia were also done in this period, recognising migrant contributions to a range of industries.[24] In this book, I will consider how racism impacted Chinese factories, but I will concentrate more closely on how Chinese migrants and their descendants succeeded and failed in the industry. We will see that manufacturers were not normally specialists, but that factory worker dormitories and other practices did indeed lead to success. Limited capital investment often did impede manufacturers, as did market downturns, workers' higher earnings and discriminatory industry regulations.

The book forms part of a recent surge of historical interest in Chinese Australian economic activity as well. Influenced especially by China's ascent as an economic power, and aiming to analyse Chinese business and labour on its own terms, historians have undertaken a series of groundbreaking studies during the past two decades. Several have examined the methods of Chinese entrepreneurs, including their dealings with non-Chinese businesses and customers. Sophie Loy-Wilson has used accounts from Chinese shopkeepers and shopworkers to move beyond the 'whimsical detail' often seen in non-Chinese reflections on Chinese shops in rural Australia. She has shown how these shops were important sites of both economic and cultural exchange.[25] In his general study of industrial entrepreneurialism on Melbourne's Little Lonsdale Street between 1860

---

23 Bon-Wai Chou, 'The sojourning attitude and the economic decline of Chinese society in Victoria, 1860s–1930s', in Paul Macgregor, ed., *Histories of the Chinese in Australasia and the South Pacific* (Melbourne: Museum of Chinese Australian History, 1995), 59–74.
24 See, for example, Sucheng Chan, *This Bittersweet Soil: Chinese in California Agriculture, 1860–1910* (Berkeley: University of California Press, 1986); Thomas Tsu-wee Tan, *Chinese Dialect Groups: Traits and Trades* (Singapore: Opinion Books, 1990); Lynn Pan, *Sons of the Yellow Emperor: A History of the Chinese Diaspora* (New York: Kodansha, 1994).

Introduction

and 1950, John Leckey explored Chinese furniture production. He has identified industrial clusters and market niches as having been crucial to Chinese factories there.[26] Historians have also revisited the lives of Chinese workers, highlighting how they were not the 'coolies' that were imagined by the racist authorities and other proponents of 'white labour'.[27] Mei-fen Kuo has investigated Chinese labour activism in Melbourne's furniture industry using Australian Chinese-language newspapers, stressing the significance of Chinese diasporic nationalism and civic organisation.[28] Studies set in other migration destinations have also proliferated during recent years. Elizabeth Sinn and Ching-hwang Yen, for instance, have considered Chinese business in California and South-East Asia respectively, emphasising its origins in Chinese culture and networks.[29] Mae Ngai and others have

---

25 Sophie Loy-Wilson, 'Rural Geographies and Chinese Empires: Chinese Shopkeepers and Shop-Life in Australia', *Australian Historical Studies*, 45:3 (2014), 407-424. Notable studies of other industries include Joanna Boileau, *Chinese Market Gardening in Australia and New Zealand: Gardens of Prosperity* (Cham: Palgrave Macmillan, 2017); Warwick Frost, 'Migrants and Technological Transfer: Chinese Farming in Australia, 1850-1920', *Australian Economic History Review*, 42:2 (2002), 113-131; Barry McGowan, 'The economics and organisation of Chinese mining in Colonial Australia', *Australian Economic History Review*, 45:2 (2005), 119-138.
26 John Leckey, 'Low, Degraded Broots? Industry and Entrepreneurialism in Melbourne's Little Lon, 1860-1950' (PhD Thesis: University of Melbourne, 2003), 305-309, 313-323, 326-329. See also Jock Collins, 'Chinese Entrepreneurs: The Chinese Diaspora in Australia', *International Journal of Entrepreneurial Behaviour & Research*, 8:1/2 (2002), 113-133.
27 See, for example, *International Labor and Working-Class History*, 91 (2017) and *Labour History*, 113 (2017).
28 Mei-fen Kuo, 'Reframing Chinese Labour Rights: Chinese Unionists, Pro-Labour Societies and the Nationalist Movement in Melbourne, 1900-10', *Labour History*, 113 (2017), 133-155. See also Marilyn Lake, 'Challenging the "Slave-Driving Employers": Understanding Victoria's 1896 Minimum Wage through a World-History Approach', *Australian Historical Studies*, 45:1 (2014), 87-102.
29 Elizabeth Sinn, *Pacific Crossing: California Gold, Chinese Migration and the Making of Hong Kong* (Hong Kong: Hong Kong University Press, 2012);

concentrated more on workers, including their accounts of their own activities.[30] This book extends these recent avenues of investigation further into the domain of Chinese overseas industrial manufacturing, which is little known relative to other endeavours. Guided principally by the personal accounts of Chinese furniture manufacturers and workers, we will see that they were adaptable and resilient. Chinese manufacturers dealt extensively with non-Chinese businesses for their supplies and had wide customer bases. They needed to compete energetically for business. Their workers had a complex and dynamic factory culture, centred on southern China but also incorporating principles espoused by the broader Australian labour movement.

Along with histories of Chinese migration, the book builds on recent explorations of economic and business history in Australia and globally. Simon Ville's and Glenn Withers' *Cambridge Economic History of Australia* has provided a thorough overview of Australian economic development, and other scholars have completed a range of comparable

---

Ching-hwang Yen, *Ethnic Chinese Business in Asia: History, Culture and Business Enterprise* (Singapore: World Scientific, 2013). See also, to take another landmark study, Adam McKeown, *Chinese Migrant Networks and Cultural Change: Peru, Chicago, Hawai'i, 1900–1936* (Chicago: Chicago University Press, 2001).

30 See, for instance, Mae M. Ngai, 'The True Story of Ah Jake: Language, Labor, and Justice in Late-Nineteenth-Century Sierra County, California', in Daniel T. Rogers, Bhavani Raman and Helmut Reimitz, eds., *Cultures in Motion* (Princeton: Princeton University Press, 2014), 197–214; Lisa Yun, *The Coolie Speaks: Chinese Indentured Laborers and African Slaves in Cuba* (Philadelphia: Temple University Press, 2008).

Introduction

work in Australia and worldwide.[31] This focused history of Chinese Australian furniture factories complements these studies.

Historical evidence

Historical source material that captures the words spoken and written by Chinese furniture industry participants is at the heart of this book, and most of it has never been seen before. Foremost are the bankruptcy records for Chinese factories in Sydney and Melbourne. These records include testimony given by factory proprietors and employees, financial ledgers, claims regarding unpaid debts from more than 200 workers, receipts and factory inventories. I also draw on Chinese testimony from various civil, criminal and industrial court proceedings, and from a Royal Commission held in Sydney. Additionally, records associated with the *Immigration Restriction Act* of 1901 are vital. These files contain information provided by migrants about their birthplaces, birthdates, travel, places of residence, businesses and occupations, assets and earnings, and their associates and family members. I also draw on five Chinese-language newspapers: the *Tung Wah News* (1898–1902), its successor newspaper the *Tung Wah Times* (1902–36), the *Chinese Australian Herald* (1894–1923) and the *Chinese Republic News* (1914–37), all printed in Sydney, and the *Chinese Times* (1902–22), printed in Melbourne. English-language booklets and

---

31 Simon Ville and Glenn Withers, eds., *The Cambridge Economic History of Australia* (Melbourne: Cambridge University Press, 2014). Refer further to Simon Ville and Claire Wright, 'Neither a Discipline nor a Colony: Renaissance and Re-imagination in Economic History', *Australian Historical Studies*, 48:2 (2017), 152–168. See also Franco Amatori and Geoffrey Jones, eds., *Business History around the World* (Cambridge: Cambridge University Press, 2003); Franco Amatori and Andrea Colli, *Business History: Complexities and Comparisons* (London: Routledge, 2013); Robert Gardella, Andrea McElderry and Jane K. Leonard, eds., *Chinese Business History: Interpretive Trends and Priorities for the Future* (New York: Routledge, 2017).

pamphlets published by Chinese furniture industry representatives are also key sources, as are letters from these spokespeople to editors of English-language newspapers.

We must exercise care with the Chinese voices that form the basis of this book. Court records and transcripts from the Sydney Royal Commission in particular are the direct outcomes of racialising and marginalising legal processes in which Chinese involvement was mediated.[32] Because these processes were dominated by people of European – mostly British – descent, Chinese participants probably felt that they had to speak and act in certain ways, especially in formal courtroom settings. They often needed to rely on interpreters, who might not have communicated the nuances of their views. The goal of such processes was typically to ascertain how businesses operated and what working conditions were like according to fixed procedures, like those governing bankruptcy. Thus, the resultant records only cover part of the industry, generally its leading manufacturers and their employees, and these records tend to reduce people who once lived and breathed to little more than the money that they earned and spent.[33] Even Chinese-language newspapers, which allow unmediated access to Chinese perspectives, neglected the voices of workers. This was because they were presided over by community elites such as John Hoe (冼俊豪

---

32 On court mediation of Chinese voices, see Nadia Rhook, '"The Chief Chinese Interpreter" Charles Hodges: mapping the aurality of race and governance in colonial Melbourne', *Postcolonial Studies*, 18:1 (2015), 1–18; Sophie Loy-Wilson, 'Coolie Alibis: Seizing Gold from Chinese Miners in New South Wales', *International Labor and Working-Class History*, 91 (2017), 36–37; Ngai, 'The True Story of Ah Jake', 197–214. On bias in court records more generally, see also Metin Coşgel and Boğaç Ergene, 'The selection bias in court records: settlement and trial in eighteenth-century Ottoman Kastamonu', *Economic History Review*, 67:2 (2014), 517–534.
33 Even bankruptcy legislation was normally only applied to failed manufacturers who had significant assets, meaning that numerous factories failed without leaving much trace.

Introduction

Xian Junhao), who presided over both a furniture factory and the *Tung Wah Times* in Sydney.³⁴

While I prioritise evidence that offers an inside view of Chinese factories, non-Chinese accounts are also important for context and comparison. The book therefore makes use of the bankruptcy files created for non-Chinese furniture factories in Sydney and Melbourne. It relies on non-Chinese testimony given in civil, criminal and industrial court cases as well, along with testimony from the Royal Commission in Sydney, Royal Commission in Melbourne and a Victorian parliamentary inquiry. Industrial legislation and reports compiled by factory inspectors appointed to enforce it are also critical sources. Others include census reports, writings by non-Chinese observers in English-language newspapers, trade union materials and the records of Victoria's Anti-Chinese League. We must exercise caution with this material as well, since much of it contains negative descriptions of Chinese furniture industry participants consistent with the 'White Australia' principle.

Book outline

Chapter One addresses the origins of Chinese involvement in Australia's furniture industry between 1800 and 1880. It begins with the earliest Chinese woodwork experts who migrated to Australia over the first half of the nineteenth century. It next turns to the Chinese gold seekers who arrived for gold rushes from the 1850s, and thereafter entered the furniture industry. It then focuses on post-gold rush industry specialists who began work in the 1870s. We will see in this

---

34 On the agendas of Chinese-language newspapers in Australia, see Mei-fen Kuo, *Making Chinese Australia: Urban Elites, Newspapers and the Formation of Chinese-Australian Identity, 1892–1912* (Clayton: Monash University Publishing, 2013); Yong, *The New Gold Mountain*, 120–156.

chapter how economic development within Australia was the main factor behind Chinese involvement in this specific industry.

We will consider how Chinese factories were set up in Chapter Two, focusing on the period between 1880 and 1930. The chapter initially describes arrangements relating to proprietorship and financing. Next, it discusses the actual factory premises. It will then look at the tools and machinery used in Chinese factories, followed by the materials, such as timber, glass, nails, glue and varnish. We will discover that while imported cultural resources were important in setting up furniture factories, Chinese Australian furniture manufacturers did not limit themselves to particularly 'Chinese' ways of approaching this task. Chinese factory operators used methods seen more widely in Australian industry, and were aided in doing so by non-Chinese Australians.

In Chapter Three, we will explore the world of Chinese factory workers through their own words. After a brief overview of workforce sizes and compositions, the chapter looks at Chinese factory workers' skill sets, their rates of pay and hours of work, and their social class. The presence of a vibrant and distinctive work culture in the factories is revealed. This work culture was informed chiefly by life and work around the Pearl River Delta, from where most of the workers had come, but also incorporated elements of the wider Australian labour movement's struggle for workers' rights. Its existence indicates that assertions of Chinese 'cheap labour', and the measures instituted to contain it, were not taken as seriously by Chinese workers as we might expect.

Chapter Four deals with the market for Chinese Australian furniture. It addresses Chinese manufacturers' sales scopes, that is, to whom they sold items and what they sold. The chapter also explores manufacturers' promotional strategies and their profit margins. We will see that rather than confining their activities to safe, empty niche markets in efforts to avoid conflict, Chinese factories competed

Introduction

energetically against both their non-Chinese equivalents and each other in the broader Australian marketplace. Indeed, they were bold, and industry conditions encouraged their competitive behaviour.

Chapter Five explains how Chinese furniture factories were restricted, and how Chinese industry participants resisted these efforts. We will look initially at the 'white labour' activism that led to the first legislation directed against Chinese factories in Melbourne in 1885. We next consider ongoing labour movement protests and two public inquiries that saw new anti-Chinese regulations adopted in 1896 and 1900. We will then address the marked expansion of racialised furniture industry regulations after Australia became a federated nation in 1901. Lastly, the chapter addresses the political opportunism that led to the final and most severe restrictions on Chinese factories in Sydney in 1927. We will recognise that there was substantial variability across the impediments put in place for Chinese factories – and in Chinese strategies of resistance – under 'White Australia'.

The book presents a nuanced picture of the history of Chinese migration to Australia. We will see Chinese Australian furniture makers as entrepreneurs and workers in their own right, as meaningful actors in Australian history. We will also see how, despite the racism directed against them, they were able to engage in the furniture industry effectively, aided in many instances by European Australians.

1
Industry Beginnings

In the 1850s, four Cantonese men, Lee Fee, Ack Chow, Ah Hing and Lee Kum (李錦 Li Jin), migrated to Australia for the gold rushes.[1] Their exact origins are uncertain, but it is likely that they came from the same place in the Pearl River Delta of Guangdong. They all knew each other and Lee Fee and Lee Kum were 'cousins', according to Lee Kum.[2] In Australia, they were not simply gold miners. They also supported gold-mining operations through the provision of goods and services to miners on different goldfields. Lee Fee kept general stores in Moruya and Mudgee in New South Wales, both near sites of gold-mining activity.[3] Lee Kum also supported gold miners by, as he put it, 'keeping a brothel' in the Victorian gold town of Beechworth.[4] The four were part

---

1 Lee Kum Testimony, 28 May 1883, Ack Chow Insolvency File, New South Wales State Records (NSWSR), 13654-2/9993-17928, 147; Ah Hing Testimony, 28 May 1883, Ack Chow Insolvency File, 154–155.
2 Lee Kum Testimony, 3 July 1883, The Queen v. Johnny Ah Ehing, Supreme Court of New South Wales, NSWSR 9/6690-83/134, 38.
3 Lee Kum Testimony, Ack Chow Insolvency File, 158.
4 Lee Kum Testimony, The Queen v. Johnny Ah Ehing, 49.

of a movement by hundreds of thousands of gold seekers to Australasia and North America in the mid-nineteenth century.[5]

In 1879, after the largest gold rushes had finished, the four 'old friends' – to borrow Ah Hing's words – became involved in a Sydney furniture factory.[6] Lee Fee and Ack Chow acquired an existing furniture production operation, Loon Cheong and Co. on George Street, with a third partner, Cheung Yen. They were soon joined there by Ah Hing and Lee Kum.[7] Originally opened in 1867, the Loon Cheong and Co. factory had been among the earliest Chinese furniture factories in the city, operating alongside a mere handful of comparable Chinese establishments.[8] By 1879, however, when the four friends assumed control of it, Chinese furniture makers were challenging their non-Chinese counterparts for primacy in the Australian furniture industry.

Furniture making was limited among Chinese migrants in European settler societies other than Australia. While there were many Chinese furniture factories in British Malaya, and smaller numbers elsewhere around South-East Asia, they were only rarely recorded in North and South America or the Pacific Islands, including New Zealand. Indeed, mining, agriculture, retailing, laundry work and outdoor labouring attracted substantial Chinese involvement in these places, as in Australia. Yet, furniture production did not, making Chinese Australian furniture factories unique.[9] This activity was also one of a handful of Chinese manufacturing activities around the Pacific

---

5 Mae M. Ngai, 'Chinese Gold Miners and the "Chinese Question" in Nineteenth-Century California and Victoria', *Journal of American History*, 101:4 (2015), 1082–1105.
6 Ah Hing Testimony, Ack Chow Insolvency File, 157.
7 Ack Chow Petition, 26 April 1883, Ack Chow Insolvency File, 3; Ah Hing Testimony, Ack Chow Insolvency File, 157; Lee Kum Testimony, The Queen v. Johnny Ah Ehing, 51.
8 Loon Cheong and Co. Promissory Note, 20 February 1883, Lee Fee Insolvency File, NSWSR, 13654-2/10017-18229, 24; *Sands Commercial Directory 1865*, 337–338; *Sands Commercial Directory 1870*, 460.

1 Industry Beginnings

Rim, other examples being garment, footwear and cigar production in San Francisco.[10]

This chapter investigates the beginnings of Chinese involvement in Australian furniture manufacturing between 1800 and 1880. The chapter's first section deals with the small number of Chinese woodwork experts who migrated to Australia in the first half of the nineteenth century, when there were dire skills shortages. Next, it looks at the larger number of Chinese migrants who travelled to Australia during the gold rushes of the 1850s and 1860s, who started making furniture afterwards amid strong demand from an Australian population dramatically increased by the gold rushes. The final section discusses newly arrived migrants who entered the industry over the 1870s, whose principal interest was in furniture production at a time of sustained urban growth. We will see that Australian economic development, that is, a strong demand for furniture combined with a small industrial base, was the key reason why Chinese migrants and some of their descendants entered the furniture industry.

Early woodwork experts

Chinese woodwork is traditionally attributed to Lu Ban (魯班). Like Confucius, Lu Ban lived in the duchy of Lu, now in the north-eastern province of Shandong, during the Zhou Dynasty (around 500 BCE). Centuries later, the Chinese thinker Mencius represented him as a pioneering engineer and craftsman, responsible for creating fearsome siege engines and advanced wooden automata. Thereafter, Lu Ban

---

9   There was some Chinese bamboo furniture marking in Hawai'i. See Ta Chen, *Chinese Migrations, with Special Reference to Labor Conditions* (Washington: Government Printing Office, 1923), 124.
10 Yong Chen, *Chinese San Francisco: A Trans-Pacific Community, 1850–1943* (Stanford: Stanford University Press, 2000), 52–69.

became the most revered figure among Chinese woodworkers, and the ideal artisan of China's traditional four-class social system, which comprised scholars, peasants, artisans and merchants (士農工商 *shinonggongshang*). The significance that he came to assume is perhaps most clearly illustrated by his deification in the fifteenth-century classic *Lu Ban Jing* (魯班經), a standard instructional manual for Chinese woodworkers for centuries to follow. It is said here that Lu Ban travelled the world on a cloud, inspiring woodworkers to achieve great feats.[11]

Chinese woodworkers, heirs to the rich legacy of Lu Ban, travelled the world in sizeable numbers from the thirteenth century and were seen in European colonies in Asia from the sixteenth century. China's highly developed handicraft and shipbuilding industries afforded it an important place in East Asian and Indian Ocean trade from around 1200 CE, during the Song Dynasty.[12] Chinese settlements were constructed along the trade routes and woodworkers migrated there in order to earn a living in construction and by repairing ships.[13] In the sixteenth century, during the Ming Dynasty, European colonies were founded in Asia, first by Portuguese and then by Spanish colonists, and Chinese and European trade networks became intertwined. Woodworkers and other migrants from China then travelled to the new European colonies. In Spanish Manila, to take one example, Chinese craftsmen from Fujian were common.[14] Bishop Domingo de Salazar wrote admiringly of their skill, which extended to the manufacture of

---

11 Klaas Ruitenbeek, *Carpentry and Building in Late Imperial China: A Study of the Fifteenth-Century Carpenter's Manual Lu Ban Jing* (Leiden: Brill, 1993), 15–24, 152–154.
12 Zhuang Guotu, 'China's Policies on Chinese Overseas: Past and Present', in Tan Chee-Beng, ed., *Routledge Handbook of the Chinese Diaspora* (London: Routledge, 2013), 31.
13 Zhu Jieqin (朱杰勤), *Dongnanya huaqiao shi* [A history of overseas Chinese in Southeast Asia] (Beijing: Zhonghua Book Company, 2008), 26, 164–166; Yow Cheun Hoe, *Guangdong and Chinese Diaspora: The changing landscape of qiaoxiang* (London: Routledge, 2013), 18–21.

1 Industry Beginnings

European-style items, in the late sixteenth century.[15] Chinese migrants met 'race'-, religion- and language-based discrimination within these migration destinations, which closed off opportunities to them.[16] Nevertheless, the expertise of artisans was prized. In European colonies, geographic isolation from the industrial centres of Europe resulted in skills shortages and created an urgent need for their services. Even so, consumer populations in these outposts could not support large-scale furniture production, limiting the numbers of Chinese furniture makers.[17]

China became a minor manufacturer of furniture for European export markets in the seventeenth century. Production of furniture in China for domestic use was advanced at the start of the seventeenth century, during the late-Ming Dynasty.[18] Yet, Portuguese and Spanish traders focused on the Asian spice trade in this period, so little Chinese furniture was sent to Europe.[19] As the century progressed and China's Ming Dynasty was replaced by the Qing, Dutch, English and French

---

14   Huang Zisheng (黄滋生) and He Sibing (何思兵), *Feilvbin huaqiao shi* [Philippine overseas Chinese history] (Guangzhou: Guangdong Higher Education Press, 1987), 73–80.
15   Lynn Pan, *Sons of the Yellow Emperor: A History of the Chinese Diaspora* (New York: Kodansha, 1994), 30–34, 130.
16   Els van Dongen, 'Entangled Loyalties: *Qiaopi*, Chinese community structures, and the state in Southeast Asia', in Gregor Benton, Hong Liu and Huimei Zhang, eds., *The Qiaopi Trade and Transnational Networks in the Chinese Diaspora* (London: Routledge, 2018), 10.
17   Chinese woodworkers also migrated in small numbers to other European settlements in Asia, as well as to South Africa and Central and South America. Refer to Pan, *Sons of the Yellow Emperor*, 34–37, 61–67; Zhu, *Dongnanya huaqiao shi*, 53.
18   Wang Shizhen (王世襄) and Yuan Wei (袁荃猷), *Mingshi jiaju yanjiu* [Ming-style furniture research] (Hong Kong: Joint Publishing, 2007); Antonia Finnane, 'Chinese Domestic Interiors and "Consumer Constraint" in Qing China: Evidence from Yangzhou', *Journal of the Economic and Social History of the Orient*, 57 (2014), 112–113.
19   James Boyajian, *Portuguese Trade in Asia under the Habsburgs, 1580–1640* (Baltimore: Johns Hopkins University Press, 2008), 1–17.

merchants became increasingly active in Asia. Along with spices, they exported more manufactures, especially those from China. These manufactured goods, including furniture, were eagerly received in Europe. They could not be supplied in quantities large enough to meet demand, however, due to restrictions within China on foreign trade.[20] This contributed to the inception of chinoiserie products in Europe from the mid-1600s: Chinese styles were imitated by European craftspeople to compensate for shortages in genuine articles.[21]

In the eighteenth century, more Chinese wares began to flow onto European markets. This owed much to the easing of China's official restrictions on foreign commerce from the late seventeenth century, namely the opening of Guangzhou as an international trading port.[22] Thanks to its special status, Guangzhou became China's manufacturing hub for the European export trade. Pieces of furniture were among the numerous items produced there for export – in both Chinese and European styles – in a section of the city known as 'Carpenter Square'.[23] Europe was the principal market, but the North American market assumed greater importance from the late eighteenth century.[24] Small

---

20 David Mungello, *The Great Encounter of China and the West, 1500–1800* (Plymouth: Rowman and Littlefield, 2013), 5–6, 15–16.
21 Dawn Jacobson, *Chinoiserie* (London: Phaidon, 1993), 9–59.
22 Paul A. Van Dyke, *The Canton Trade: Life and Enterprise on the China Coast, 1700–1845* (Hong Kong: Hong Kong University Press, 2005), 5; Paul A. Van Dyke, *Merchants of Canton and Macao: Success and Failure in Eighteenth-Century Chinese Trade* (Hong Kong: Hong Kong University Press, 2016), 7–30.
23 Carl Crossman, *The China Trade: Export Paintings, Furniture, Silver & Other Objects* (Princeton: Pyne Press, 1972), 142–152. On traditional Cantonese furniture, see Xue Yongjun (薛拥军), 'Guangshi mudiao yishu jiqi zai jianzhu he shinei zhuangshi zhong de yingyong yanjiu' [Cantonese-style woodcarving craft and its architecture centring on applied research in interior decoration] (PhD Thesis: Nanjing Forestry University, 2012), 9–52; Zhu Yun (朱云), 'Guangdong chuantong jiaju de tese fenxi' [Analysis of the characteristics of Guangdong traditional furniture], *Baozhuang gongcheng* [Packaging engineering], 39:16 (2018), 236–242.

amounts of furniture were exported to Australia at the beginning of the nineteenth century. There they made up part of what James Broadbent, Suzanne Rickard and Margaret Steven have described as a 'cosmopolitan and polyglot' colonial culture.[25] Furniture manufacturing for export in China declined over the early nineteenth century due to the waning popularity of Chinese styles in Europe and North America, and as a result of rapid industrialisation on these continents, which rendered Chinese manufacturing for export less competitive.[26]

As manufacturing declined in China, Chinese woodworkers began migrating to Britain's new Asian colonies. Driven by the need to seek out new opportunities overseas, Cantonese furniture makers in particular travelled to Penang in the late eighteenth century, and then Singapore in the early nineteenth century. In both colonies, they were engaged principally in making furniture for large Chinese migrant populations, and in construction. They also erected temples to Lu Ban.[27] On a much smaller scale, Chinese furniture makers and other woodworkers migrated to India, where they found work servicing British Calcutta's colonial elite.[28] Chinese migrant occupations in all

---

24 Wang Gungwu, *Anglo-Chinese Encounters since 1800: War, Trade, Science and Governance* (Cambridge: Cambridge University Press, 2003), 43–74.
25 James Broadbent, Suzanne Rickard and Margaret Steven, *India, China, Australia: Trade and Society 1788–1850* (Glebe: Historic Houses Trust of New South Wales, 2003), 22.
26 Ulrike Hilleman, *Asian Empire and British Knowledge: China and the Networks of British Imperial Expansion* (Basingstoke: Palgrave Macmillan, 2009), 31–34; Crossman, *The China Trade*, 3–4. On industrialisation and furniture, see Manfred Bale, *Woodworking Machinery: Its Rise, Progress and Construction with Hints on the Management of Saw Mills and the Economical Conversion of Timber* (London: Crosby, Lockwood and Co., 1880), 6–11, 71–87.
27 Khoo Su Nin, *Streets of George Town, Penang: An Illustrated Guide to Penang's City Streets & Historic Attractions* (Penang: Phoenix Press, 2007), 119–120; Thomas Tsu-wee Tan, *Chinese Dialect Groups: Traits and Trades* (Singapore: Opinion Books, 1990), 11–12; Ching-hwang Yen, *Ethnic Chinese Business in Asia: History, Culture and Business Enterprise* (Singapore: World Scientific, 2013), 67.

these colonies were influenced by British colonial hierarchies that kept Chinese people out of higher levels of government. However, Chinese migrants were not otherwise constrained by British restrictions, so woodworkers probably chose their industry based on demand for their skills. In Penang and Singapore, dialect and native place origins determined their activities as well. Cantonese migrants concentrated on artisanal pursuits in these locales.[29]

Chinese woodworkers started migrating to Australia in small numbers during the early nineteenth century. The first to arrive in the new British colony of New South Wales, and the first Chinese person to be recorded in a colonial muster was 'Ahuto', a 'carpenter' who arrived in 1803 on the *Rolla*.[30] Mak Saiying (麥世英 Mai Shiying) was another early Chinese woodworker in New South Wales, arriving in 1818. A 'carpenter' as well, he was employed by wealthy landholder John Blaxland on the outskirts of Sydney, and later by the Macarthur family, also wealthy landholders.[31] In the 1820s, more woodworkers travelled to New South Wales. As Kate Bagnall has described, 'carpenters' Ahehew, Ahoun and Awage appeared in the Colonial Secretary's correspondence between 1822 and 1825.[32] Two Chinese furniture makers, Quong and Tchiou, also worked for Scottish pastor

---

28 Bijoy Kumar Bose, 'A Bygone Chinese Colony in Bengal', *Bengal Past and Present*, 47:2 (1934), 120–122. See also Warwick Oakman, 'Influence of Anglo-Indian and Anglo-Chinese Furniture in Colonial Australia', in Greg Peters and Jim Kennedy, eds., *Proceedings of the Inaugural Australian Furniture History Symposium* (Canberra: Furniture History Society of Australasia, 2007), 18–22.
29 Tan, *Chinese Dialect Groups*, 11–12.
30 Kate Bagnall, 'Man Sue Bach, 1790–1862: the "oldest Chinese colonist" in New South Wales', *The Tiger's Mouth: Thoughts on the History and Heritage of Chinese Australia*, 23 February 2013, accessed 1 July 2018, http://chineseaustralia.org/tag/john-shying/.
31 Ian Jack, 'Some Less Familiar Aspects of the Chinese in 19th-Century Australia', in Henry Chan, Ann Curthoys and Nora Chiang, eds., *The Overseas Chinese in Australasia: History, Settlement and Interactions* (Canberra: Centre for the Study of the Chinese Southern Diaspora, 2001), 47.

1 Industry Beginnings

John Dunmore Lang in Sydney from 1827.[33] Woodworkers were occasionally seen in the other Australian colonies. Furniture historian Warwick Oakman has noted how Hookam Chan, 'an esteemed Chinese cabinetmaker from India', worked for Lieutenant-Governor James Stirling in 1829 in the Swan River Colony (Western Australia).[34] Most of these woodworkers were Cantonese.[35] They also constituted a substantial part of the total Chinese population of Australia in the early nineteenth century.

Chinese woodworkers arriving in Australia found their expertise to be in high demand regarding production of good-quality furniture. Industrialisation in Europe and North America was underway, with sizeable volumes of furniture and other products manufactured there in major cities.[36] Australia was far removed from this activity, however, and shipping services linking it to these centres were insufficient for regular shipments of bulky, fragile furniture.[37] As seen in the earliest European colonies in Asia, skills shortages also hindered Australian

---

32　Bagnall, 'Man Sue Bach, 1790–1862'. Awage went to Sydney from Calcutta. See Index to New South Wales Colonial Secretary's Papers 1788–1825, NSWSR Indexes, accessed 1 July 2018, https://www.records.nsw.gov.au/archives/collections-and-research/guides-and-indexes/colonial-secretarys-papers.

33　Eric Rolls, *Sojourners: The Epic Story of China's Centuries-Old Relationship with Australia* (St. Lucia: University of Queensland Press, 1992), 32–33.

34　Oakman, 'Influence of Anglo-Indian and Anglo-Chinese Furniture in Colonial Australia', 18–22. No Chinese furniture industry participants were listed in the 1828 Census of NSW. See Kevin Fahy, Christina Simpson and Andrew Simpson, *Nineteenth Century Australian Furniture* (Sydney: David Ell Press, 1985), 43. Nine Chinese furniture makers arrived in Tasmania in 1830. See 'An Era', *Launceston Advertiser*, 26 July 1830.

35　The predominance in names of 'Ah' (亞 *ya*), an informal term of address in Cantonese dialects, as well as Cantonese woodworkers' presence in the British colonies of Penang and Singapore, suggest that most were Cantonese.

36　Margaret Macdonald-Taylor, *English Furniture from the Middle Ages to Modern Times* (London: Evans Brothers, 1965), 31–35; Elizabeth Bidwell Bates and Jonathan L. Fairbanks, *American Furniture: 1620 to the Present* (New York: Richard Marek Publishers, 1981), 195–280.

domestic industry. The transportation of convicts from Britain guaranteed that Australia's European population grew much faster than in these other colonies, but it also meant a colonial workforce of predominantly unfree, unskilled labourers. Their ability to produce manufactured products was limited and their labour was used principally for public works. According to the furniture historians Kevin Fahy, Christina Simpson and Andrew Simpson, convicts were able to make 'survival furniture'.[38] While functional, this was undesirable to wealthy landholders, political powerbrokers and even free settlers with respectable incomes. Hence, there were opportunities for Chinese woodworkers to make more attractive articles.[39] Colonial hierarchies centred on the convict system, so there was little antagonism towards Chinese migrants in these early years.[40] Nonetheless, opportunities to create a cohesive Chinese furniture sector, as seen in Penang or Singapore, were limited by woodworkers' modest numbers, their isolation from each other and Australia's small consumer population.

Over the 1830s, the demand for furniture shifted somewhat from good-quality pieces to reasonably priced ones. Australia's European population had expanded significantly since New South Wales was established in 1788 – to approximately 130,000 by the year 1841 –

---

37   David Hainsworth, 'The New South Wales shipping interest 1800–1821: a study in colonial entrepreneurship', *Australian Economic History Review*, 8:1 (1968), 17–30.
38   Fahy, Simpson and Simpson, *Nineteenth Century Australian Furniture*, 38–41. There were exceptions, described throughout David St L. Kelly, *Convict and Free: The Master Furniture-Makers of New South Wales 1788–1851* (North Melbourne: Australian Scholarly Publishing, 2014).
39   On desirable pieces, see Clifford Craig, Kevin Fahy and E. Graeme Robertson, *Early Colonial Furniture in New South Wales and Van Diemen's Land* (Melbourne: Georgian House, 1972), 3–8; Oakman, 'Influence of Anglo-Indian and Anglo-Chinese Furniture in Colonial Australia', 18–22.
40   John Hirst, *Freedom on the Fatal Shore: Australia's First Colony* (Melbourne: Black Inc., 2008), 139–157.

and an increasing proportion of the population comprised free settlers of modest means.⁴¹ Cabinetmakers among these settlers campaigned successfully to limit the employment of convict labour in the production of basic, cheap furniture, causing furniture prices to rise.⁴² Chinese woodworkers started to produce cheaper, yet still good-quality, alternative pieces. They faced minimal competition since, as historian Godfrey Linge has described, very few 'good [European] craftsmen and skilled operatives' went to work in the Australian colonies. Prospects were better for them in Europe and the United States.⁴³ Technical skills shortages remained a serious problem in the Australian colonies over the 1830s. Agriculture, especially wool cultivation for spinning mills in Britain, emerged as the main economic activity.⁴⁴

As the decade ended, the First Opium War (1839–42) between Britain and China profoundly changed the nature of Chinese manufacturing, trade and overseas migration. Trading outposts were forcibly established by the British in ports along China's coastline.⁴⁵ According to historian Carl Crossman, this led to a state of cutthroat competition among industrialists in different regions, including the manufacturers of furniture, for the already depressed export trade.

---

41 *Australian Historical Population Statistics, Population by sex, state and territories, 31 December, 1788 onwards*, Australian Bureau of Statistics, cat. no. 3105.0.65.001, accessed 1 July 2018, http://www.abs.gov.au/ausstats/ abs@.nsf/INotes/3105.0.65.0012008Data%20Cubes?opendocument&T.
42 Fahy, Simpson and Simpson, *Nineteenth Century Australian Furniture*, 49–50. It is also likely that prices rose due to increasing extravagance as the Regency period ended and the Victorian era began. See Edward T. Joy, *The Country Life Book of English Furniture* (London: Country Life, 1964), 77–79.
43 Godfrey J. R. Linge, *Industrial Awakening: A Geography of Australian Manufacturing 1788 to 1890* (Canberra: Australian National University Press, 1979), 54.
44 Simon Ville, 'Business Development in Colonial Australia', *Australian Economic History Review*, 38:1 (1998), 21, 26.
45 Song-Chuan Chen, *Merchants of War and Peace: British Knowledge of China in the Making of the Opium War* (Hong Kong: Hong Kong University Press, 2017), 126–149.

Further industrialisation in Europe and North America, as well as the importation of foreign goods through the 'treaty ports', reduced the profitability of manufacturing in China and ended Guangzhou's dominance as an industrial and trade hub.[46] This forced thousands out of work. These economic conditions, and a challenge to law and order resulting from the Qing government's weakened position, increased the attractiveness of overseas migration.[47] Migrating abroad also became more viable because of easier access to foreign shipping in the treaty ports.

After the First Opium War, a moderate number of additional Chinese woodworkers began work in Australia. Most, like their forerunners, were Cantonese. Louis Ah Mouy (雷亞妹 Lei Yamo), who had originated in Xinning (新寧) in Guangdong, was one of these woodworkers. He arrived in Melbourne as a carpenter via Penang in 1851.[48] There were also two furniture manufacturers operating in Adelaide in the 1840s, Sang Tim and Zick Zong.[49] Some Chinese indentured labourers transported to Australia from the newly established British trading outpost in Xiamen between 1847 and 1853 were woodworkers as well. One was an unidentified 'carpenter' hired by E. Hamilton of Black Creek in New South Wales in 1852.[50] The majority of the 3500 Chinese indentured labourers sent to the colonies from

---

46 Crossman, *The China Trade*, 3–4; Jiang Wei (蔣茜), '1700–1840 nian Zhong Ying maoyi beijing xia de sheji jiaoliu yanjiu' [Design exchange research on the background of Sino-British trade, 1700–1840] (PhD Thesis: Nanjing Arts Institute, 2017), 113–116.
47 Yow has noted many bankruptcies in the manufacturing sector. See Yow, *Guangdong and Chinese Diaspora*, 22. On the widespread use of opium, see Dai Yi, *Concise History of the Qing Dynasty*, V4 (Singapore: Enrich Professional Publishing, 2012), 285–288.
48 Yong Ching Fatt, 'Louis Ah Mouy', *Australian Dictionary of Biography*, accessed 1 July 2018, http://adb.anu.edu.au/biography/ah-mouy-louis-2872.
49 Eric Rolls, *Citizens: Continuing the Epic Story of China's Centuries-Old Relationship with Australia* (St. Lucia: University of Queensland Press, 1996), 111.

Xiamen, however, were merely intended to alleviate agricultural labour shortages brought on by the end of convict transportation to New South Wales in 1840.[51] The descendants of some of the first Chinese woodworkers in Australia also became woodworkers in this period. Mak Saiying's sons with his wife Sarah – John, George, James and Thomas Shying – worked as carpenters, undertakers (coffin makers) and cabinetmakers in Sydney.[52] Australia's total Chinese population did not increase far beyond the 3500 labourers who had arrived from Xiamen under contract.[53]

In the 1840s, the demand for good-quality furniture re-emerged and intensified in Australia. Due to the advent of steamships and the establishment of regular cargo services between British and American industrial centres and Australian ports, the local market was flooded with manufactured products from Britain and the United States. In 1840, Australia became the largest export market for British furniture, and one of the largest for American.[54] Yet, as noted by Linge, nearly all of this was end-of-season stock 'dumped' in the colonies: furniture that was out-of-fashion and often damaged.[55] Generally, it was also

---

50   Maxine Darnell, 'Indentured Chinese Labourers and Employers Identified, New South Wales, 1828–1856', *Chinese Heritage of Australian Federation Project*, accessed 1 July 2018, https://arrow.latrobe.edu.au/store/3/4/5/1/public/indentured.htm.
51   Maxine Darnell, 'The Chinese Labour Trade to New South Wales, 1783–1853: An Exposition of Motives and Outcomes' (PhD Thesis: University of New England, 1997), 190–289; Margaret Slocomb, *Among Australia's Pioneers: Chinese Indentured Pastoral Workers on the Northern Frontier 1848 to c. 1880* (Bloomington: Balboa Press, 2014), 89–206.
52   Neera Sahni, 'Mak Sai Ying Aka John Shying', *Research Services, City of Paramatta Council*, 27 January 2017, accessed 3 July 2018, http://arc.parracity.nsw.gov.au/blog/2017/01/27/mak-sai-ying-aka-john-shying/.
53   *Census of New South Wales 1856*, 4.
54   Fahy, Simpson and Simpson, *Nineteenth Century Australian Furniture*, 9, 50–51.
55   Linge, *Industrial Awakening*, 410.

exported in individual parts to make efficient use of cargo space. Therefore, a significant portion of Australia's furniture industry was realigned to assemble imported furniture components.[56] High-quality pieces became rarer and more coveted. Chinese woodworkers thus helped to supply furniture to the growing ethnic European population, which had reached over 400,000 by 1850.[57] Yet, they continued to operate in modest numbers and largely in isolation from one another. In this era, for the first time, agitation against so-called 'coolies' had become a feature of Australian colonial society. Chinese migrants were depicted negatively as 'cheap labour', which began to constrain their occupational choices.[58]

Gold seekers to furniture makers

Over the 1850s, commercial quantities of gold were discovered in the south-east of Australia, prompting extensive inbound migration from around the globe. Australia's official population increased from around 400,000 at the beginning of this decade to 1,150,000 by the 1860s. The most dramatic population growth occurred in the new colony of Victoria, site of the richest goldfields.[59] Mass migration to Australia was part of a broader movement of people around the Pacific Rim in this

---

56 Fahy, Simpson and Simpson, *Nineteenth Century Australian Furniture*, 182.
57 *Australian Historical Population Statistics, Population by sex, state and territories, 31 December, 1788 onwards*, Australian Bureau of Statistics, cat. no. 3105.0.65.001, accessed 1 July 2018, http://www.abs.gov.au/ausstats/abs@.nsf/INotes/3105.0.65.0012008Data%20Cubes?opendocument&T.
58 Margaret Slocomb, 'Preserving the Contract: The Experience of Indentured Labourers in the Wide Bay and Burnett Districts in the Nineteenth Century', *Labour History*, 113 (2017), 106–107.
59 *Australian Historical Population Statistics, Population by sex, state and territories, 31 December, 1788 onwards*, Australian Bureau of Statistics, cat. no. 3105.0.65.001, accessed 1 July 2018, http://www.abs.gov.au/ausstats/abs@.nsf/INotes/3105.0.65.0012008Data%20Cubes?opendocument&T.

1 Industry Beginnings

era, driven by gold discoveries in California in the early 1850s, Canada in the late 1850s and New Zealand in the early 1860s.

Chinese migrants travelled in large numbers to the Australian goldfields. By the 1860s, there were over 50,000.[60] Chinese gold-rush migrants had originated almost entirely in the counties of the Pearl River Delta, a map of which is shown below (Figure 1.1).[61] Like many thousands of non-Chinese migrants who travelled to Australia, they were attracted by gold, which offered them and their families the hope of a better life. Crises in China stemming from the weakening of the Chinese government following the First Opium War (1839–42), and then the Second Opium War (1856–60), were key drivers of Chinese overseas migration. The close proximity of the Pearl River Delta to Hong Kong, ceded to Britain in 1842 and a major international port by the 1850s, encouraged mobility as well. From Hong Kong, Chinese migrants travelled to Australia and other Pacific Rim locales, although California was by far the most popular of these destinations.[62]

Australia's sudden population growth led to urgent demand for large quantities of manufactured items, including furniture, which domestic manufacturers scrambled to meet; yet, there was little

---

60 Keir Reeves and Benjamin Mountford, 'Sojourning and Settling: Locating Chinese Australian History', *Australian Historical Studies*, 42:1 (2011), 113; Michael Williams, 'Destination Qiaoxiang: Pearl River Delta Villages and Pacific Ports, 1849–1949' (PhD Thesis: University of Hong Kong, 2002), 42–46.
61 Zhongshan was formerly Xiangshan; the Siyi counties are Enping, Kaiping, Xinning, Taishan (formerly Xinning) and Xinhui; the Sanyi counties are Nanhai, Panyu and Shunde. The source of this map is Michael Williams, *Returning Home with Glory: Chinese Villagers around the Pacific, 1849–1949* (Hong Kong: Hong Kong University Press, 2018), 38. I thank Michael Williams and Hong Kong University Press for their permission to publish it here.
62 Ngai, 'Chinese Gold Miners and the "Chinese Question"', 1086–1088; Keir Reeves, 'Sojourners or a New Diaspora? Economic Implications of the Movement of Chinese Miners to the Southwest Pacific Goldfields', *Australian Economic History Review*, 50:2 (2010), 178–192.

Figure 1.1 Map of Pearl River Delta, Guangdong, China.

additional Chinese involvement in the furniture industry over the 1850s. In Melbourne, the furniture industry consisted of less than 100 people in 1850, but it had expanded fourfold to over 400 almost entirely ethnic European participants by 1861.[63] Demand, however, was not met by manufacturers in Australia, so imports made up shortfalls, although even these were stretched. Millions of pounds worth of furniture was imported by the Australian colonies in the 1850s, supplied chiefly by British and American furniture factories, but also by those in China.[64]

---

63 *Census of Victoria 1861*, 13, 16; *Census of Victoria 1871*, 15, 106; 'Colonial Furniture Trade', *Age*, 4 August 1862; 'The Melbourne Furniture Trade', *Age*, 27 August 1862; 'The Condition of Labour', *Argus*, 28 November 1863.
64 Fahy, Simpson and Simpson, *Nineteenth Century Australian Furniture*, 149. Chinese furniture also went to California in small amounts. See Elizabeth Sinn, *Pacific Crossing: California Gold, Chinese Migration and the Making of Hong Kong* (Hong Kong: Hong Kong University Press, 2013), 309–310.

Most Chinese gold-rush migrants neglected the opportunities in Australian manufacturing at this time owing to their focus on mining and support activities. There was at least one exception. Ah Toy arrived in Sydney in 1854, more than likely from Dongguan (東莞) given his later association with leading Dongguan merchants in Sydney, and opened a furniture factory there almost immediately.[65]

While Chinese participation in Australian furniture production did not increase much over the 1850s, numerous woodworkers were to be found in Chinese mining and supporting workforces. Beginning with carpenter Louis Ah Mouy, who was in Melbourne engaged in construction when the Victorian rush started, woodworkers went to the goldfields with other migrants.[66] They stabilised mining shafts with wooden beams, built and maintained mining equipment, erected structures in mining camps and made wooden boxes in which to transport gold.[67] Chinese woodworkers on the diggings also made furniture for use in Chinese camps and for non-Chinese consumers, such as a chair gifted to a pastoralist near Camperdown, Victoria, during the gold rushes, now held in the Art Gallery of South Australia.[68] Goldfield woodworkers were inspired by the text *Lu Ban Jing*. That is clear in this particular chair, which bears hallmarks of both the 'official chair' (牙轎 *ya jiao* [lit. 'tooth chair']) and the 'meditation chair' (禪轎 *chan jiao*) in the treatise.[69] It is also evident in certain other

---

65 Ah Toy Testimony, 10 September 1891, *Report of the Royal Commission on Alleged Chinese Gambling and Immorality and Charges of Bribery against Members of the Police Force* (*NSWRC*) (Sydney: Government Printer, 1892), 37; 'Ah Toy', *Evening News*, 26 March 1878.
66 Yong, 'Louis Ah Mouy'.
67 Jack, 'Some Less Familiar Aspects of the Chinese in 19th-Century Australia', 47.
68 'Chinese cabinet-maker, Victoria, Australia, Armchair, c. 1870', Art Gallery of South Australia, 898F11A, accessed 1 September 2018, http://www.artgallery.sa.gov.au/agsa/home/Collection/detail.jsp?accNo=898F11A.

objects, like the gold-rush wheelbarrow identified by historian Juanita Kwok in the New South Wales mining town of Hill End.[70] That these designs were used suggests that a number of goldfield woodworkers were experts, having studied this traditional woodworkers' manual.[71] It is also highly likely that they passed knowledge on to others on the goldfields. Skill in woodwork was widespread, too, among non-Chinese miners in Australia and elsewhere.[72]

Chinese migrants were met with anti-Chinese sentiment on the Australian goldfields. Historian Barry McGowan in particular has shown that while it did not define their activities, Chinese migrants were the targets of violence. Riots at Buckland River in Victoria in 1857 and Lambing Flat in New South Wales over 1860–61 resulted in injury for many, and death for some, at the hands of thugs.[73] Incidents such as these were closely associated with the institution of racist legislation intended to limit Chinese migration to the colonies. In 1855, Victoria enacted such laws, as did South Australia in 1857 and New South Wales in 1861.[74] Similar developments were seen across the Pacific, but

---

69 'Sedan chair for official use' and 'Meditation chair', *Lu Ban Jing*, II 30, II 40, in Ruitenbeek, *Carpentry and Building in Late Imperial China*, 224. 'Tooth' (牙 ya) is a homonym of 'official' (衙 ya).
70 'Chinese Bag Cart', History Hill Museum Collection, Hill End, New South Wales, photograph courtesy of Juanita Kwok, 15 August 2015; 'Wheelbarrow', *Lu Ban Jing*, II 90, in Ruitenbeek, *Carpentry and Building in Late Imperial China*, 275. Refer also to Wing-Fai Wong, 'The significance of Lu Ban Jing, the carpenter's and builder's geomancy manual, in Chinese Australian heritage conservation', paper presented at Dragon Tails, the Fourth Australasian Conference on Overseas Chinese History and Heritage, Cairns Sheridan Hotel, 2–5 July 2015.
71 Wang has argued the same of Hakka miners in West Borneo. See Tai Peng Wang, *The Origins of the Chinese Kongsi*, (Selangor: Pelanduk Publications, 1994), 47–53.
72 Ralph Birrell, 'The Development of Mining Technology in Australia 1801–1945' (PhD Thesis: University of Melbourne, 2005), 35–64.
73 David Kent, 'Small Businessmen and their Credit Transactions in Early Nineteenth-Century Britain', *Business History*, 36:2 (1994), 47–64.

violence was most pronounced in California, where Chinese migrants could not expect to be protected under criminal law, unlike those in the British colonies of Australia, Canada and New Zealand.[75]

As the gold fever of the 1850s and early 1860s abated, Chinese migrants started returning to China, but some remained and moved from gold mining and related activities into other, mostly agricultural, pursuits. Rural towns and major cities alike became sites of Chinese market gardens from the 1860s onwards. Over 1000 market gardeners operated in Australia by 1871.[76] Clearing land for pastoralists was another pursuit, occurring mostly in New South Wales.[77] Chinese migrants also became involved in tobacco and banana growing, working on vineyards and shearing sheep.[78] In the 1870s, after the short-lived Palmer River gold rush in Queensland, Chinese migrants began growing sugar in the Cairns area as well.[79] Woodwork expertise was useful in a number of post-rush agricultural pursuits, into which goldfield woodworkers were most likely recruited. Following the gold rushes elsewhere around the Pacific Rim, Chinese migrants who remained in their migration destinations entered similar industries.[80] A special case, explored by historian Sue Fawn Chung in the United

---

74   Barry McGowan, 'Reconsidering Race: The Chinese experience on the goldfields of southern New South Wales', *Australian Historical Studies*, 36:124 (2004), 312–331.
75   Joseph Lee, 'Anti-Chinese Legislation in Australasia', *Quarterly Journal of Economics*, 3:2 (1889), 218.
76   Sun Sing Loong Testimony, 11 December 1891, NSWRC, 388–389.
77   *Census of Victoria, 1871*, 106.
78   Barry McGowan, 'Ringbarkers and Market Gardeners: A Comparison of the Rural Chinese of New South Wales and California', *Chinese America: History and Perspectives*, 19 (2006), 31–46.
79   Michael Williams, *Chinese Settlement in NSW: A Thematic History* (Sydney: Heritage Office of New South Wales, 1999), 41–44; Rod Lancashire, 'Blanche Street, Wahgunyah: A Pre-Federation Australian Chinese Community on the Border', in Sophie Couchman, John Fitzgerald and Paul Macgregor, eds., *After the Rush: Regulation, Participation and Chinese Communities in Australia, 1860–1940* (Fitzroy: Otherland Literary Journal, 2004), 191–202.

States, was the timber industry. Chinese migrants harvested and processed timber, much of which was used in railway construction, on a vast scale across America's western states.[81] The same was not seen in Australia, most likely because of its markedly smaller timber industry, rail networks and Chinese population.[82]

Chinese migrants from goldfield areas also established furniture factories in Australian cities in the post-rush years.[83] Some became well known during the late 1860s, such as those operated by Kem Wah in Melbourne and Loon Cheong and Co. in Sydney, which won prizes in trade exhibitions.[84] Migrants from most Pearl River Delta counties entered the furniture industry. As manufacturer Yuen Tah explained, by 1891 Sydney's furniture sector included Chang Sing (增邑 Zengcheng/yi), Toon Goon (東莞 Dongguan), Heung Shan (香山 Xiangshan), See Yip (四邑 Siyi) and Sam Yip (三邑 Sanyi) migrants.[85] Yet, Chinese furniture makers remained few in the 1860s. Fifty people made up Melbourne's Chinese sector in 1871, and this was roughly the same case in Sydney.[86] Across the Pacific, Chinese migrants also

---

80 Cathie May, *Topsawyers: The Chinese in Cairns, 1870 to 1920* (Townsville: James Cook University Press, 1984), 42–48.
81 Cecilia Tsu, *Garden of the World: Asian Immigrants and the Making of Agriculture in California's Santa Clara Valley* (New York: Oxford University Press, 2013), 15–52; Adam McKeown, *Chinese Migrant Networks and Cultural Change: Peru, Chicago, Hawai'i, 1900–1936* (Chicago: Chicago University Press, 2001).
82 Sue Fawn Chung, *Chinese in the Woods: Logging and Lumbering in the American West* (Chicago: University of Illinois Press, 2015). Refer, in addition, to Wen Zhengde, 'Breaking Racial Barriers: Wo Kee Company', *Chinese America: History and Perspectives*, 19 (2006), 13–17.
83 Lay Jong Testimony, 393.
84 A small number also began work in rural locales, but they are not covered here. On Chinese factories in the former gold-rush town of Bendigo, for instance, see Amanda Rasmussen, 'The Chinese in Nation and Community Bendigo 1870s–1920s' (PhD Thesis: La Trobe University, 2009), 103–105.
85 Fahy, Simpson and Simpson, *Nineteenth Century Australian Furniture*, 188.
86 Yuen Tah Testimony, 2 October 1891, *NSWRC*, 119.

1 Industry Beginnings

moved away from the gold diggings and into industrial manufacturing, especially in San Francisco, where a relatively large Chinese community – 12,000 by 1870 – could support a greater diversity of enterprise. There, Chinese migrants became involved in clothing, footwear and cigar production in their hundreds over the 1860s, yet mostly ignored furniture manufacturing.[87]

As Chinese furniture factories opened during the 1860s, there was still strong demand for furniture from Australia's rapidly growing population, although by this time consumers had become increasingly settled, urbanised and discerning.[88] People from all backgrounds moved from the goldfields to live in Sydney and Melbourne in particular. Simultaneously, migrants travelled from overseas, primarily Britain, to settle in Australia's cities and towns. The population rose to 1,700,000 over the 1860s.[89] As Linge has noted, tens of thousands of residences, along with a commensurate number of new schools, hotels, offices and churches, were built throughout the colonies.[90] All these new buildings required furniture. However, while consumers might have accepted mass-produced British and American imports at the peak of the rushes, many saw this as inconsistent with long-term settlement in Australia. They demanded a degree of quality better suited to their permanent homes and premises.[91] Furniture production

---

87 *Census of Victoria, 1861*, 13; *Census of Victoria, 1871*, 106; *Sands Commercial Directory 1865*, 337–338; *Sands Commercial Directory 1870*, 460.
88 Ye Hing Testimony, 18. See also Return of Premises Occupied by Chinese within the City of Sydney, *NSWRC*, 487–493; War Lee Testimony, 23; Joe Sing Testimony, 63; Leun Chong Testimony, 30.
89 Simon Ville, 'Colonial Enterprise', Simon Ville and Glenn Withers, eds., *The Cambridge Economic History of Australia* (Melbourne: Cambridge University Press, 2015), 207.
90 *Australian Historical Population Statistics, Population by sex, state and territories, 31 December, 1788 onwards*, Australian Bureau of Statistics, cat. no. 3105.0.65.001, accessed 1 July 2018, http://www.abs.gov.au/ausstats/abs@.nsf/INotes/3105.0.65.0012008Data%20Cubes?opendocument&T.
91 Linge, *Industrial Awakening*, 212, 417.

among European Australians advanced rapidly during the 1860s. Melbourne's industry doubled from 400 to 800 participants.[92] Yet, manufacturers could not produce enough of the furniture required.[93]

Chinese furniture industry entrants of the 1860s worked to help satisfy the demand. They were guided sometimes by skills acquired in China and used initially on the diggings, sometimes by skills learned on the goldfields, and occasionally by non-Chinese consultants.[94] It is also likely that the furniture industry entrants of the 1860s learned of opportunities there from the pre-gold rush Chinese woodworkers and their descendants. Anti-Chinese sentiment, magnified by gold-rush violence and racialised legislation, probably contributed to migrants feeling the need to band together in this industry for mutual support as well. Nevertheless, this cannot explain why the furniture industry was selected in Australia and eschewed in North America, where circumstances were similar. The underdeveloped state of Australia's furniture industry compared with that on the East Coast of the United States, a net exporter, was the principal reason for the choice.[95]

There was a marked expansion of Chinese Australian furniture production in the 1870s, primarily in Sydney. The Chinese sector there grew to some 350 people by 1878.[96] Many of these furniture makers

---

92 This was also due to a move towards more extravagance in mid-Victorian British furniture styles, largely a reaction against mass-produced articles. See Macdonald-Taylor, *English Furniture from the Middle Ages to Modern Times*, 41–44.
93 *Census of Victoria, 1861*, 16; *Census of Victoria, 1871*, 15. See also 'Colonial Furniture Trade', *Age*, 4 August 1862; 'The Melbourne Furniture Trade', *Age*, 27 August 1862; 'The Condition of Labour', *Argus*, 28 November 1863.
94 *NSW FSA Report 1897–1930*; *VIC FSA Report 1897–1930*.
95 Andrew Markus, 'Divided We Fall: The Chinese and the Melbourne Furniture Trade Union, 1870–1900', *Labour History*, 26 (1974), 1.
96 Ah Yet Schedule, 14; Ack Chow Schedule, 29 August 1883, Ack Chow Insolvency File, 132; Wat A. Che Schedule, 22 November 1883, Kum Leong Insolvency File, NSWSR 13654-2/10028-18374, 54; Quong Lee Schedule, 142; Sue Gay Statement, 12.

1 Industry Beginnings

were former gold-rush participants, including 'old friends' Lee Fee, Ack Chow, Ah Hing and Lee Kum, and Australian-born descendants of such migrants. Melbourne's Chinese furniture sector expanded only slightly, and there remained few or no Chinese factories elsewhere.[97]

From the 1870s, progressively more ostentatious Australian homes increased the demand for premium furniture. The dramatic spike in economic activity that followed the first gold rushes evolved into more consistent, long-term economic development. Consequently, householders, as well as being more settled, urbanised and discerning than at the height of the gold rushes, became more concerned with extravagant displays of prosperity. One of their main interests, in addition to more sophisticated buildings, became, as Linge put it, 'increasingly ornate displays of furniture'.[98] Furniture manufacturers in Australia, however, although their numbers increased further in the 1870s, could still not meet the demand. A limitation of the Australian furniture industry became apparent to observers in this period. While the call for premium furniture from a population that had reached 2,230,000 by 1880 was considerable, this consumer base was not wide enough to justify an extensive rollout of machinery as in Britain and the United States.[99] Handwork prevailed, and, as was seen in previous decades, less attractive imports continued to make up for deficits in domestic output, and many manufacturers were occupied with assembling and repairing imported furniture components.[100]

---

97 'Chinese Increase', *Newcastle Morning Herald and Miners' Advocate*, 18 November 1878.
98 'New Furniture Factory', *Age*, 8 August 1874; Victorian Factory Registration Notices, 1897–1930.
99 Linge, *Industrial Awakening*, 418. See also Lionel Frost, 'Urbanisation', Simon Ville and Glenn Withers, eds., *The Cambridge Economic History of Australia* (Melbourne: Cambridge University Press, 2015), 250. English furniture of the late-Victorian era was also typified by extravagance. See Joy, *The Country Life Book of English Furniture*, 79–86; Macdonald-Taylor, *English Furniture from the Middle Ages to Modern Times*, 44–46.

Chinese furniture factories that opened in the 1870s did so largely in answer to the evolving economic situation. They sought to provide discerning customers alternatives to cheap imports and, to some degree, other, overly expensive domestic items. New Chinese manufacturers and factory workers of this period were probably also influenced by their woodwork experience, advice from earlier industry entrants and anti-Chinese sentiment, which re-emerged in force during the 1870s owing to fears of Chinese 'cheap labour'.[101] Another factor informing Chinese involvement in the furniture industry in this period, described by Bon-Wai Chou, was the low levels of capital investment that it required. Handwork prevailed, so costly technology and the financial constraints that it would have placed on migrants were not pressing concerns.[102]

Post-rush specialists

In the late 1860s, the disruption from the Opium Wars in China subsided and, as part of a broad push to match European industrial powers on their own terms, a new generation of Chinese manufacturers and industrial workers emerged. Qing authorities encouraged the establishment of large, mechanised manufacturing concerns, including

---

100 Fahy, Simpson and Simpson, *Nineteenth Century Australian Furniture*, 71. See further Diane Hutchinson, 'Manufacturing', in Simon Ville and Glenn Withers, Eds., *The Cambridge Economic History of Australia* (Melbourne: Cambridge University Press, 2015), 287–308; *Australian Historical Population Statistics, Population by sex, state and territories, 31 December, 1788 onwards*, Australian Bureau of Statistics, cat. no. 3105.0.65.001, accessed 1 July 2018, http://www.abs.gov.au/ausstats/abs@.nsf/INotes/ 3105.0.65.0012008Data%20Cubes?opendocument&T.
101 A few Chinese manufacturers had insurance, with non-Chinese insurance companies. See Yuen Gar Ledger, 1 October 1912 to 24 August 1914, Yuen Gar Bankruptcy File, 12–17; Lim Juen Statement, 49–51.
102 Phil Griffiths, '"This is a British Colony": The Ruling-Class Politics of the Seafarers' Strike, 1878–79', *Labour History*, 105 (2013), 131–152.

around Guangdong. Foreign capital, chiefly British, provided a critical stimulus.[103] Chinese industrial ambitions, however, went unrealised in this period. Yet, as historians like Xiong Yuezhi have described, novel approaches to industrial manufacturing in China from the 1860s marked the next stage in its development and sparked an enthusiasm for industrialism.[104] Such enterprise among Chinese overseas migrants, including in the furniture industries of Penang and Singapore – and in the other Californian industries mentioned, as well as in Canadian salmon canning – also increased.[105]

Even though China's economic and political circumstances improved markedly, migrating abroad was still deemed worthwhile by many. Migration from Guangdong to Australia and other locations for post-rush economic activities replaced gold-rush migration. Restrictions on the numbers of Chinese migrants travelling to Victoria and New South Wales were repealed in 1865 and 1867 respectively.[106] The freedom allowed arrivals from overseas to join those who had moved out of gold mining and into alternative occupations during the 1860s and 1870s. More than 20,000 Chinese people travelled to Australia over the period from 1872 to 1881: a mixture of new and returning migrants. The total Chinese population rose from close to 30,000 in 1871 to almost 40,000 in 1881.[107] Post-rush migration like

---

103 *Sands & McDougall's Directory 1870–1930*; Victorian Factory Registration Notices, 1897–1930,
104 Du Xuncheng (杜恂诚), *Minzu zibenzhuyi yu jiu Zhongguo zhengfu, 1840-1937* [National capitalism and the old Chinese government, 1840–1937] (Shanghai: Shanghai Academy of Social Sciences Press, 1991); David Pong, 'Government Enterprises & Industrial Relations in Late Qing China', *Australian Journal of Politics and History*, 47:1 (2001), 4–23.
105 Xiong Yuezhi, *Eastward Dissemination of Western Learning in the Late Qing Dynasty* (Singapore: Enrich Professional Publishing, 2013), 111–150.
106 Diane Hutchinson, 'Manufacturing', in Simon Ville and Glenn Withers, eds., *The Cambridge Economic History of Australia* (Melbourne: Cambridge University Press, 2015), 290; Linge, *Industrial Awakening*, 11–18.
107 Lee, 'Anti-Chinese Legislation in Australasia', 219–220.

this occurred around the Pacific Rim. However, California remained the most popular destination, having had the largest Chinese communities with the broadest scope of economic activity.[108] San Francisco alone was home to some 30,000 Chinese people by 1879.[109]

Among the new Chinese migrants to Australia were those who travelled specifically to participate in furniture manufacturing. These consisted, firstly, of entrepreneurs who set up and ran furniture factories. Two such entrepreneurs were Tack Lee and Yee Lee (義利 Yi Li), who migrated to Sydney in 1876 and 1878 respectively and established a factory together in 1878.[110] The new industry entrants consisted of workers as well. Sun Sing Loong was one, arriving in Sydney in 1878 to work at Ah Toy's factory in Sydney.[111] In certain situations, migrants went to work in factories, and then became proprietors. Lay Jong (鹿童 Lu Tong) and his three brothers, for instance, as Lay Jong explained, 'came out' to Australia in 1876, 'worked three years for wages' in factories, then became 'employers' themselves in 1880.[112] These arrivals, in addition to Chinese former gold seekers, contributed to the expansion of Chinese Australian furniture manufacturing during the 1870s. Statistics do not indicate the percentages of these different industry entrants, nor whether new migrant entrants went to Australia directly from China or first participated in furniture production in South-East Asia. The latter is

---

108 Choi Chingyan, *Chinese Migration and Settlement in Australia* (Sydney: Sydney University Press, 1975), 22.
109 Henry Yu, 'Mountains of Gold: Canada, North America and the Cantonese Pacific', in Tan Chee-Beng, ed., *Routledge Handbook of the Chinese Diaspora* (London: Routledge, 2013), 108–121.
110 Leckey, 'Low, Degraded Broots?', 325.
111 Tack Lee Testimony, 18 November 1890, Tack Lee Bankruptcy File, NSWSR, 13655-10/22672-02959, 19; Yee Lee Testimony, 11 April 1892, Yee Lee Bankruptcy File, NSWSR, 13655-10/22771-4833, 304. See also Wong Sum Ling Testimony, 3 May 1889, Wong Sum Ling Bankruptcy File, NSWSR 13655-10/22559-1039, 24.
112 Sun Sing Loong Testimony, 11 December 1891, *NSWRC*, 389–390.

possible, as shown by the experience of Louis Ah Mouy, who arrived in Victoria as a carpenter from Penang before the gold rushes.

Industry specialists migrated to Australia amid demand for increasingly extravagant articles of furniture. The production of such articles required complex skill sets, which are unlikely to have been available among former gold seekers to the level required in Chinese Australian furniture production on the scale seen from the 1870s.[113] This was despite factories having been able to draw on the experience of Chinese goldfield woodworkers and non-Chinese experts. Chinese specialists came from overseas in response to this situation. Some factory proprietors had been personally involved in, or were at least eyewitnesses to, China's drive for industrialisation. Some factory employees, Sun Sing Loong for example, had completed furniture making apprenticeships in China.[114] These specialists drew on industry knowledge to answer Australia's demand for premium-quality furniture. Specialists could have been encouraged to enter the industry by some of the same factors as Chinese former gold seekers as well. Even so, they are likely to have been influenced more by backgrounds and aspirations in furniture production specifically.

Conclusion

A confluence of factors led to the inception of Chinese Australian furniture production. Chinese woodworkers of the early nineteenth century appear to have entered the Australian furniture industry with reference to a rich tradition of Chinese woodwork and events in China

---

113 Fitzgerald, *Red Tape Gold Scissors*, 154–157.
114 This need was probably exacerbated by the heavier emphasis on finely crafted furniture during this period stemming from the Arts and Crafts Movement in Britain. See Joy, *The Country Life Book of English Furniture*, 79–86; Macdonald-Taylor, *English Furniture from the Middle Ages to Modern Times*, 44–46.

(and Asia more broadly) that encouraged overseas migration. Skills shortages and demand in Australia for good-quality and inexpensive furniture also seem to have informed these early experts. The next group of Chinese furniture industry entrants from the 1860s were guided by the same tradition, along with events in China stemming from the Opium Wars that rendered overseas migration more attractive and accessible. The main Australian gold rushes of the 1850s and early 1860s, which lured many thousands of Chinese migrants in search of wealth, also created openings in the furniture industry. There was a post-rush construction boom and strong demand for considerable quantities of increasingly ornate furniture. Advice offered by established manufacturers and the modest outlays necessary for industry entry probably influenced Chinese furniture makers to begin work at this time as well, and discrimination closed other avenues of opportunity to them. Chinese migrants who migrated to Australia over the 1870s and became involved in furniture production directly were motivated to a greater extent by specific industry expertise and ambition than those from the goldfields.

Among the reasons that Chinese migrants took an interest in Australia's furniture industry, economic development within Australia was key. Migrants' and their descendants' choices to participate in this particular economic activity reveal that they were mostly responding to opportunities afforded by economic expansion and consumerism in their migration destination.

2
Setting Up Shop

In March 1885, Yee Wye established a furniture manufacturing operation in Melbourne. Although he had 'cousins' or 'blood relations', as he called them, living in Australia – Weng Hap, Quong Lee and Yen Leung – they did not take part. The business was his own. He had a modest sum of cash to invest, his personal savings of 'a few pounds'. 'I worked … made a little money and then started for myself', he explained regarding his financing.[1] Yee Wye leased a factory site, just off Little Bourke Street in Chinatown, from a non-Chinese landlord. The premises were substantial, at a rent of £14 every month, large enough for at least fifteen men to work, eat their meals and sleep, and room to store vast amounts of timber, other materials and finished furniture. Yee Wye also owned a 'plant', that is, a steam boiler and machinery. This and most of his manufacturing supplies he bought from non-Chinese businesspeople near the factory. Because he only had 'a little money', he depended largely on trade credit. By 1889, he was more than £2000 in debt.[2]

---

1 Yee Wye Testimony, 8 July 1889, Yee Wye Insolvency File, Public Record Office of Victoria (PROV) 762/P/0-335-5786, 6–14.
2 Yee Wye Schedule, 13 May 1889, Yee Wye Insolvency File, 27–37.

This chapter addresses how Chinese furniture manufacturers like Yee Wye set up furniture factories in Sydney and Melbourne. It begins with how proprietorship was organised, and how manufacturers raised finance. It then turns to the actual sites of production: the physical spaces of furniture factories. The chapter then explores the tools and machines used in factories, and the materials and other supplies needed. We will see here that manufacturers drew on imported cultural resources to organise their operations, but also used the methods of Australian industry more broadly, usually in concert with non-Chinese Australians.

Proprietorship

Sole trading was the most common form of proprietorship in Chinese Australian furniture manufacturing. Yee Wye was a sole trader, even though his 'cousins' in Australia could have helped him. Sing Lee, who had a factory in Sydney in the 1880s, was another operator who started business by himself. 'I am not nor was I ever in partnership with any person whomsoever', he declared on an affidavit in 1888. Like Yee Wye, Sing Lee had relatives in Australia. Two of his brothers had also migrated to Sydney, and one of these, Sing War, was working at a rival factory.[3] Yee Wye and Sing Lee were facing bankruptcy when they described trading alone, so it is possible that they were lying to protect partners, yet this is unlikely. Numerous other Chinese furniture manufacturers described owning businesses independently, and not only in court.[4] Such arrangements were not without precedent in

---

3   Sing Lee Affidavit, 5 May 1888, Sing Lee Bankruptcy File, New South Wales State Records (NSWSR) 13655-10/2250-00112, 6.
4   See, for instance, Victorian Factory Registration Notices, 1897–1930, PROV 1399/P/0-1-4; Victorian Register of Firms, 1893–1926, PROV 12342; New South Wales Register of Firms, 1903–1922, NSWSR 12961.

2 Setting Up Shop

southern China. The extended family was the traditional industrial unit in the Ming and Qing Dynasties, but there were always exceptions to this broad trend, as historians Xu Dixin and Wu Chengming have discussed.[5] Sole trading, especially in market gardening, retailing and food service, was also seen in other 'Cantonese Pacific' migration destinations, according to historian Henry Yu.[6] Such operators were usual in the European Australian furniture sector as well.[7] In fact, sole trading was the standard form of proprietorship in Australian manufacturing in the late nineteenth century, a defining feature of Australia's early industrialisation discussed by historian Simon Ville.[8] This standard started to change from the early twentieth century owing to the proliferation of companies with extensive financial resources, referred to collectively as 'big business' by historian David Merrett.[9] However, the same pattern was not seen within the Chinese furniture sector. As Fitzgerald has noted, Chinese Australian 'big business' generally invested offshore, so the prevalence of sole trading in the sector remained constant.[10]

---

5   Xu Dixin and Wu Chengming, *Chinese Capitalism, 1522–1840* (London: Palgrave Macmillan, 2000), 14–16, 378–379. On the Cantonese furniture industry specifically, refer to Xue Yongjun (薛拥军), 'Guangshi mudiao yishu jiqi zai jianzhu he shinei zhuangshi zhong de yingyong yanjiu' [Cantonese-style woodcarving craft and its architecture centring on applied research in interior decoration] (PhD Thesis: Nanjing Forestry University, 2012), 37–39.
6   Henry Yu, 'Unbound Space: Migration, Aspiration, and the Making of Time in the Cantonese Pacific', in Warwick Anderson, Miranda Johnson and Barbara Brookes, eds., *Pacific Futures: Past and Present* (Honolulu: University of Hawai'i Press, 2018), 186–190.
7   Victorian Factory Registration Notices, 1897–1930; Victorian Register of Firms, 1893–1926; New South Wales Register of Firms, 1903–1922.
8   Simon Ville, 'Colonial Enterprise', in Simon Ville and Glenn Withers, eds., *The Cambridge Economic History of Australia* (Melbourne: Cambridge University Press, 2015), 218.
9   David Merrett, 'Big Business and Foreign Firms', in Simon Ville and Glenn Withers, eds., *The Cambridge Economic History of Australia* (Melbourne: Cambridge University Press, 2015), 309–329.

Most sole traders took direct responsibility for their factories. This was the case with Yee Wye and Sing Lee, and Charles Lum who operated a factory in Sydney during the 1910s. 'I always looked after the business myself', Lum said in court in 1914 of his hands-on style.[11] Owner-operators were former furniture factory employees in the vast majority of cases, which may explain their preference for direct involvement in the day-to-day operations. According to Charles Fahey and André Sammartino, the average industrialist operating in late nineteenth century Melbourne 'emerged from the factory floor as a skilled tradesman', and often assumed personal control of their businesses.[12] A few sole traders hired managers to take charge of their factories for them. 'I don't work in the carpentering shop at all', testified Woo Lung in Sydney in 1873 of his decision to delegate all tasks to his manager.[13]

In addition to sole traders, small partnerships of friends were widespread. Loon Cheong and Co. in Sydney consisted of three friends from 1879: Lee Fee, Ack Chow and Cheung Yen. Ack Chow stated on an affidavit in 1883 that Lee Fee had been 'a partner and personal friend of mine for a long time'.[14] Another such partnership was that comprising Tin Yow (陳天佑 Chen Tianyou), Leong Tong and Low Wing in the

---

10 John Fitzgerald, *Big White Lie: Chinese Australians in White Australia* (Sydney: University of New South Wales Press, 2007), 179.
11 Charles Lum Testimony, 26 October 1914, Charles Lum Bankruptcy File, NSWSR 13655-10/23741-20077, 122. See further Wong Sum Ling Testimony, 3 May 1889, Wong Sum Ling Bankruptcy File, NSWSR 13655-10/22559-1039, 23–24; Ah Chee Schedule, 19 January 1891, Ah Chee Insolvency File, PROV 765/P/0-12-90/140, 9; Shung Yem Testimony, 9 February 1903, Shung Yem Insolvency File, PROV 766/P/0-36-819, 55.
12 Charles Fahey and André Sammartino, 'Work and Wages at a Melbourne Factory, The Guest Biscuit Works 1870–1921', *Australian Economic History Review*, 53:1 (2013), 27; Ville, 'Colonial Enterprise', 218.
13 Woo Lung Testimony, 23 May 1873, Woo Lung Insolvency File, NSWSR 13654-2/9488-11460, 65.
14 Ack Chow Affidavit, 26 April 1883, Ack Chow Insolvency File, NSWSR 13654-2/9993-17928, 3.

2 Setting Up Shop

Sun Tong War and Co. factory in Sydney.[15] 'We are good friends', testified Low Wing of his partners in 1901.[16] These partnerships, however, in spite of the warm feelings expressed by members towards each other, were regularly reinforced using written agreements. A detailed contract was drawn up by the members of Loon Cheong and Co. in 1879. This proved useful in Ack Chow's defence when Lee Fee absconded to Hawai'i after stealing all the factory's money (apparently in collaboration with Cheung Yen), leaving Ack Chow to face their creditors alone.[17] As well as having been formalised through contracts like this, such partnerships were often registered under Australian colonial and state firm law.[18] These arrangements illustrate how implicit bonds of trust, frequently attributed to Chinese businesses in China and abroad, were not always seen as sturdy enough foundations for the formation of firms.[19] Non-Chinese furniture manufacturers created similar partnerships in Sydney and Melbourne, especially prior to the

---

15   Leong Tong Testimony, 14 October 1901, Tin Yow and Low Wing Bankruptcy File, NSWSR 13655-10/23338-14814, 58. See also Man Sing Testimony, 23 March 1891, Man Sing Bankruptcy File, NSWSR 13655-10/22675-3020, 68; Yee Lee Testimony, 11 April 1892, Yee Lee Bankruptcy File, NSWSR 13655-10/22771-4833, 304; Low Lum and Leong Dong Affidavit, 17 March 1893, Leong Dong Bankruptcy File, NSWSR 13655-10/22844-6266, 28; Lee Gow and Man Hing Affidavit, 13 January 1902, Lee Gow Insolvency File, PROV 765/P/0-321-90/3865, 5-7; Leun Chong Testimony, 10 November 1925, Leun Ah Chong Bankruptcy File, NSWSR 13655-10/24188-25180, 28.
16   Low Wing Testimony, 3 November 1901, Tin Yow and Low Wing Bankruptcy File, 73.
17   Ack Chow Affidavit, 3.
18   Victorian Register of Firms, 1893-1926; New South Wales Register of Firms, 1903-1922.
19   Fitzgerald, *Big White Lie*, 65; Faure, 'Beyond Networking', 31; Ching-hwang Yen, *Ethnic Chinese Business in Asia: History, Culture and Business Enterprise* (Singapore: World Scientific, 2013), 135-172; Jungying Jia, 'The evolution of the *qiaopi* trade: a case study of the Tianyi firm', in Gregor Benton, Hong Liu and Huimei Zhang, eds., *The Qiaopi Trade and Transnational Networks in the Chinese Diaspora* (London: Routledge, 2018), 115.

entry of 'big business' into their industry. Many also sought to cement their partnerships in writing.[20]

Larger, less tight-knit teams existed in the Chinese furniture sector as well. In Sydney in the 1910s, the Sun Kwong Loong and Co. factory involved nine friends and associates, Yew Gwong (耀光 Yao Guang), Jan Way (威象 Wei Xiang), Jan Chick (贊澈 Zan Che), George Foy, Waig Young, Lee Chun, Gen Bong, Lew Di and Jip Tin (洽典 Qia Dian).[21] Partnerships of this size were unique to the Chinese furniture sector. Most other partnerships were either smaller or became corporate entities with much larger numbers of shareholders. Corporations were all but non-existent among Chinese Australian furniture manufacturers.[22] Even so, such partnerships appear not to have been large worker cooperatives like those noted by Mae Ngai on the goldfields of Victoria and California.[23]

Besides friendship, partners came together on the basis of complementary skill sets. Tin Yow of Sun Tung War and Co. said in court in 1901 that he was 'overseer over the men' and that he also needed to 'look after the banking'. One of his two partners, Leong

---

20   See, for instance, John Penman Affidavit, 4 May 1896, John Penman Insolvency File, PROV 765/P/0-221-90/2508, 51–53. See further Victorian Register of Firms, 1893–1926; New South Wales Register of Firms, 1903–1922.
21   Partner Testimony, 1915, Jan Way Bankruptcy File, NSWSR 13655-10/23778-20439, 98–180. See further Joe Sing Testimony [re Joe Sing, Hor Poi, Wing Ching, Git Song, Moo Din, Ah Ling and You Shoung], 17 November 1914, Joe Sing Hong Bankruptcy File, NSWSR 13655-10/23741-20068, 59–60; Partner Testimony [re Harry Yuen Gar, Low Chan, Rose Choy York, Yip See and Chew Tar], 1916, Harry Yuen Gar Bankruptcy File, NSWSR 13655-10/23807-20778, 1–11. Consult also Victorian Register of Firms, 1893–1926; New South Wales Register of Firms, 1903–1922.
22   Documents lodged under Companies Acts, NSWSR 12951; Register of Miscellaneous Companies, 1853–1959, PROV 8279.
23   Mai M. Ngai, 'Chinese Gold Miners and the "Chinese Question"', in Nineteenth-Century California and Victoria', *Journal of American History*, 101:4 (2015), 1091–1092.

Tong, handled 'the outside work' of buying and selling goods, and his other partner, Low Wing, acted as a 'bookkeeper and general hand'.[24] The members of Sun Kwong Loong and Co. were also a mix of woodworkers, administrators and merchants with commercial expertise, and most had a personal role in the operation of the factory.[25] The same was seen throughout Australian industrial manufacturing. Diverse industrial technologies and business approaches necessitated disparate expertise, and increasingly so over time.[26]

Native place connections informed Chinese partnerships as well, though operators tended not to mention their places of origin on record, presumably because they assumed these to be irrelevant to audiences in courtrooms and other public forums. Several of the Sun Kwong Loong and Co. partners were migrants from Xiangshan (香山), now Zhongshan (中山) – in the Pearl River Delta of Guangdong. Having a common place of origin was vital, alongside partners' complementary skill sets, for this firm's proprietorship arrangements.[27] Historian Mei-fen Kuo has noted how most Chinese firms in Australia were organised thusly, particularly during the nineteenth century, although they became far more flexible over time.[28] It was unusual, nevertheless, for there to be European partners in Chinese furniture factories and vice versa. In 1925, the Yon Brothers and Co. furniture factory in Melbourne had a European partner, Ernest Blanchfield, but there were few other cases.[29]

---

24 Tin Yow Testimony, 14 October 1901, Tin Yow and Low Wing Bankruptcy File, 51.
25 Partner Testimony, Jan Way Bankruptcy File, 98–180. See also Joe Sing Testimony, 59–60.
26 Fahey and Sammartino, 'Work and Wages at a Melbourne Factory', 41–42.
27 Lee Chun Testimony, 10 August 1915, Jan Way Bankruptcy File, 103–105.
28 Mei-fen Kuo, *Making Chinese Australia: Urban Elites, Newspapers and the Formation of Chinese-Australian Identity, 1892–1912* (Clayton: Monash University Publishing, 2013), 17–51.

There were also family industrial concerns, owned and operated by family members. One was Go Bo Brothers in Sydney, presided over by the four Go brothers. The firm's 1905 registration certificate lists Go Kee, Go Yow, Go Di and Go Song as partners in the venture.[30] Another operation was that of Yon Brothers and Co. in Melbourne during the 1920s. 'Business [was] carried on by my brothers and myself', explained Rupert Yon in 1925.[31] Blanchfield appears to have acted as a silent partner. These family furniture firms perhaps most closely resembled the traditional Chinese industrial outfit mentioned by Xu and Wu.[32] Even so, Chinese family firms in the Australian furniture industry were often also registered under colonial and state firm legislation with all family members listed individually, as seen with Go Bo Brothers. This protected individual interests and it further illustrates how bonds of trust, even within families, were formalised in writing. Non-Chinese family furniture factories, including that of the Solomon brothers in Melbourne, were relatively common as well.[33] Registering individual interest was also usual for them.[34]

---

29   Rupert Yon Testimony, 10 June 1925, Rupert Yon Insolvency File, PROV 766/P/0-186-A4224, 15. See also 'H. L. & S. Simpson and Company Limited', *TWT*, 1 October 1921. Chan King Testimony, 31 March 1913, Willie King Bankruptcy File, NSWSR 13655-10/23691-19488, 66.
30   Go Kee Application for Permission [for Go Chock] to Enter the Commonwealth, 19 January 1911, Go Chock and Chong Ah Wong File, National Archives of Australia (NAA) Sydney SP42/1-C1912/7152, 41.
31   Rupert Yon Testimony, 15.
32   Xu and Wu, *Chinese Capitalism, 1522-1840*, 14-16, 378-379. See further Wellington Chan, 'Personal Styles, Cultural Values and Management: The Sincere and Wing On Companies in Shanghai and Hong Kong, 1900-41', *Business History Review*, 70:2 (1996), 141-166.
33   'New Furniture Factory', *Age*, 8 August 1874; Kevin Fahy and Andrew Simpson, *Australian Furniture: Pictorial History and Dictionary* (Sydney: Casuarina Press, 1998), 18-138.
34   Victorian Register of Firms, 1893-1926; New South Wales Register of Firms, 1903-1922.

2 Setting Up Shop

Most Chinese Australian furniture firms were continually changing their proprietors. 'That partnership has dissolved and my brother is still carrying on that business whilst I am in business on my own account', stated Go Kee, a former partner in Go Bo Brothers, in 1911.[35] Often, operations changed hands due to migrants' return trips to China. War Lee, who ran a factory in Sydney, said in court in 1914 that he had 'started in business with a partner at first, Ah Kee', but had then 'bought out Ah Kee's share' because 'Ah Kee went home to China'.[36] War Lee then became a sole trader. Michael Williams has shown how change was normal in Chinese overseas firms because of constant movement between migration destinations and places of origin in China.[37] Yu has called this a 'recurring cycle of investment and return'.[38] Ethnic European firms were more stable in this regard, a significant point of difference between the two sectors of the Australian furniture industry.[39]

Raising finance

Chinese manufacturers typically had modest sums of cash when setting up furniture factories. Yee Wye personally invested what he referred to as 'a few pounds' in his operation in 1885. 'I can't remember how much', he stated in 1889, but it was unlikely to have far exceeded £200.[40]

---

35 Go Kee Letter to the Minister of External Affairs, 19 January 1911, Go Chock and Chong Ah Wong File, 35.
36 War Lee Testimony, 9 November 1914, Sam War Lee Bankruptcy File, NSWSR 13655-10/23744-20102, 22. See also Harry Kow Testimony, 18 February 1908, Harry Kow Bankruptcy File, NSWSR 13655-10/23541-17604, 45; Yuen Gar Testimony, 18 November 1914, Yuen Gar Bankruptcy File, NSWSR 13655-10/23743-20093, 40; Ernest Quong Testimony, 4 September 1917, Ernest Quong Bankruptcy File, NSWSR 13655-10/23844-21213, 17.
37 Michael Williams, *Returning Home with Glory: Chinese Villagers around the Pacific, 1849–1949* (Hong Kong: Hong Kong University Press, 2018), 98–119.
38 Yu, 'Unbound Space', 187.
39 Fahy and Simpson, *Australian Furniture*, 18–138.
40 Yee Wye Testimony, 10.

This scale of investment was the most common in the Chinese furniture sector.[41] Even the largest partnerships that enabled individuals to pool their resources, including Sydney's Sun Kwong Loong and Co., seldom involved substantially more than this sum, £500 in the case of these nine partners.[42] Only a handful of manufacturers had over £1000, such as Chow Kum (周錦 Zhou Jin) and Ah Garb in Sydney and Sue Gay in Melbourne.[43] Two hundred pounds was a lot for an individual in late nineteenth- and early twentieth-century Australia, enough to buy several fine horses, for instance, but investments like this pale in comparison with those made by some of the foremost European Australian furniture manufacturers.[44] Anthony Hordern and Sons, to take perhaps the clearest example of 'big business' in the furniture industry, erected a new furniture factory in Sydney worth over £15,000 in 1901.[45] Modest investments were viable, nevertheless, since furniture production did not necessitate substantial sums of capital, least of all before the rollout of capital-intensive machinery in the twentieth century.[46] Bon-Wai Chou has contended that this was the most

---

41 Charles Lum Testimony, 4. See also Shung Yem Testimony, 59–60; Sidney Jack Testimony, 18 March 1909, Jack Lem Bankruptcy File, NSWSR 13655-10/23574-17992, 114; Henry Louey Testimony, 15 March 1910, Henry Louey Bankruptcy File, NSWSR 13655-10/23603-18391, 97; Chan King Testimony, 66; Ernest Quong Testimony, 17. Historian Michael T. W. Tsin has argued that Cantonese entrepreneurs in China underreported their assets, although this carried the risk of imprisonment in Australian bankruptcy courts. See Michael T. W. Tsin, *Nation, Governance, and Modernity in China: Canton, 1900–1927* (Stanford: Stanford University Press, 2000), 209.
42 Partner Testimony, Jan Way Bankruptcy File, 98–180.
43 Chow Kum Testimony, 12 December 1891, *Report of the Royal Commission on Alleged Chinese Gambling and Immorality and Charges of Bribery against Members of the Police Force (NSWRC)* (Sydney: Government Printer, 1892), 395; Tung Wai Hee File, 5 May 1920, NAA Sydney A1/1925/22539, 56. I thank Kate Bagnall for this file.
44 On horses, see 'Clearing Sale', *Argus*, 24 January 1887; 'Albury Special Horse Sale', *Argus*, 5 July 1888; 'The Colonial Buggy Trade', *Singleton Argus*, 18 May 1889.
45 'Our Industrial Expansion', *Sydney Morning Herald (SMH)*, 20 August 1903.

appealing aspect of furniture production for Chinese migrants and their families in Australia, as it enabled them to return easily to China, that is, without binding financial commitments.[47] On the other hand, limited capital was the leading complaint made by bankrupt Chinese manufacturers.[48] They were also discouraged from investing larger amounts by anti-Chinese laws, such as the Australia-wide immigration restrictions from 1888 and the *Factories and Shops Acts* in Victoria from 1887 and New South Wales from 1896, to be discussed in Chapter Five.

Furniture manufacturers, many of whom were former factory employees, regularly relied on their own savings for investment. 'I worked … made a little money and then started for myself', said Yee Wye of his capital.[49] 'I saved it up [£54] from my wages when I was working', Lew Di similarly stated of his investment in Sun Kwong Loong and Co.[50] Transitioning from worker to business proprietor with saved wages was a common practice in early European Australian manufacturing, as Fahey and Sammartino have noted.[51] This gradually became less viable, however, owing to the proliferation of large industrial concerns. Yet, because Chinese sole traders were not displaced by large Chinese companies, which avoided the Australian

---

46   Godfrey J. R. Linge, *Industrial Awakening: A Geography of Australian Manufacturing 1788 to 1890* (Canberra: Australian National University Press, 1979), 271. On mechanisation in Sydney furniture factories, see *Report on the Working of the Factories and Shops Act (NSW FSA Report) 1897–1930*.
47   Bon-Wai Chou, 'The sojourning attitude and the economic decline of Chinese society in Victoria, 1860s–1930s', in Paul Macgregor, ed., *Histories of the Chinese in Australasia and the South Pacific* (Melbourne: Museum of Chinese Australian History, 1995), 59–74.
48   Peter Gibson, 'Australia's Bankrupt Chinese Furniture Manufacturers, 1880–1930', *Australian Economic History Review*, 58:1 (2018), 87–91.
49   Yee Wye Testimony, 10.
50   Lew Di Testimony, 127. See also Yuen Gar Testimony, 39; Kwong Song Testimony, 10 November 1925, Leun Ah Chong Bankruptcy File, 30.
51   Fahey and Sammartino, 'Work and Wages at a Melbourne Factory', 27.

furniture industry, this approach to financing remained feasible and widespread in the Chinese sector over time.

Manufacturers often also borrowed cash from small groups of friends and relatives. Henry Louey, who carried on business in Sydney over the 1900s, was one such manufacturer. 'I had £175', he testified in 1910 in relation to his own cash, which he had saved chiefly by working in other furniture factories in Sydney and Melbourne. 'George Louey is my cousin', Henry Louey elaborated, 'I borrowed £150 from him'. 'Wong is a friend of mine', he added, 'I borrowed £75 from him'. 'I borrowed £20 from Leong', Louey concluded of his combined cash total of £420.[52] While this and similar cases amounted to a type of collective financing, which has regularly been understood as a defining feature of Chinese business organisation, these were only ever small groups.[53] They were unlike the large networks used by Australia's Chinese commercial elite to mobilise financing for the 'Four Great Companies' of Shanghai – the Sincere, Wing On, Sun Sun and Sun Company department stores.[54] Friends and relatives who loaned cash also asked for written assurances from time to time, as did George Louey (雷永洪 Lei Yonghong) from Henry Louey.[55] Other manufacturers, too, sought loans from friends and

---

52   Henry Louey Testimony, 97–99.
53   See also Quong Lee Schedule, 28 May 1889, Quong Lee Insolvency File, PROV 762/P/0-338-71/5816, 20; Shung Yem Testimony, 59–60; Wong Ah Leet Schedule, 14 November 1911, Wong Ah Leet Insolvency File, PROV 765/P/0-437-90/5527, 41; Sidney Jack Testimony, 114; Chan King Testimony, 66; Charles Lum Ledger, 12 September 1912 to 17 September 1914, Charles Lum Bankruptcy File, 10–50; Ernest Quong Testimony, 17. Historian Michael Ng has suggested that Chinese 'loans' in Hong Kong bankruptcy cases were often investments disguised as loans in order to exploit British bankruptcy legislation, but there was never any suggestion of this in Australia. See Michael Ng, 'Dirt of whitewashing: re-conceptualising debtors' obligations in Chinese business by transplanting bankruptcy law to early British Hong Kong', *Business History*, 57:8 (2015), 1233.
54   Andrew Godley and Haiming Hang, 'Collective financing among Chinese entrepreneurs and department store retailing in China', *Business History*, 58:3 (2016), 1–14; Fitzgerald, *Big White Lie*, 177–209.

relatives. Yet, they also tended to borrow large sums from banks, unlike their Chinese counterparts.[56] Chinese manufacturers could have been denied the same access to bank capital as a consequence of anti-Chinese sentiment, though they typically maintained bank accounts.[57] Some disliked banks. Henry Louey reported a negative banking experience, theft of £50 by a bank clerk. He said that he became 'afraid after that' to deal with banks.[58] Not taking out bank loans could have also been, as Faure has suggested, one result of the widespread reliance on interpersonal rather than institutional finance in late nineteenth- and early twentieth-century China.[59] Chinese factories did not float shares on the stock market, either, as other factories often did.[60]

Some proprietors raised finance through other business ventures as well. Tin Yow of Sydney's Sun Tong War and Co. had diverse interests on which he drew to help raise his £50 contribution to the factory's £150 total cash investment. 'I go to the markets and buy and sell vegetables in the morning', he stated. 'In the afternoon and evening, I am in a gambling room. I am a croupier in a gambling shop in Wexford Street',

---

55   Henry Louey Bankruptcy File, 51.
56   See, for instance, Charles Servante Schedule, 21 July 1891, Charles Servante Insolvency File, PROV 765/P/0-36-90/399, 19; John Penman Schedule, 4 January 1896, John Penman Insolvency File, 5.
57   Loon Moon Testimony, 30 October 1913, Loon Moon Bankruptcy File, NSWSR 13655-10/23707-19673, 5; Yuen Gar Testimony, 14; Lew Di Testimony, 27 July 1915, Jan Way Bankruptcy File, 126.
58   Henry Louey Testimony, 97. 'Foreign' banks were also depicted as unreliable by Australia's Chinese press. See 'Mujiang xin yi' [Woodworker news], *CAH*, 15 September 1894.
59   David Faure, 'Beyond Networking: An Institutional View of Chinese Business', in Medha Kudaisya and Ng Chin-keong, eds., *Chinese and Indian Business: Historical Antecedents* (Leiden: Brill, 2009), 35. Seung-joon Lee, on the other hand, has argued that Cantonese merchants in Guangzhou were very comfortable with European and American banking services. Seung-joon Lee, *Gourmets in the Land of Famine: The Culture and Politics of Rice in Modern Canton* (Stanford: Stanford University Press, 2011), 50.
60   Documents lodged under Companies Acts, NSWSR 12951; Register of Miscellaneous Companies, 1853–1959, PROV 8279.

he further explained.[61] Mobilising capital via other business pursuits was more common within partnerships than among sole traders, who tended to focus their efforts on the furniture industry.

Trade credit was another means of raising finance for Chinese furniture concerns in Sydney and Melbourne, and the single most crucial means for many. Yon Brothers and Co. in Melbourne is arguably the most striking example of how manufacturers often utilised trade credit. 'I put no cash into the business', pointed out Rupert Yon in 1925. 'Neither did Blanchfield', Yon added regarding his partner.[62] Yet, despite this lack of cash, Yon Brothers and Co. amassed a total debt of close to £4000 over the early 1920s with firms that had offered them trade credit.[63] While other Chinese factories did not normally use it so extensively, and also used other types of financing, nearly all relied heavily on trade credit.[64] This was not specific to Chinese factories, however. Indeed, Chinese furniture manufacturers were participating in a general practice within Australian enterprise of using trade credit to help mitigate uncertainty associated with its vast distances from world financial centres.[65] Even so, Chinese manufacturers may have been more willing to rely on other Chinese businesses in this regard where practical. 'Chinese firms give long credit and the general custom is to make demand from time to time for payment but they are put

---

61 Tin Yow Testimony, 12.
62 Rupert Yon Testimony, 15.
63 Rupert Yon List of Creditors, 7 May 1925, Rupert Yon Insolvency File, 223.
64 Ah Chee Schedule, 9; Sidney Jack Statement, 15 February 1909, Jack Lem Bankruptcy File, 129; Sun Kwong Loong and Co. Statement, 9 August 1915, Jan Way Bankruptcy File, 36–37; Yuen Gar Statement, 28 October 1914, Yuen Gar Bankruptcy File, 44; Joe Sing Statement, 2 October 1914, Joe Sing Hong Bankruptcy File, 68; War Lee Statement, 20 October 1914, Sam War Lee Bankruptcy File, 28; Lim Juen Statement, 6 December 1926, Lim Juen Insolvency File, PROV 10246/P/0-111-15/197049, 112; Sue Gay Statement, 7 July 1927, George Sue Gay Insolvency File, PROV 10246/P/0-124-15/2216, 6–9.
65 Ville, 'Colonial Enterprise', 215–217.

off and they usually accept any sums that are offered', testified Lee Chun, one member of the Sun Kwong Loong and Co. partnership in Sydney, in 1915.[66] This was common among Chinese businesspeople in South-East Asia, as historians such as Carl Trocki and Phillip Kuhn have shown, but less so in China, according to Michael Ng.[67]

A reliance on trade credit often led to instability in Chinese industrial operations stemming from constant pressure to pay off creditors. 'I am pressed by numerous creditors', testified Low Wing in Sydney when he went bankrupt in 1887.[68] Bong Shue in Melbourne also lamented 'pressure of creditors' when he found himself in the same position in 1907.[69] Under pressure to pay creditors, Chinese factories were compelled to sell furniture cheaply, had production materials repossessed and goods confiscated, and were subject to litigation, all of which were detrimental to business.[70] Gambling was also common in Sydney in last-ditch efforts to find cash for creditors, although it was uncommon in Melbourne, most likely because of gambling's stricter treatment in Victorian bankruptcy legislation.[71] None of these varied complications, however, were specific to the Chinese furniture sector. Instability stemming from reliance on trade credit, including that

---

66 Lee Chun Testimony, 10 August 1915, Jan Way Bankruptcy File, 137.
67 Carl Trocki, 'Boundaries and Transgressions: Chinese Enterprise in Eighteenth- and Nineteenth-Century Southeast Asia' [1997], in Hong Liu, ed., *The Chinese Overseas*, V3 (London: Routledge, 2006), 45–68; Philip A. Kuhn, 'Three Cultures of Migration', in Leo Suryadinata, ed., *Migration, Indigenization and Interaction: Chinese Overseas and Globalization* (Singapore: World Scientific, 2014), 43–44; Ng, 'Dirt of whitewashing', 1219–1247.
68 Low Wing Testimony, 31 May 1887, Low Wing Insolvency File, NSWSR 13654-2/10351-22105, 3.
69 Bong Shue Affidavit, 18 October 1907, Bong Shue Insolvency File, PROV 765/P/0-402-90/5084, 6.
70 Yee Lee complained of having to 'make up extra cheap furniture for auction sale' when pressed by creditors. Refer to Yee Lee Affidavit, 15 August 1893, Yee Lee Bankruptcy File, NSWSR 13655-10/22771-4833, 5.
71 *Bankruptcy Act 1887* (NSW), 45–47; *Insolvency Act 1890* (VIC), 140.

associated with gambling, was often noted by ethnic European furniture manufacturers as well.[72] Historian David Kent has also described how a reliance on trade credit often led to instability in nineteenth-century British manufacturing.[73]

Across the sector, remittances and returns to China were often prioritised before capital investment. Yuen Gar (蔡元加 Cai Yuanjia) was one Sydney furniture manufacturer who remitted most of his earnings to his wife, child and extended family members in China, 'two or three pounds at a time', as he said, rather than reinvesting them back into the business.[74] Many manufacturers, including Lay Jong (鹿童 Lu Tong) and his four brothers in Sydney, were also saving money instead of reinvesting it, in order to return to China permanently. 'About £300 or £400 would be enough', he explained to the 1891 Royal Commission in Sydney, for each brother to go back and live there in comfort.[75]

Factory premises

Factory premises varied greatly in size. In 1891, Sun Sing Loong, a long-time factory worker who had just gone into business on his own account, told the Royal Commission in Sydney that his factory was 'a little place in a shed … twenty feet by twelve feet' in the suburb of Waterloo, in the city's south, for himself and an employee.[76] Sun's former boss, Ah Toy, spoke in contrast about his own two-storey

---

72 Alfred Garner and George Boulton Schedule, 2; Alfred Graham Testimony, 3–4; Albert Attwells Testimony, 4–5; 'Gambling', *SMH*, 2 March 1921.
73 David Kent, 'Small Businessmen and their Credit Transactions in Early Nineteenth-Century Britain', *Business History*, 36:2 (1994), 47–64.
74 Yuen Gar Testimony, 39. See also Loon Moon Testimony, 5; War Lee Testimony, 24; Joe Sing Testimony, 63; Partner Testimony, Jan Way Bankruptcy File, 98–180; Kwong Song Testimony, 30.
75 Lay Jong Testimony, 12 December 1891, *NSWRC*, 393. See also Chow Kum Testimony, 395.
76 Sun Sing Loong Testimony, 11 December 1891, *NSWRC*, 388–389.

2 Setting Up Shop

Figure 2.1 Chung Lee's Factory, Crown Street, Sydney, 1901.

factory complex in the heart of the city, off George Street. 'I have one [work]shop ... a store next door ... and a big yard', he boasted, which altogether could accommodate a workforce of around 'sixty men'.[77] Dimensions of Chinese furniture factories differed according to operators' financial resources, workforces and use of machinery, and in Sydney there was a native place aspect to factory size as well. Operators from Gao/yaoming (高/要明) county, including Sun Sing Loong, typically used smaller premises than manufacturers who had migrated from other counties, a pattern that was not repeated in Melbourne, where there were only a few Gao/yaoming migrants.[78] One of the larger Chinese furniture factories, that of Chung Lee in Sydney, is shown in Figure 2.1.[79]

---

77 Ah Toy Testimony, 10 September 1891, *NSWRC*, 37–38.
78 Sun Sing Loong Testimony, 389. See also Kuo, *Making Chinese Australia*, 22–39, 185.
79 City of Sydney Archives, NSCA CRS 51/99.

While the smaller Chinese factories had a single workspace, larger establishments contained several work areas, intended to limit outsourcing and to maximise self-sufficiency. In 1885, Ye Hing talked about the layout of his factory on Little Bourke Street in Melbourne at the trial of one of his employees, Ah Toy, for the murder of another worker, Chung Chee. As he testified, there was the 'office', a 'workshop', a 'polishing room', the 'kitchen' and a 'shed'.[80] Similar workspaces were regularly mentioned by other Chinese manufacturers.[81] Offices were where administrative tasks such as bookkeeping were carried out in-house. Woodwork was done in workshops arranged according to different processes, or processes were spread out across several workshops, sometimes in more than one building.[82] The result was that manufacturers could, for example, run their own lathes and their own circular saws, and co-operate less with other factories. Polishing needed to be done away from woodwork, since sawdust and fragments of timber could adhere to wet polish and ruin furniture. Hence, factories having their own polishing rooms made sense in terms of self-sufficiency as well. Kitchens and associated dining areas, where cooks worked and most others in the factory ate, similarly kept meals for factory employees on-site. Sheds were multipurpose work areas

---

80 Ye Hing Testimony, 9 April 1885, The Queen v. Ah Toy, Supreme Court of Victoria, Public Record Office of Victoria (PROV) 30/P/29-650-9, 18. Ah Toy was acquitted by reason of insanity.
81 Lee Kum Testimony, 28 May 1883, Ack Chow Insolvency File, 153; Ah Toy Testimony, 37-38; Lay Jong Testimony, 393; Chow Kum Testimony, 394; Tye Shing Testimony, 17 April 1903, The King v. Ah Chuck, Supreme Court of Victoria, PROV 30/P/0-1323-208, 25; Victorian Factory Registration Notices, 1897-1930, PROV 1399/P/0-1-4.
82 Ah Yet Schedule, 22 December 1882, Ah Yet Insolvency File, PROV 762/P/0-193-71/4046, 65; Ah Wong Testimony, 6 March 1906, Furniture Trade Union v. Ah Wong, New South Wales Court of Arbitration, NSWSR 5340-2/74-18, 142-147; Quong Wing Testimony, 18 October 1926, Pennell v. Quong Wing, trading as W. Rising and Co., Supreme Court of New South Wales, NSWSR 2713-6/1309, 32-38; Edgar Cutler Testimony, 9 March 1906, Furniture Trade Union v. Ah Wong, 4.

likewise geared towards making factories self-sufficent. Many were makeshift structures, little more than back yards covered over in corrugated iron.[83] Configuring factory premises for more tasks, thereby making factories more self-contained, was also standard outside the Chinese sector.[84] Kitchens and yards, however, were particular to the Chinese factories, suggesting an even stronger push by the Chinese manufacturers towards self-sufficiency.[85] That they approached factory premises in this way, driven by the idea of self-reliance, problematises the notion raised by historians Eric Rolls and John Leckey that specialisation and co-ordination among Chinese furniture firms characterised their operation in Australia.[86]

Dormitories were another typical feature of Chinese Australian furniture factories. 'They lived in the shop', said Sydney's Woo Lung of his twenty or so employees in 1873.[87] Ye Hing also described three bedrooms on the second floor of his Melbourne factory used by workers in the 1880s.[88] Manufacturers sleeping in the factories was usual as well. Sydney's Lay Jong, who went to work for Sun War Hop when his own business foundered in 1893, discussed the 'boss's cabin' at his new workplace. It was a room on the ground floor where Sun War Hop slept and kept valuables, especially 'brassware' (brass furniture fittings), which could be easily stolen.[89] Factory living in most instances meant

---

83 Lay Jong Testimony, 393.
84 'New Furniture Factory', *Age*, 8 August 1874; Victorian Factory Registration Notices, 1897–1930.
85 *NSW FSA Report 1898*, 23–24; *NSW FSA Report 1908*, 21.
86 Eric Rolls, *Citizens: Continuing the Epic Story of China's Centuries-Old Relationship with Australia* (St. Lucia: University of Queensland Press, 1996), 111–114; John Leckey, 'Low, Degraded Broots? Industry and Entrepreneurialism in Melbourne's Little Lon, 1860–1950' (PhD Thesis: University of Melbourne, 2003), 336.
87 Woo Lung Testimony, 65.
88 Ye Hing Testimony, 18. See also Return of Premises Occupied by Chinese within the City of Sydney, *NSWRC*, 487–493; War Lee Testimony, 23; Joe Sing Testimony, 63; Leun Chong Testimony, 30.

high-density living.⁹⁰ This was a useful cost-saving measure, but also posed a health risk, as noted by Sydney manufacturer Leong Tong. In 1901, he had to evacuate his factory due to 'the plague' (bubonic), which spread rapidly through the densely occupied rooms.⁹¹ With the 1896 *Factories and Shops Act* in Victoria, factory dormitories were made illegal in Melbourne, prompting manufacturers to house factory staff in nearby buildings.⁹² Boarding and feeding employees was widespread among Chinese firms in China, a cultural practice imported by Chinese migrants to Australia and other migrant destinations.⁹³ The practice was unusual in other Australian workplaces.⁹⁴

Storage spaces were also standard in most factories. In 1893, Yee Lee (義利 Yi Li) from Sydney testified: 'I have a lot of timber in the shop worth more than £150'.⁹⁵ Other operators reported similar and sometimes larger quantities, as much as £400 or £500 worth of timber.⁹⁶ Timber needed to be dried before production to ensure quality, and

---

89   Lay Jong Testimony, 27 July 1893, Lay Jong Bankruptcy File, NSWSR 13655-10/22864-6597, 47–50. See further Ah Ling Testimony, 17 April 1903, The King v. Ah Chuck, 24; Tye Shing Testimony, 25.
90   Visits of Inspection, *NSWRC*, 475–481; Return of Premises Occupied by Chinese within the City of Sydney, *NSWRC*, 487–493; Shirley Fitzgerald, *Red Tape Gold Scissors: The Story of Sydney's Chinese* (Sydney: Halstead, 2008), 106.
91   Leong Tong Testimony, 59.
92   Wing Young and Co., Banana Wholesalers and Cabinet Makers, 1920s, Chinese Museum plaque, Melbourne; Witness Testimonies, 17 October 1901, The King v. Shing Duck, Supreme Court of Victoria, PROV 30/P/0-1270-529, 6–29; Witness Testimonies, 29 September 1903, The King v. Wong Dew Duck, Supreme Court of Victoria, PROV 30/P/0-1338-469, 5–24. See also *Report of the Chief Inspector of Factories, Workrooms, and Shops (VIC FSA Report) 1899*, 31.
93   Sun Sing Loong Testimony, 389; Him Mark Lai, 'Chinese Guilds in the Apparel Industry of San Francisco', *Chinese America: History and Perspectives*, 21 (2008), 20–21; Brett Sheehan, *Industrial Eden: A Chinese Capitalist Vision* (Cambridge: Harvard University Press, 2015), 120.
94   *NSW FSA Report 1897–1930*; *VIC FSA Report 1897–1930*.
95   Yee Lee Testimony, 306.
96   Ah Yet Schedule, 14; Ack Chow Schedule, 29 August 1883, Ack Chow Insolvency File, 132; Wat A. Che Schedule, 22 November 1883, Kum Leong

drying in storage spaces at the factories enabled manufacturers to avoid buying the more expensive pre-dried timber. Melbourne's Ye Hing said that he stacked timber above his shed. Completed furniture was also often stored in the factories while it awaited sale and/or delivery to customers.[97] Storage areas for timber and finished furniture were usual across the furniture industry more broadly.[98] In fact, since factories stored so much timber and furniture, along with flammable liquids, they faced the common risk of catastrophic fire.[99] This was particularly the case during the late nineteenth century, when kerosene lanterns, which could explode if knocked over, were an important source of artificial illumination.[100] Smoking in factories (mainly tobacco, and to a lesser extent opium in Chinese factories) was widely practised and increased the risk of fire considerably.[101]

Factory sites were almost always located centrally. The most common addresses in Sydney were Pitt Street, Goulburn Street, Sussex Street, George Street and Elizabeth Street, within the city centre. Botany Road, traversing the southern suburbs of Alexandria and Waterloo

---

Insolvency File, NSWSR 13654-2/10028-18374, 54; Quong Lee Schedule, 142; Sue Gay Statement, 12.
97 Ye Hing Testimony, 18. See also Sun Sing Loong Testimony, 391.
98 'New Furniture Factory', *Age*, 8 August 1874; Victorian Factory Registration Notices, 1897–1930.
99 On factory fires, see, for instance, Wat A. Che Affidavit, 4 December 1883, Kum Leong Insolvency File, 58; 'Great Fire at Circular Quay', *Daily Telegraph (DT)*, 12 November 1883; [Ah Sin, Melbourne, 1896] 'Series of Fires in City and Suburbs', *Age*, 9 March 1896; [Go Bo Bros., Sydney, 1912] 'A City Fire', *DT*, 5 November 1912; [Chung War and Co.] 'Chinese Factory Burned', *Australasian*, 4 January 1913; [Gee Wah, Melbourne, 1914] 'Furniture Factory Damaged', *Argus*, 1 April 1914; [John Hoe, Sydney, 1921] 'Furniture Factory Fire', *Evening News (EN)*, 14 July 1921.
100 'Kerosene Lamp Explosion', *EN*, 17 February 1876; 'Lamp Explosions', *Sydney Mail and New South Wales Advertiser*, 23 May 1885; 'Kerosene Lamp Explosions', *Argus*, 3 September 1901.
101 A few Chinese manufacturers had insurance, with non-Chinese insurance companies. See Yuen Gar Ledger, 1 October 1912 to 24 August 1914, Yuen Gar Bankruptcy File, 12–17; Lim Juen Statement, 49–51.

and not far from the city centre, was another common address.[102] Chinese manufacturers in Melbourne also carried on work in central locations, particularly Little Bourke and Little Lonsdale Streets in the heart of the city.[103] Sites were often within 'Chinatown' precincts. This afforded manufacturers ready access to the services of other Chinese entrepreneurs and cheaper rents, since these locations were regularly shunned by non-Chinese businesses and residents.[104] 'Chinatowns' also offered some safety in numbers from racist harassment and violence. Even so, these locations were by no measure critical to Chinese industry. Arguably a more important consideration in the location of factory sites was their proximity to ethnic European suppliers and customers. Being close to them enabled manufacturers to save on transport costs, and was especially important to help guarantee the safe delivery of furniture.[105] Operating near suppliers and customers was why practically all Australian industrial manufacturing was located centrally within Sydney and Melbourne, as inadequate inter- and intra-urban/colonial/state freight services made it difficult for manufacturing operations to span long distances.[106]

Chinese factory sites also tended to be leased from non-Chinese landlords. Ah Yet, whose Melbourne operation spanned multiple sites,

---

102 *Sands Commercial Directory 1870–1930*; Sydney Assessment Books, 1870–1930, City of Sydney Archives, accessed 1 October 2018, http://photosau.com.au/CosRates/scripts/home.asp; Return of Premises Occupied by Chinese within the City of Sydney, *NSWRC*, 487–493.
103 *Sands & McDougall's Directory 1870–1930*; Victorian Factory Registration Notices, 1897–1930,
104 Leckey, 'Low, Degraded Broots?'; Fitzgerald, *Red Tape Gold Scissors*, 95–98, 112–121, 157–159.
105 See also Peter Scott, 'Mr Drage, Mr Everyman, and the creation of a mass market for domestic furniture in interwar Britain', *Economic History Review*, 62:4 (2009), 805.
106 Diane Hutchinson, 'Manufacturing', in Simon Ville and Glenn Withers, eds., *The Cambridge Economic History of Australia* (Melbourne: Cambridge University Press, 2015), 290; Linge, *Industrial Awakening*, 11–18.

rented seven buildings from one landlord, Mr. Raphael, on Market Lane during the 1880s.[107] Yee Wye had a similar arrangement with a landlord.[108] Lay Jong leased his Sydney factory from a non-Chinese property owner as well. 'My landlord', he told the Royal Commission in 1891, 'is the Honourable John Lucas, MLC' (Member of the Legislative Council).[109] Leckey has noted how Chinese manufacturers on Melbourne's Little Lonsdale Street were sometimes vulnerable and exploited by powerful landlords.[110] However, this was not a standard practice. Chinese furniture manufacturers were often desirable tenants, taking out long-term leases – for over ten years in some cases – and paying for building maintenance and improvements. Lay Jong even extended the space that he leased from Lucas, adding another level on the roof at his own expense.[111] As such, Chinese operators regularly endeared themselves to their influential landlords and received political favours. Lucas was accused of using his influence in order to protect his tenant and frustrate the efforts of the anti-Chinese lobby.[112] Municipal governments benefited from such lease agreements in terms of rate payments by Chinese operators as well, which helped offset racialised agitation.[113] Chinese landlords were less common, and few Chinese manufacturers owned factories, in part owing to restrictions on non-naturalised migrants buying property.[114] Without property to offer as collateral, bank loans would have been harder for them to secure. As

---

107 Ah Yet Schedule, 65. See further Melbourne Rate Books, 1870–1930, Ancestry.com, accessed 1 October 2018, https://search.ancestry.com.au/search/db.aspx?dbid=60706.
108 Yee Wye Schedule, 33.
109 Lay Jong Testimony, 1891, 393. See further Sydney Assessment Books, 1870–1930.
110 Leckey, 'Low, Degraded Broots?', 325.
111 Lay Jong Testimony, 1891, 393. See also Loon Moon Testimony, 6; George Joy Certificate Exempting from Dictation Test Application (CEDT), 31 August 1903, George Joy File, NAA Sydney SP42/1-C/1917/208, 23.
112 Report, *NSWRC*, 22.
113 Fitzgerald, *Red Tape Gold Scissors*, 154–157.

leaseholders, manufacturers would have also been much less likely to install machines, since doing so often required structural modification to existing buildings.

Tools and machinery

European hand tools were the most common tools used in factories. Sun Sing Loong explained to the Royal Commission in Sydney that nearly all tools in the Chinese sector – hammers, mallets, chisels, files, planes, drills, saws, axes and so on – were European tools. 'Very little comes from China', he said, 'perhaps a little saw, or an occasional tomahawk'.[115] Manufacturers may have felt public pressure to be seen as contributing to Australian society, so they could have tried to downplay the significance of Cantonese woodwork tools. Indeed, historian Kevin Chamberlain has catalogued eleven different varieties of Australian-made Chinese planes in Melbourne's Chinese Museum and Bendigo's Golden Dragon Museum, and in his own collection, that differ markedly from European planes. He has also identified distinctive frame saws and sloping workbenches used in Chinese factories in Melbourne.[116] These are all similar to those held in the Museum of Dr. Sun Yat-sen in Cuiheng, Zhongshan, Guangdong, and to Cantonese traditional woodwork equipment described by historian Xue Yongjun.[117] Certain tools involved workers using their feet as well

---

114 Sydney Assessment Books, 1870–1930; Melbourne Rate Books, 1870–1930. See also Tye Shing Factory and Sue Gay Factory, *The Architecture of Arthur Purnell*, Culture Victoria, accessed 15 September 2017, https://cv.vic.gov.au/stories/built-environment/the-architecture-of-arthur-purnell/.
115 Sun Sing Loong Testimony, 391.
116 Kevin Chamberlain, 'Chinese Woodworking Tools in Victoria', *The Tool Chest*, 52 (1999), 6–18.
117 Xue, 'Guangshi mudiao yishu jiqi zai jianzhu he shinei zhuangshi zhong de yingyong yanjiu', 60–64. I thank Natalie Fong for a photograph of woodwork tools held in the Museum of Dr. Sun Yat-sen. See further Li Zhen (李渽),

as their hands, a technique that can be seen, along with frame saws, in an 1880 depiction of a Melbourne Chinese factory printed in the *Australasian Sketcher* (Figure 2.2). Contrary to the suggestion of this drawing, however, such specialised equipment and techniques are unlikely to have been used generally in Australia. They were probably the preserve of experts schooled in traditional approaches, which numerous furniture workers were not, as will be demonstrated in the next chapter. Chinese tools and methods were also invariably used in combination with European tools, and, in the case of Chinese planes, English plane blades.[118]

European tools came entirely from ethnic European ironmongers and hardware dealers. Quong Lee in Melbourne purchased a range of saws, screwdrivers, hammers, chisels, files, clamps, planes and blades, sharpening stones, measuring squares, compasses and pencils from A. and J. Boyes in 1889.[119] 'All the tools are bought here from the ironmongers', explained Sun Sing Loong in 1891 of his experience in Sydney's Chinese sector.[120] Usually, however, factory operators did not purchase tools, leaving workers to buy their own. 'The men bring their own tools with them', stated Woo Lung of the practice in his factory.[121] Lay Jong testified the same: 'the tools belonged to the workmen … I had none of my own'.[122] Workers themselves revealed that they called on hardware merchants to buy

---

Zhongguo chuantong jianzhu mu zuo gongju [Chinese traditional construction and woodwork tools] (Shanghai: Tongji University Press, 2004); Chen Ming (陈铭), '20 shiji Zhongguo jiaju jiagong jishu yu shebei fazhan yanjiu' [20th century Chinese furniture processing technology and equipment development research] (PhD Thesis: Nanjing Forestry University, 2011), 11–39.
118 Chamberlain, 'Chinese Woodworking Tools in Victoria', 9.
119 Quong Lee Schedule, 86–88.
120 Sun Sing Loong Testimony, 391.
121 Woo Lung Testimony, 65.
122 Lay Jong Testimony, 1893, 40.

Figure 2.2 Furniture Makers, *Australasian Sketcher*, 24 April 1880.

tools, as well as work clothes. References provided by these ethnic European businesspeople describing workers' long-term patronage were often placed in their applications for ' Certificates Exempting from Dictation Test' (CEDTs), required for re-entering Australia when returning from overseas.[123] Throughout the Australian furniture industry, factory workers bringing their own hand tools

---

123 Chun Lit CEDT Application, 20 June 1911, Chun Lit File, NAA Sydney SP42/1-C1939/201, 40; Ding Larn CEDT Application, 7 July 1913, Ding Larn File, NAA Sydney SP42/1-C1930/247, 38; Ah Cheong CEDT Application, Ah Cheong File, NAA Melbourne B13-1914/21688, 9; Wong Hop CEDT Application, 9 November 1922, Wong Hop File, NAA Melbourne B13-1922/22357, 9–10; Wong Ah Chew CEDT Application, 13 September 1925, Wong Ah Chew File, NAA Sydney SP42/1-C1929/6422, 10; Quong Chor CEDT Application, 24 February 1927, Quong Chor File, NAA Melbourne B13-1927/7411, 7. This is also evident in a section on European tools in a Chinese–English phrase book published for Chinese

was the norm, as indeed it was for the workers in China.[124] Edgar Cutler from Sydney's United Furniture Trade Society stated in the New South Wales Court of Arbitration in 1904 that cabinetmakers' toolkits cost them between £10 and £14 for 'machine shops' and more for 'hand shops'.[125]

Woodworkers made any Chinese tools that they needed or purchased these from Chinese toolmakers in Australia. Several catalogued by Chamberlain have makers' marks, particularly those of Louey Woon and Lim Toon, toolmakers operating in Melbourne.[126] Chinese workers also brought some tools – 'perhaps a little saw, or an occasional tomahawk', as Sun Sing Loong put it – with them from China.[127]

Machinery was also used regularly in the Chinese furniture sector. In 1906, Ah Wong and a number of his factory employees testified in the New South Wales Court of Arbitration that his Sydney factory had circular saws and lathes powered by a coal-fired steam boiler.[128] From 1914, Sue Gay ran an 'electric polishing plant', 'circular saws', a 'groover' and a 'buzzer' (planer) in his Melbourne establishment, worth approximately £500 altogether.[129] Woodwork machinery enabled manufacturers to save on labour and avoid purchasing machine-made components from other factories. Its rollout was encouraged in Australia's Chinese-language newspapers, part of a broader effort to encourage

---

migrants in Australia. See Sun Johnson, *The Self Educator* (Sydney: Sun Johnson, c. 1892), 57–64.

124 Edgar Cutler Testimony, 8 November 1904, United Furniture Trade Society of New South Wales v. Anthony Hordern and Sons, New South Wales Court of Arbitration, NSWSR 5340-2/5714, 42. On Cantonese tradition, refer to Xue, 'Guangshi mudiao yishu jiqi zai jianzhu he shinei zhuangshi zhong de yingyong yanjiu', 60–64.
125 Edgar Cutler Testimony, 1904, 42.
126 Chamberlain, 'Chinese Woodworking Tools in Victoria', 8–9.
127 Sun Sing Loong Testimony, 391.
128 Ah Wong Testimony, 142–147; Willie Wing Testimony, 9 March 1906, Furniture Trade Union v. Ah Wong, 167–175.
129 Sue Gay Statement, 10, 12.

Chinese migrants to embrace 'modernity', as described by Kuo.[130] It was more common, nevertheless, for Chinese furniture manufacturers to indicate that they had not mechanised at all. 'I did not use machines [apart from two lathes]', stated Lay Jong in court in 1893, to take one example.[131] Machine work was often outsourced, typically to non-Chinese factories. Ah Yet in Melbourne, for example, purchased table legs from furniture manufacturers Cohen Brothers and Co. in the 1880s.[132]

Machine use in Chinese furniture factories increased over time. This is illustrated in Figure 2.3, a graph of data gathered by factory inspectors on machine horsepower used in the Sydney furniture industry.[133] According to these statistics, ethnic European manufacturers mechanised their factories to a higher degree, and the gap between Chinese and non-Chinese establishments only ever widened. Less mechanisation in the Chinese factories was a consequence of their modest capital. Even so, relative to Europe and the United States, Australian industrial manufacturing generally, including furniture manufacturing, involved 'minimal technology', as noted by Simon Ville. This was because of Australia's comparatively small consumer base.[134] Cabinetmaker William Holman also testified in 1904 regarding the limits of machines in the furniture industry: 'from week

---

130 Mei-fen Kuo, 'Confucian Heritage, Public Narratives and Community Politics of Chinese Australians at the Beginning of the 20th Century', in Sophie Couchman and Kate Bagnall, eds., *Chinese Australians: Politics, Engagement and Resistance* (Leiden: Brill, 2015), 156.
131 Lay Jong Testimony, 1893, 41.
132 Ah Yet Schedule, 14, 105. See also Yee Wye Schedule, 29; Lee Gow and Man Hing Schedule, 13 January 1902, Lee Gow Insolvency File, 765/P/0-321-90/3865, 10, 46–53; Charles Lum Ledger, 10–50; Woo Lung Ledger, 8 April 1872 to 29 March 1873, Woo Lung Insolvency File, 18–45; Man Sing Ledger, 27 January 1890 to 29 October 1890, Man Sing Bankruptcy File, 8–28; Yuen Gar Ledger, 12–17; Shung Yem Testimony, 58.
133 Author's graph using data from *NSW FSA Report 1897–1928*. No such data was collected on factories in Sydney prior to 1897, and none was collected in Melbourne.
134 Ville, 'Colonial Enterprise', 207.

2 Setting Up Shop

to week, from month to month, the designs from which the men have to work are constantly altered'.[135] Historian Peter Scott has described this in early twentieth-century London, too, arguing that this was the reason why 'true mass production' was never witnessed in the furniture industry there.[136] By the 1920s, nevertheless, it had become evident to Samuel Tye of the Quong Yick factory in Melbourne that his workers' hand tools could no longer match his non-Chinese rivals' 'up-to-date and labour-saving machinery', which his own modest finances precluded and which he blamed for his bankruptcy in 1926.[137]

Machines were sourced from non-Chinese machine dealers. Charles Lum in Sydney stated in 1914 that he purchased machines 'on time payment' from Gibson, Battle and Co.[138] It is possible that he was influenced to do so by this company's advertisements in Sydney's *Tung Wah Times* (東華報 *Donghuabao*).[139] Other machine merchants advertised in the Chinese-language press, too, and could have inspired other proprietors to do as Lum did.[140] There do not appear to have been

---

135 William Holman Testimony, 8 November 1904, United Furniture Trade Society of New South Wales v. Anthony Hordern and Sons, New South Wales Court of Arbitration, 16–17.
136 Scott, 'Mr Drage, Mr Everyman', 805. The Arts and Crafts Movement also stressed finely crafted furniture over mass-produced articles. See See Edward T. Joy, *The Country Life Book of English Furniture* (London: Country Life, 1964), 87–90. Art Nouveau furniture involved intricate carving, which needed to be done by hand or using expensive machinery. See Margaret Macdonald-Taylor, *English Furniture from the Middle Ages to Modern Times* (London: Evans Brothers, 1965), 45–46.
137 Samuel Tye Affidavit, 26 October 1926, Quong Yick Insolvency File, PROV 10246/P/0-108-15/1915, 20.
138 Charles Lum Testimony, 4.
139 'Haigh's Brand Moulding Machines', *TWT*, 18 November 1911.
140 'Eliza Tinsley', *CT*, 3 June 1905; 'Parke, Lacy & Co., Ltd.', *TWT*, 15 March 1913; 'Roderick Gilles', *TWT*, 24 October 1925; 'Marrickville Machine and Motor Co.', *Chinese Republic News*, 26 March 1927. On similar advertisements for sewing machines and laundry appliances in California, see, for example, 'Jiqi gongsi bugao' [Machine company notice], *Chung Sai Yat Po* (San Francisco), 23 January 1901.

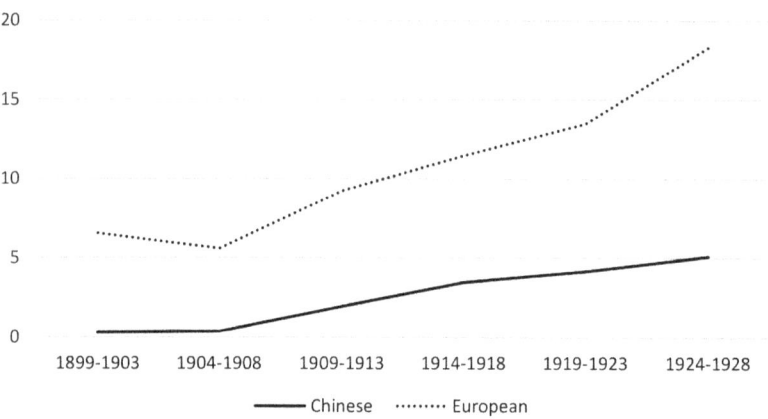

Figure 2.3 Machine horsepower per Sydney furniture factory.

Chinese machine dealers within Australia, and machines were never imported from China. One Brisbane manufacturer, Zhong Tongxing (鐘同興) from Zengyi county (增邑), invented an oil-powered woodwork machine in 1906. He then sent timber models of his invention to a steel foundry.[141] The device could have been used in Sydney and Melbourne factories, but this was the only case where they might have employed woodwork machines from a Chinese source. Manufacturers had no choice but to purchase coal, gas, water, oil and electricity for machinery outside the Chinese community.[142]

---

141 'Huaren zhizao xinshi jiqi' [Chinese invents new machine], *TWT*, 29 September 1906; 'Huaren xin kuan jiqi zhi faming' [Chinese invents new machine], *TWT*, 23 January 1909.
142 Ah Nim Ledger, 28 October 1882 to 28 April 1883, Sun Ying Tiy Insolvency File, NSWSR 13654-2/9994-17931, 1–27; Yee Lee and Co. Ledger, 1 January 1890 to 26 January 1892, Yee Lee Bankruptcy File, 7–280; Charles Lum Ledger, 10–50; Sun Kwong Loong and Co. Statement, 36–37; Rupert Yon Statement, 17 September 1925, Rupert Yon Insolvency File, 113–115.

Manufacturing materials

Chinese furniture makers used a range of timber. Australian native timber was used widely, particularly during the nineteenth century. Ack Chow from Loon Cheong and Co. in Sydney reported £400 worth of red cedar in the factory when their business failed in 1883.[143] Ah Yet had been utilising red cedar, too, along with white cedar, when he closed his factory in Melbourne that year.[144] Australian red cedar, however, had been virtually depleted by the early twentieth century and ceased being used.[145] Queensland kauri was popular among Chinese factory operators as well. Hing Pound and War Lee, to take two Sydney examples, each purchased sizeable amounts during the early 1900s.[146] New Zealand kauri replaced the Queensland variety in factories as supplies of that also dwindled and became more expensive over the twentieth century.[147] Then New Zealand kauri became scarcer and dearer in turn.[148] Other imported timber, chiefly from North America – such as walnut, ash, oak and Oregon – was used by Chinese

---

143 Ack Chow Schedule, 132. See also Woo Lung Ledger, 18–45; Ah Kum Schedule, 21 August 1884, Ah Kum Insolvency File, NSWSR 13654-2/10087-19025, 9; Wong Sum Ling Schedule, 18 March 1889, Wong Sum Ling Bankruptcy File, NSWSR 13655-10/22559-1039, 44.
144 Ah Yet Schedule, 14. See also Quong Lee Schedule, 77–80, 100–102; Yee Wye Schedule, 29–30.
145 'Timber Resources', *SMH*, 1 November 1912.
146 Hing Pound Statement, 18 February 1909, Hing Pound Bankruptcy File, NSWSR 13655-10/23578-18024, 38, 52; War Lee Ledger, 20 October 1914, Sam War Lee Bankruptcy File, 9–11. See also Sing Lee Statement, 10 March 1888, Sing Lee Bankruptcy File, 21; Quong Lee Schedule, 20–21; Ah Chee Schedule, 44–49; Lim Juen Statement, 73–76; Sue Gay Statement, 70–83.
147 Pon Kee Schedule, 29 October 1914, Pon Kee Insolvency File, PROV 766/P/0-118-90/2797, 19–20. See also Ernest Lin Schedule, 5 July 1907, Ernest Lin Insolvency File, PROV 765/P/0-399-90/5033, 84–89; Lim Juen Statement, 43–46; 'Timber Resources', *SMH*, 1 November 1912.
148 'The Passing of the Kauri', *Mercury*, 3 January 1908. See also 'Timber Resources', *SMH*, 1 November 1912. Chow Kum denied staining pine to look like cedar. See Chow Kum Testimony, 396.

manufacturers as well. 'We go in for walnut and ash a good deal', remarked Chow Kum in 1891.[149] His records reveal that he also purchased American oak.[150] Timber from East and South-East Asia was seldom used in furniture factories, even though species such as gingko, Chinese elm, China-fir and teak would have been more familiar to China-trained woodworkers.[151] This timber was too costly in Australia.[152] Chinese factories utilised the same timber as most others. Furniture historians Kevin Fahy, Christina Simpson and Andrew Simpson have described how both Australian native timber and timber imported from North America and New Zealand were widespread in Australian furniture production owing to demand for articles made from all such varieties.[153]

Chinese factories sourced timber almost entirely from ethnic European timber dealers. Ack Chow recorded that he sourced red cedar from James Wright, a major dealer, in 1883.[154] Similarly, Chow Kum stated that he purchased his timber 'from Allen and Walker and the Kauri Timber Company principally': another two important timber merchants in Sydney.[155] The same was seen in Melbourne. Chinese operators often purchased from Alcock and Co.'s timberyard on Little Bourke and Lonsdale Streets. Another dealer referred to regularly by Melbourne

---

149 Chow Kum Testimony, 395.
150 Chow Kum Statement, 30 June 1890, Chow Kum Bankruptcy File, NSWSR 13655-10/22648-2524, 13, 15. See also Chan King Statement, 3 March 1913, Willie King Bankruptcy File, 17, 72; Sue Gay Statement, 70–83.
151 Klaas Ruitenbeek, *Carpentry and Building in Late Imperial China: A Study of the Fifteenth-Century Carpenter's Manual Lu Ban Jing* (Leiden: Brill, 1993), 7–15. For exceptions, refer to Ernest Quong Statement, 10 July 1917, Ernest Quong Bankruptcy File, 5–14, 21; Sue Gay Statement, 70–83; Quong Lee Schedule, 101.
152 See, for instance, 'The Value of Teak', *DT*, 9 June 1890.
153 Kevin Fahy, Christina Simpson and Andrew Simpson, *Nineteenth Century Australian Furniture* (Sydney: David Ell Press, 1985), 38–53.
154 Ack Chow Schedule, 132–133. Refer also to Henry Louey Ledger, 15 January 1909 to 24 January 1910, Henry Louey Bankruptcy File, 4–47; Charles Lum Ledger, 10–50.

2 Setting Up Shop

Chinese manufacturers, was James Moore and Sons.[156] Timber merchants, like machine dealers, advertised in the Chinese-language press. H. McKenzie from Sydney did so in the *Chinese Australian Herald* (廣益華報 *Guangyihuabao*), and J. C. Edington and Son from Melbourne did likewise in the *Chinese Times* (愛國報 *Aiguobao*).[157] Chinese operators sometimes also sourced timber from non-Chinese manufacturers and one another.[158] There were few Chinese timber dealers in Australia, and furniture factories did not branch out into harvesting and milling timber.[159] Further, timber harvested and milled by large numbers of Chinese people in North America only ever arrived in Chinese Australian furniture factories via non-Chinese intermediaries such as H. McKenzie and J. C. Edington.

Furniture production also required several other materials. Ack Chow recorded in the 1880s that, apart from timber, the factory used knobs, locks, hinges, catches, handles, nails, screws, bolts, glue, putty, glass, mirrors, tiles and polish.[160] Sydney's Yee Lee and partner Tack Lee similarly required locks, nails, screws, hooks, glue, methylated spirits, varnish, polish, paint, glass, marble, tiles, slate and shellac.[161] Stationery

---

155 Chow Kum Testimony, 395. See further Man Sing Ledger, 8–28; Toong Hing Ledger, 12 March 1921 to 10 February 1923, Toong Hing Bankruptcy File, NSWSR 13655-10/24025-23254, 4–90.
156 Ernest Lin Schedule, 22; Pon Kee Schedule, 19–20; Quong Lee Schedule, 77–80, 100–102.
157 'H. McKenzie', *Chinese Australian Herald*, 23 March 1901; 'J. C. Edington', *Chinese Times (CT)*, 13 June 1908.
158 Ah Yet Schedule, 7–11, 105, 125, 179, 188; Ah Nim Ledger, 8, 22; Man Sing Ledger, 8–28.
159 I have found only two instances of Chinese furniture manufacturers shipping timber to Sydney or Melbourne from elsewhere in Australia. Refer to Sing Lee Statement, 8; Lay Jong Statement, 30 June 1893, Lay Jong Bankruptcy File, 34. I have identified two Australian-born Chinese working as agents for European Australian timber dealers in the 1920s. See Lim Juen Statement, 43–46; Sue Gay Statement, 136–138.
160 Ack Chow Schedule, 233–236.
161 Yee Lee and Co. Ledger, 7–280.

was required to support manufacturing activities as well: materials used for bookkeeping and promotional purposes, for instance.[162] In Melbourne from 1896, and then Sydney from 1927, all furniture factories were also legally obliged to buy rubber stamps for stamping their furniture.

Other production necessities, much like timber, came almost without exception from non-Chinese suppliers. Ack Chow noted that he sourced nails, screws, handles and knobs from ironmongers such as W. C. Fallick, as did Chow Kum and other manufacturers in Sydney and Melbourne.[163] Bong Shue of Lonsdale Street, to take a Melbourne example, purchased methylated spirits, polish, varnish and other solutions from hardware merchants Campbell, Stone and Co. and Robert Tucker and Co. in the early 1900s.[164] Chinese factories often also sourced materials from specialist suppliers such as marble merchant Ernest Braby and stationers Hart Printing.[165] There were practically no Chinese firms in these supplying industries.[166] European Australian purveyors of most other factory necessities advertised in the pages of Australia's Chinese-language newspapers as well. Melbourne ironmongers A. and J. Boyes placed advertisements in the *Chinese*

---

162 Charles Lum Statement, 8 October 1914, Charles Lum Bankruptcy File, 126–132; Toong Hing Ledger, 4–90; Rupert Yon Statement, 126–129.
163 Ack Chow Schedule, 100–101; Chow Kum Statement, 15. See further Quong Lee Schedule, 148; Ah Chee Schedule, 8.
164 Bong Shue Schedule, 18 October 1907, Bong Shue Insolvency File, PROV 765/P/0–402–90/5084, 8. See also Quong Lee Schedule, 110–113; Yee Wye Schedule, 54–58; Ah You Schedule, 5 October 1904, Ah You Insolvency File, PROV 766/P/0–49–1133, 14–22.
165 Sun Tong War and Co. Schedule, 4 March 1902, Tin Yow and Low Wing Bankruptcy File, 4; Lee Gow and Man Hing Schedule, 10; Ah Nin Schedule, 5 February 1903, Ah Nin Insolvency File, PROV 766/P/0–36-A818, 8; Rupert Yon Statement, 62–64, 126–129.
166 *Census of the Commonwealth of Australia 1911*, 899–1073. However, on British Columbia, see 'Ming Wo Hardware Co.', *Chinese Times* (Vancouver), 1 August 1922.

2 Setting Up Shop

Times for over twenty years.[167] Rubber stamp makers were also consistent advertisers in Melbourne.[168]

Food ingredients were the only items purchased primarily from Chinese suppliers. Chow Kum's records show that he bought Cantonese salted fish, black fungus, lychee nuts (dried lychees), dried vegetables, soy sauce, bean paste, noodles, tofu and rice from Gee War, a grocer in Sydney, in the late nineteenth century.[169] Lim Juen, who operated under the name Wing On in Little Lonsdale Street in Melbourne in the 1920s, made comparable transactions. He purchased 'lap chong', or Cantonese sausage, 'fat choy', or 'hair vegetable', 'foo chook', or dried tofu skin sticks, Cantonese salted fish, rice and tea from the grocer Sun Wah Loong (新華隆 Xin Hualong) in Melbourne.[170] Most such items had been imported, typically from Hong Kong, and were sent to factories along native place lines. The Sun Kwong Loong and Co. factory in Sydney, for example, which had partners from Xiangshan county, purchased most of its food from Xiangshan firm Kwong War Chong (廣和昌 Guanghechang) in Sydney, Hong Kong and Xiangshan.[171] Doing this was important for workforces recruited chiefly on the basis of native place, since, in this manner, workers could be kept satisfied with familiar cuisine from their home areas.[172] Other

---

167 'Boyes Bros.', *CT*, 26 March 1902 to 15 July 1922. See further 'E. H. Allen & Co.', *CT*, 15 April 1903; 'London & American Hardware Supply Store', *CT*, 13 May 1903; 'William Hartley, Importer of General Hardware', *CT*, 23 March 1904; 'Blockey, Stone & Co. Pty. Ltd.', *CT*, 30 October 1920.
168 See, for example, 'W. L. Swift', *CT*, 24 April 1909; 'G. G. Roeszler & Son', *CT*, 29 June 1912.
169 Chow Kum Statement, 19–34. See also Yee Lee Testimony, 307; Joe Sing Statement, 30–35.
170 Lim Juen Statement, 20–22, 112.
171 Lee Chun Testimony, 10 August 1915, Jan Way Bankruptcy File, 103–105. Refer also to Tin Yow Testimony, 3 March 1902, Tin Yow Bankruptcy File, NSWSR 13655-10/23335-14768, 3.
172 On the importance of food culture around Guangzhou, see Lee, *Gourmets in the Land of Famine*, 55.

than what was supplied by chickens and ducks in factory yards, meat and eggs also came from the Chinese grocers of Sydney and Melbourne, as did fresh vegetables.[173]

Chinese manufacturers tended to contract non-Chinese carters to deliver their goods. In 1893, Yee Lee mentioned that he contracted 'a carter named Jacques' for the purpose of 'carting cedar', and indeed other manufacturers noted similar relationships.[174] Some also had suppliers deliver items, such as Chow Kum regarding ironmongery from W. C. Fallick in Sydney.[175] Chinese factory workers collected items on a less frequent basis. Ah Yet dispatched his employees to collect materials in Melbourne using a factory horse and cart in the 1880s.[176]

Conclusion

Chinese Australian furniture manufacturers regularly set up their factories using cultural resources imported from China. Family and native place formed the bases of many furniture firms. Manufacturers often also raised finance collectively, using money from other Chinese migrants in Australia for their industrial ventures. Chinese furniture manufacturers drew on imported approaches when configuring factory spaces as well, having uniquely Chinese factory kitchens and

---

173 Ah Yet Schedule, 8; Quong Lee Schedule, 21–22; Chow Kum Statement, 19–34; Yee Lee and Co. Ledger, 7–280; You Kee Young Schedule, 10 December 1894, You Kee Young Insolvency File, PROV 765/P/0-187-90/2095, 8; Charles Wing Schedule, 6 November 1901, Charles Wing Insolvency File, PROV 765/P/0-319-90/3845, 8. On chickens and ducks in factory sheds, refer to Man Sing Testimony, 70.
174 Yee Lee Testimony, 272, 306. See also Ah Nim Ledger, 14, 17; Man Sing Ledger, 11; Lay Jong Testimony, 1893, 50; Joe Sing Statement, 18–28.
175 Chow Kum Statement, 15. See further Quong Lee Schedule, 20–21; Ah Chee Schedule, 44–49; Leun Chong Statement, 1 October 1925, Leun Ah Chong Bankruptcy File, 16–17.
176 Ah Yet Schedule, 14, 55.

dormitories and selecting sites in 'Chinatown' in order to be able to utilise Chinese business networks more easily. Tools of the Cantonese tradition, too, were purchased from Chinese toolmakers in Australia and occasionally brought from China. Manufacturers also sometimes sourced timber from each other, and they relied heavily on native place ties to import staples of Cantonese cuisine for factory meals. Setting up Chinese factories in these ways consistently, yet not completely, set them apart from their non-Chinese equivalents in the furniture industry. Doing so was a means of mitigating the constraints of their Australian industrial settings. In the face of anti-Chinese discrimination, these approaches offered manufacturers a sense of familiarity and security.

Numerous Chinese factories were set up in accordance with different principles. There were many sole traders (mainly owner-operators), along with partnerships defined by friendship and complementary skill sets. Proprietors financed firms through their own savings (normally saved wages), modest loans from close associates, earnings from other businesses, and trade credit. Factories were also configured with a view to maximising self-sufficiency, centrally located close to non-Chinese suppliers and customers and leased principally from non-Chinese landlords. European tools and machines from non-Chinese hardware dealers, ironmongers and machine merchants were critically important in Chinese furniture factories. This was the case, too, with most manufacturing supplies, including Australian native timber and timber imported from North America and New Zealand. Virtually all of these materials were sourced from European Australian firms in Sydney and Melbourne. Such features of Chinese establishments made them strikingly similar to other factories in the Australian furniture industry.

There was a clear tailoring of Chinese operations to Australian industrial conditions. Several features – like the protection of individual interests via firm registration (even among family members), widespread use of trade credit from non-Chinese firms, and reliance on supplies and equipment from these firms – were never seen to the same extent around the Pearl River Delta. Setting up furniture factories accordingly appears in certain cases to have related to the use of 'modern' methods, encouraged in Chinese Australian newspapers. In other instances, Chinese proprietors may have been trying to offset the discrimination of 'White Australia', conforming to practices that might have been viewed as more typically 'Australian'. In most situations, however, Chinese factory operators seem to have set up factories in these ways as per their requirements and preferences for making furniture, probably because they thought these approaches would yield the best results in business. More often than not, such practices required close co-operation with European Australians, who, if for no other reason than commercial pragmatism, assisted the Chinese manufacturers.

3
Workers

Cabinetmaker Ding On (定安 Ding An) was working at the Sun Kwong Loong and Co. factory in Sydney in 1915. Before that, he explained, he had lived and worked locally for 'over twenty years'. At the beginning of 1915, he was paid a weekly wage of £3, or the mandated minimum wage for cabinetmakers that year. When his employers encountered financial difficulty later on in the year, however, his wage was reduced to £2/16/-. Ding On lived at the factory with up to thirty other employees. They ate Cantonese food prepared by factory cook Yit Yung (葉姜 Ye Jiang). Living and eating his meals at the factory cost him 'ten shillings a week', said Ding On. He further explained that he was 'not a pieceworker'. His working week was most likely the forty-eight-hour week laid down in New South Wales industrial legislation, since his earnings met legal requirements, at least at the start of 1915. Ding On worked and lived alongside his employers, who were once workers themselves. Together, they discussed financial and other matters at the breakfast table each morning.[1]

---

1   Ding On Testimony, 10 August 1915, Jan Way Bankruptcy File, New South Wales State Records (NSWSR) 13655-10/23778-20439, 142–153; Gen Bong Testimony, 10 August 1915, Jan Way Bankruptcy File, 198; Yit Yung Testimony, 10 August

Ding On reflected on factory work at his employers' bankruptcy hearing in an era when the opinions of Chinese Australian furniture factory workers were drowned out by the controversial claims that were made about them. Chinese workers were regularly accused by 'white labour' agitators of being so-called 'cheap labour'. This charge had several different elements, including that they lacked skill, that they were both overworked and underpaid and that they constituted an underclass, or 'coolie' class.[2] Chinese community leaders such as Sydney furniture manufacturer John Hoe (冼俊豪 Xian Junhao) disputed assertions that Chinese workers were 'cheap labour', arguing that they and European Australian workers shared the same working conditions and ideals.[3] Very rarely, however, were the voices of Chinese workers themselves audible in this debate, even though it centred on their personal experiences.

In this chapter, we will hear how Chinese furniture workers narrated their own lives in Sydney and Melbourne during the period between 1880 and 1930. Following a discussion of workforce compositions, the chapter addresses Chinese workers' reflections on aspects of their

---

1915, Jan Way Bankruptcy File, 156; Sun Kwong Loong and Co. Statement, 9 August 1915, Jan Way Bankruptcy File, 75–98; 'Industrial Registrar's Office', *New South Wales Government Gazette*, 20 November 1912. Some material from this chapter has been published as Peter Gibson, 'Voices of Sydney's Chinese Furniture Factory Workers, 1890–1920', *Labour History*, 112 (2017), 99–117.

2   Edgar Cutler Testimony, 6 December 1891, *Report of the Royal Commission on Alleged Chinese Gambling and Immorality and Charges of Bribery against Members of the Police Force (NSWRC)* (Sydney: Government Printer, 1892), 428–432; William Holman Testimony, 17 December 1891, *NSWRC*, 432–437; *Factories Act Inquiry Board, Second Progress Report* (Melbourne: Government Printer, 1894); *Evidence Taken by the Royal Commission Appointed to Investigate and Report on the Operation of the Factories and Shops Law of Victoria* (Melbourne: Government Printer, 1903).

3   'The Chinese Question', *Sydney Morning Herald (SMH)*, 1 July 1908; 'Chinese in Waterloo', *SMH*, 2 July 1908; 'The Chinese Question', *SMH*, 27 July to 15 August 1908; 'Kedai mugong' [Harshly treated woodworkers], *Tung Wah Times (TWT)*, 9 January 1901.

3 Workers

activities that were deemed threatening to other workers and were thus the subject of negative claims: their skills, their rates of pay and work hours, and their social class.[4] The chapter will show that Chinese furniture workers had a unique work culture, one which was informed principally by their experiences, responsibilities and ambitions in China. Yet, this work culture was also influenced by the Australian labour movement, not by its 'cheap labour' rhetoric, but by its efforts to improve workers' rights more generally.

Factory workforces

Chinese furniture factories employed fewer than twenty workers in most cases. Sydney's Woo Lung had between fifteen and twenty men engaged in the early 1870s.[5] Yee Wye in Melbourne had a comparable workforce, around fifteen workers, throughout the 1880s.[6] These were normal workforce sizes in the Chinese sector over the late nineteenth century. With a few exceptions like Ah Toy's factory in Sydney, which employed over sixty men, non-Chinese factory workforces tended to be larger.[7] Some of the largest, including that of Solomon Brothers and Co. in Melbourne in the 1870s, involved more than 100 employees.[8] In the early twentieth century, workforces in both sectors became smaller and

---

4   Chinese workers' reflections are extremely rare. See Judy Yung, Gordon Chang and Him Mark Lai, eds., *Chinese American Voices: From the Gold Rush to the Present* (Berkeley: University of California Press, 2006), 6.
5   Woo Lung Testimony, 23 May 1873, Woo Lung Insolvency File, NSWSR 13654-2/9488-11460, 65.
6   Yee Wye Schedule, 13 May 1889, Yee Wye Insolvency File, Public Record Office of Victoria (PROV) 762/P/0-335-5786, 50.
7   Ah Toy Testimony, 10 September 1891, *NSWRC*, 41. See also *Report of the Chief Inspector of Factories, Workrooms, and Shops (VIC FSA Report) 1897–1930*; *Report on the Working of the Factories and Shops Act during the year (NSW FSA Report) 1897–1930*; Victorian Factory Registration Notices, 1897–1930, PROV 1399/P/0-1-4.

closer in size. Ten became the average for the Chinese sector in Sydney, and thirteen outside the sector.[9] Workforces became smaller still in Melbourne: four in Chinese furniture factories and five in non-Chinese equivalents.[10] More machinery may help explain the reductions in workforces, although the different workforce sizes in Sydney and Melbourne are more difficult to explain. Mary Rankin suggested in her 1916 book on industrial arbitration and conciliation that the Victorian *Factories and Shops Act* of 1896 prompted all Melbourne factories to scale back workforces to avoid notice and thereby the minimum wage provisions of the legislation.[11] The New South Wales *Factories and Shops Act* would have encouraged less downsizing, since, as will be detailed in Chapter Five, it was markedly less onerous. Higher protective tariffs in Victoria also meant that small operations were more viable there than in New South Wales.[12]

Chinese furniture production firms had a mix of woodworkers and other employees. Cabinetmakers and polishers did the majority of woodwork. As factories were mechanised from the late nineteenth century onwards, sawyers, turners and other process workers like boiler attendants became increasingly important. Clerks, cooks, salespeople and managers were also needed, especially in large industrial ventures.

Family members were sometimes used to assemble factory workforces. As historian Mark Finnane has described, cabinetmaker Chung Teong Toy was recruited from China to work as a foreman by a relative in Melbourne, Chang Goey, but he was not permitted

---

8 'A Melbourne Furniture Factory', *Argus*, 17 August 1874; *VIC FSA Report 1897–1930*; *NSW FSA Report 1897–1930*; Victorian Factory Registration Notices, 1897–1930.
9 *NSW FSA Report 1897–1930*.
10 *VIC FSA Report 1897–1930*.
11 Mary Theresa Rankin, *Arbitration and Conciliation in Australasia: The Legal Wage in Victoria and New Zealand* (London: Allen and Unwin, 1916), 50–58.
12 Allan Martin, 'Free trade and protectionist parties in New South Wales', *Historical Studies: Australia and New Zealand*, 6:23 (1954), 315–323.

to leave the *Afghan* in 1888.[13] A family approach to recruitment was also used in 1911 by the Go brothers. They successfully applied for exemption from the *Immigration Restriction Act* to have their youngest brother, Go Chock, travel to Sydney from China to be trained as factory manager.[14] In both instances, the role to be filled was an important one, so this approach could have been favoured when recruiting workers for positions of authority.

Chinese factories drew more heavily on broader native place ties to recruit workers. As noted in the last chapter, operators seldom discussed Chinese places of origin on record, but there is some indication that workforces were recruited largely on this basis. Chow Kum, a representative of the Siyi community, according to one local government official in Sydney, staffed his factory entirely with 'men who come from the same village as himself'.[15] This is consistent with findings made by Kuo, Williams and Boileau, who have demonstrated that a large number of Chinese businesspeople recruited workers from the same places around the Pearl River Delta as themselves.[16] Native place ties were often also used by other firms to recruit workers.

---

13 Mark Finnane, 'Law as Politics: Chinese Litigants in Australian Colonial Courts', in Sophie Couchman and Kate Bagnall, eds., *Chinese Australians: Politics, Engagement and Resistance* (Leiden: Brill, 2015), 126.
14 Go Kee Application for Permission [for Go Chock] to Enter the Commonwealth, 19 January 1911, Go Chock and Chong Ah Wong File, National Archives of Australia (NAA) Sydney SP42/1-C1912/7152, 34–35. See also Ian Welch, 'Alien Son: The Life and Times of Cheok Hong Cheong, 1851–1928' (PhD Thesis: Australian National University, 2003), 285–286.
15 Appendix, *NSWRC*, 481.
16 Mei-fen Kuo, *Making Chinese Australia: Urban Elites, Newspapers and the Formation of Chinese-Australian Identity, 1892–1912* (Clayton: Monash University Publishing, 2013), 19–35; Michael Williams, 'Destination Qiaoxiang: Pearl River Delta Villages and Pacific Ports, 1849–1949' (PhD Thesis: University of Hong Kong, 2002), 130–133; Joanna Boileau, 'Chinese Market Gardening in Australia and New Zealand, 1860s–1960s: A Study in Technological Transfer' (PhD Thesis: University of New England, 2014), 175–182, 295.

Historian Keith Pescod has noted how Irish industrialists in Melbourne, including furniture manufacturers James Curtin and Henry Alcock, regularly hired workers from the same counties in Ireland as themselves.[17]

While native place recruitment was important, Chinese workforces also consisted of Chinese workers who had originated in other places. This is perhaps best illustrated by the turmoil in Sydney's Chinese community during the 1891 Royal Commission. Furniture manufacturers in the city centre, chiefly from Dongguan (東莞) and Xiangshan (香山) counties in the Pearl River Delta, complained to the Commissioners that some of their former workers were setting up factories and manufacturing their own furniture in the southern suburbs of Waterloo and Alexandria.[18] Chinese migrants residing in these suburbs had migrated principally from the Gao/yaoming (高/要明) counties, which indicates that many of these new factory proprietors were in fact Gao/yaoming migrants formerly employed by Dongguan and Xiangshan bosses.[19]

As among factory proprietors, it was normal for Chinese factory workforces to be in constant flux due to workers' returns to China. Thousands of workers reported having visited China for extended periods in applications for a 'Certificate Exempting from Dictation Test' (CEDT), as required under the 1901 *Immigration Restriction Act* to re-enter Australia. Cabinetmaker Ah Cheong, for instance, noted in a 1924 application that he had returned to China on three separate

---

17 Keith Pescod, *The Emerald Strand: The Irish-born Manufacturers of Nineteenth-century Victoria* (North Melbourne: Australian Scholarly Publishing, 2007), 216–232.
18 Lay Jong Testimony, 12 December 1891, *NSWRC*, 393; Chow Kum Testimony, 12 December 1891, *NSWRC*, 395; Sun War Hop Testimony, 12 December 1891, *NSWRC*, 397.
19 Kuo, *Making Chinese Australia*, 24–25, 29–35.

occasions since arriving in Melbourne in 1901, where he stayed for nine, eighteen and twenty-one months respectively.[20]

It was common for Chinese establishments to employ non-Chinese workers as well. Yee Wye engaged at least one, John Selman, in Melbourne in the 1880s.[21] Ah Yet, also in Melbourne in the 1880s, employed more – seventeen ethnic Europeans alongside thirty Chinese workers – although this high a number was fairly unusual. Most manufacturers who hired non-Chinese workers had one or two in smaller workforces.[22] While Chinese workers could expect employers to provide accommodation and meals, evidence of ethnic Europeans living and dining alongside Chinese co-workers has not surfaced. Non-Chinese factories in Australia rarely had Chinese workers, unlike the non-Chinese cigar, clothing and footwear factories operating in San Francisco, which contracted large numbers of them.[23] This could

---

20 Ah Cheong Certificate Exempting from Dictation Test (CEDT) Application, 20 March 1922, Ah Cheong File, NAA Melbourne B13-1922-6456, 11. See also, for instance, Hong Bow CEDT Application, 15 January 1925, Hong Bow File, NAA Melbourne B13-1925/10543, 15; Hong Sing CEDT Application, 20 June 1924, Hong Sing File, NAA Melbourne B13-1924/26848, 22; Louey Foo CEDT Application, 5 March 1925, Louey Foo File, NAA Melbourne B13-1925/10588, 16; Ching Yow CEDT Application, 24 March 1904, Ching Yow File, NAA Sydney SP42/1-B1907/2726, 13.
21 Yee Wye Schedule, 50.
22 Godfrey J. R. Linge, *Industrial Awakening: A Geography of Australian Manufacturing 1788 to 1890* (Canberra: Australian National University Press, 1979), 287; Ah Toy Testimony, 37; Harry Kow Testimony, 18 February 1908, Harry Kow Bankruptcy File, NSWSR 13655-10/23541-17604, 46; Sidney Jack Testimony, 30 March 1909, Jack Lem Bankruptcy, NSWSR 13655-10/23574-17992, 113; Furniture Trade Union v. Ah Wong, New South Wales Court of Arbitration, NSWSR 5340-2/74-18; Chin Youey CEDT Application, 23 September 1925, Chin Youey File, NAA Melbourne B13-1925/27576, 10; Pennell v. Quong Wing, trading as W. Rising and Co., Supreme Court of New South Wales, NSWSR 2713-6/1309; 'Chinese Master: European Servant', *Herald*, 13 July 1906.
23 Sole trader Sing Lee's brother, Sing War, worked for Mr. Pyke, although that is the only case I have found. See Sing Lee Affidavit, 3. On San Francisco, refer to Him Mark Lai, 'Chinese Guilds in the Apparel Industry of San Francisco',

have been due to industrial legislation and the leading roles that ethnic European furniture workers regularly played within the Australian labour movement, to be discussed in Chapter Five.

Worker skill

Chinese Australian furniture factory workers regularly identified themselves as 'carpenters', especially in the nineteenth century. In 1876, thirteen of fourteen workers at Chow Young's establishment in Sydney reported that they were 'carpenters' on affidavits filed for back pay when Chow Young went bankrupt.[24] Seven out of the fourteen employees at Quong Lee's establishment in Melbourne likewise specified the role 'carpenter' on their affidavits in 1889, as did all seven from Ah Chee's Melbourne factory in 1891.[25] Sun Sing Loong, a long-time employee of Ah Toy in Sydney, similarly said to the Royal Commission in Sydney in 1891: 'I am a carpenter'.[26]

As used by Chinese furniture factory workers, the term 'carpenter' had connotations of considerable woodwork skill. While suggestive in English of expertise in building, not the finer work of making furniture, 'carpenter' was the translation of the Chinese words *mujiang* (木匠) and *mugong* (木工).[27] Both of these words were used to describe furniture workers by Australia's Chinese press and were translated as 'carpenter' in Chinese–English phrase books used by Chinese migrants

---

Chinese America: History and Perspectives, 21 (2008), 17–23. On European cultural diversity in factories, see 'A Melbourne Furniture Factory', *Argus*, 17 August 1874.

24 Worker Affidavits of Debt, 7 March 1876 to 7 April 1876, Chow Young Insolvency File, NSWSR 13654-2/9598-12761, 71–96.
25 Worker Affidavits of Debt, 25 May 1889 to 27 June 1889, Quong Lee Insolvency File, PROV 762/P/0-338-71/5816, 38–129.
26 Sun Sing Loong Testimony, 11 December 1891, *NSWRC*, 388.
27 On 'carpenter' as a building trade, not a furniture trade, see *NSW FSA Report 1897*, 24; *VIC FSA Report 1897*, 3.

3 Workers

in Australia.²⁸ These words invoked a proud artisanal tradition. As Klaas Ruitenbeek has pointed out, the *mujiang*, who created all kinds of wooden articles, including houses and furniture, was the archetypal artisan of imperial China, disciple of the master Lu Ban (魯班) and the personification of *qiao* (巧), or 'technical skill'.²⁹ Australia's Chinese newspapers also linked Chinese furniture makers to this concept of *qiao*.³⁰ In selecting these words to describe themselves, workers were often making powerful statements regarding their expertise. Workers did not always endorse the traditional imperial order that made them models of artisanal skill. Indeed, historian Chi-Kong Lai has stressed that Xiangshan county in Guangdong, where many workers had originated, was a hotbed of revolutionary activity vital to the overthrow of the imperial system in 1911.³¹ They still appear to have revelled in the distinction, nevertheless, which set them apart from Chinese workers in other industries. They even celebrated Lu Ban Day in Australia.³²

The term 'carpenter' was linked by at least one worker to a period of training in China's furniture industry. Sun Sing Loong said in 1891 that he had 'served an apprenticeship of three years' making furniture in China before leaving for Sydney in 1878.³³ His home area, Gao/

---

28 Sun Johnson, *The Self Educator* (Sydney: Sun Johnson, c. 1892), 57, 66.
29 Klaas Ruitenbeek, *Carpentry and Building in Late Imperial China: A Study of the Fifteenth-Century Carpenter's Manual* Lu Ban Jing (Leiden: Brill, 1993), 15–24.
30 Refer, for instance, to 'Meilipan mu hang jianglai zhi jing tian ji di' [Melbourne wood industry bound for thorns in heaven, brambles on earth], *Chinese Australian Herald (CAH)*, 19 August 1911; 'Junhao hao mu chang guanggao' [John Hoe wood factory advertisement], *TWT*, 9 February 1924.
31 Chi-Kong Lai, 'Xiangshan County and the 1911 Revolution', *New Asia Review*, 13 (2012), 162–167. See also David Faure, *Emperor and Ancestor: State and Lineage in South China* (Stanford: Stanford University Press, 2007), 291–347.
32 Lu Ban Day was on the thirteenth of July. See 'Huaren mugong jinnian Lu Ban' [Chinese woodworkers commemorate Lu Ban], *CT*, 2 July 1910; 'Mu hang da qing hui guanggao' [Wood industry large celebration advertisement], 1 July 1911.

75

yaoming (高/要明), and other Pearl River Delta counties represented in Australia, migrants from which were all involved in the furniture industry, were mostly agricultural, with large-scale industrial production confined to parts of the Three Counties (三邑 Sanyi) directly adjacent to Guangzhou. Sun Sing Loong and other China-trained woodworkers in Australia may have needed to travel to regional centres for furniture-making apprenticeships. Guangzhou and its immediate environs had the best opportunities for such training, as China's pre-eminent manufacturing centre for Western export markets since the seventeenth century, albeit one that had declined by the nineteenth century.[34]

During the twentieth century, more Chinese workers identified with skilled European furniture trades. In 1903, when Shung Yem (常炎 Chang Yan) closed his Melbourne factory, ten employees filed claims for back pay, most in the roles of 'cabinetmaker' and 'polisher'.[35] When Sydney manufacturer Henry Louey ceased production in 1910, a 'turner', 'stainer', 'French polisher' and six 'cabinetmakers' submitted claims for pay due to them as well.[36] Chan King, a failed factory boss forced to seek work in another furniture factory also testified, in 1913: 'I am a cabinetmaker by trade'.[37]

---

33 Sun Sing Loong Testimony, 390–391.
34 Xue Yongjun (薛拥军), 'Guangshi mudiao yishu jiqi zai jianzhu he shinei zhuangshi zhong de yingyong yanjiu' [Cantonese-style woodcarving craft and its architecture centring on applied research in interior decoration] (PhD Thesis: Nanjing Forestry University, 2012), 9–52. Mae Ngai has described Siyi workers migrating to Guangzhou on a seasonal basis for factory work. See Mae M. Ngai, *The Lucky Ones: One Family and the Extraordinary Invention of Chinese America* (Princeton: Princeton University Press, 2012), 4.
35 Worker Affidavits of Debt, 10 February 1903 to 17 February 1903, Shung Yem Insolvency File, PROV 766/P/0-36-819, 3–28.
36 Worker Affidavits of Debt, 9 March 1910 to 14 March 1910, Henry Louey Bankruptcy File, NSWSR 13655-10/23603-18391, 77–89.
37 Chan King Testimony, 31 March 1913, Willie King Bankruptcy File, NSWSR 13655-10/23691-19488, 66–67.

Increasing identification with European furniture trades by Chinese factory workers, even if only in court for the benefit of non-Chinese audiences, may have been owing to the standardised terminology for furniture factory roles that came with closer regulation of the furniture industry after 1896. *Factories and Shops Acts* in New South Wales and Victoria led to the standardisation of terms for furniture trades such that industry minimum wages could be monitored and then fixed.[38] Chinese furniture workers are likely to have experienced pressure from factory inspectors appointed under the legislation to use the terms.[39] Non-Chinese co-workers and supervisors, such as foreman George Holland who worked at Lim Juen's Melbourne factory in the 1920s, could have also influenced Chinese workers in this regard.[40]

Use of European furniture trade terminology also appears to have reflected more specialisation in Chinese factories that came with increasing mechanisation. Willie Wing, who operated a saw and fed coal into a steam boiler at Ah Wong's (王金鐘 Wang Jinzhong) factory in Sydney, discussed delineation of woodwork on the factory floor based on use of machinery. In the New South Wales Court of Arbitration in 1906, Wing explained that he sawed timber with a circular saw and looked after the boiler in one room, then brought the timber to the turners working in another section of the factory so that they could turn table legs from it on machine lathes. He also described going to see the polishers in a different part of the factory

---

38 'The Furniture Board', *SMH*, 14 April 1897; *NSW FSA Report 1897*, 33; *VIC FSA Report 1897*, 3.
39 *NSW FSA Report 1897*, 24; *NSW FSA Report 1898*, 23; *VIC FSA Report 1897*, 10–13.
40 Chin Youey CEDT Application, 10; Worker Affidavits of Debt, 21 December 1926 to 30 December 1926, Lim Juen Insolvency File, PROV 10246/P/0-111-15/197049, 9–14, 29–31, 39–43, 101–108. See also Witness Testimonies, 18–19 October 1926, Pennell v. Quong Wing, trading as W. Rising and Co.

to attach handles onto drawers and doors onto wardrobes after they had finished polishing these machine-made components.[41] Ah Wong's employees might well have used terms such as 'polisher' and 'turner' instead of *mujiang/gong*, or 'carpenter', since their notions of skill were changing as machines became more common and artisanal traditions were contested. Historian Ben Maddison has noted how this was occurring among workers more widely in Australia during the early twentieth century.[42] The same was also taking place within China's furniture industry, as historian Zhou Bei has described.[43] It is possible that exhortations by Australia's Chinese-language newspapers for Chinese migrants to embrace 'modernity', particularly in relation to technology, encouraged the adoption of new terminology by Chinese workers as well.[44]

In a handful of instances, workers' identification as tradesmen in the European sense was owing to the fact that they were born and/ or had completed apprenticeships in Australia. Sidney Jack, who was employed in a number of Chinese factories in Sydney and Melbourne, testified at his bankruptcy hearing in 1909 that he was born in Australia and had undertaken 'cabinetmaking and French polishing' training in Melbourne.[45] Jack did not reveal, however, whether he was apprenticed

---

41 Willie Wing Testimony, 9 March 1906, Furniture Trade Union v. Ah Wong, 167–175.
42 Ben Maddison, '"The Skilful Unskilled Labourer": The Decline of Artisanal Discourses of Skill in the NSW Arbitration Court, 1905–15', *Labour History*, 93 (2007), 77–84.
43 Zhou Bei (周蓓), 'Ershi shiji Zhongguo jiaju fazhan licheng yanjiu' [Twentieth century Chinese furniture development process research] (MA Thesis: Nanjing Forestry University, 2004), 40–49.
44 Mei-fen Kuo, 'Confucian Heritage, Public Narratives and Community Politics of Chinese Australians at the Beginning of the 20th Century', in Sophie Couchman and Kate Bagnall, eds., *Chinese Australians: Politics, Engagement and Resistance* (Leiden: Brill, 2015), 156. See also 'Huaren xin kuan jiqi zhi faming' [Chinese invents new machine], *TWT*, 23 January 1909.
45 Sidney Jack Testimony, 111–112.

in a Chinese factory. According to Sun Sing Loong, apprentices were never taken in Chinese factories in Sydney. New employees were given 'rough work' to do for 'a few months', he explained.[46] In Melbourne factories, on the other hand, several workers, such as Yee Lim and Ah You at Yee Wye's establishment on Market Lane in the 1880s, called themselves 'apprentices'.[47] It is quite possible, therefore, that Sidney Jack was apprenticed in a Melbourne Chinese factory.

A number of Chinese woodworkers made no obvious attempt to link themselves to any conception of skill. Willie Wing talked about the skill of his co-workers at Ah Wong's factory, although he did not identify himself as a skilled worker. He said that he needed to 'saw wood' and 'put coal on and keep steam up', as well as assist the turners and polishers.[48] Many workers who lodged claims when employers went bankrupt did not specify their roles, either, including the nine from Harry Kow's Sydney factory in 1907.[49]

Not identifying themselves as skilled woodworkers probably reflected the realities of workers' roles. Factories required unskilled workers for basic tasks. Additionally, factories did not always offer woodworkers the chance to work regularly. Sing Leng (連勝 Lian Sheng) stated in a Sydney court in 1895: 'I work in a cabinetmaker's shop sometimes'.[50] In such cases, workers often needed to find employment on Sydney's Chinese market gardens or in its shops as well, so they did not necessarily consider themselves professional woodworkers, let alone highly skilled ones.

---

46 Sun Sing Loong Testimony, 391.
47 Yee Lim and Ah You Affidavits of Debt, 27 April 1889, Yee Wye Insolvency File, 123, 162.
48 Willie Wing Testimony, 167.
49 Worker Affidavits of Debt, 17 February 1908, Harry Kow Bankruptcy File, NSWSR 13655-10/23541-17604, 6–15.
50 Sing Leng Testimony, 5 March 1896, Sing Leng Bankruptcy File, NSWSR 13655-10/23072-10431, 3.

Other Chinese factory employees identified either as white-collar workers or as cooks. 'I was a sort of clerk at Loon Cheong's', said Ah Hing of his role at Loon Cheong and Co.'s Sydney operation when it failed in 1883.[51] Hoong Nam (洪南 Hong Nan) had a contract to work as 'manager' (主 zhu) at Khan Meng's (恳明 Ken Ming) Melbourne factory in 1894.[52] This contract, drawn up using red paper, suggests that a certain spiritual significance was attached to his role, as the colour red has ancient associations with good fortune in China, and since success or failure in the contract was linked to 'heaven's will' (天命 tianming).[53] Hoong's contract also suggests a need to reinforce employer–manager relations in writing. Along with white-collar workers, there were cooks. Yit Yung identified himself as the 'cook' at the Sun Kwong Loong and Co. factory in Sydney in 1915. Another cook was Bong Shue, who prepared food in a number of different Melbourne Chinese furniture factories between 1897 and 1915, and who also identified himself as a 'cabinetmaker' and 'French polisher'.[54] Non-woodworkers in Chinese factories had different understandings of skill, particularly clerks and managers, whose literacy and numeracy often differentiated them from others.[55] However, the skills of these workers were seldom challenged by 'white labour' proponents, so their stake in the 'cheap labour' debate was smaller.

---

51 Ah Hing Testimony, 28 May 1883, Ack Chow Insolvency File, NSWSR 13654-2/9993-17928, 14.
52 Hoong Nam Testimony, 1 July 1896, Hoong Nam Insolvency File, PROV 765/P/0-229-90/2610, 201.
53 Hoong Nam Contract, 1 March 1894, Hoong Nam Insolvency File, 154. On similar ritual, see John Fitzgerald, *Big White Lie: Chinese Australians in White Australia* (Sydney: University of New South Wales Press, 2007), 65.
54 Bong Shue CEDT Application, 4 May 1915, Bong Shue File, NAA Melbourne B13-1915/11306, 19.
55 Ah Fat Testimony, 9 March 1906, Furniture Trade Union v. Ah Wong, 149; Seck Fan Testimony, 9 March 1906, Furniture Trade Union v. Ah Wong, 175.

3 Workers

Rates of pay and hours of work

Chinese woodworkers often stated that they were paid a set weekly wage. All ten workers at Man Sing's Sydney factory reported receiving weekly wages on affidavits of debt in 1890.[56] The same was seen among workers at Ah Chee's Melbourne furniture establishment in 1891: all seven who filed claims against Ah Chee did so for weekly wages.[57] The eight employees at the Chong Sing and Co. factory in Sydney stated that they were paid on the same basis in 1893.[58] All eleven of the woodworkers at Charles Wing's Melbourne factory, too, recorded receiving weekly wages in 1901.[59]

Chinese woodworkers reported receiving wages that were nearly always markedly less than the minimums received outside the Chinese furniture sector. In the 1870s and 1880s, this meant under £2 each week.[60] Close to forty Chinese waged woodworkers across fourteen factories claimed back pay in bankruptcy court over these two decades, the best-paid of whom was Mok Leong Shing of Sun Hang Leong and Co. in Sydney at £1/11/6 per week, markedly less than the £2.[61] From the late 1890s onwards, however, Chinese woodworkers reported

---

56 Worker Affidavits of Debt, 28 November 1890, Man Sing Bankruptcy File, NSWSR 13655-10/22675-3020, 33-57.
57 Worker Affidavits of Debt, 6 January 1891, Ah Chee Insolvency File, PROV 765/P/0-12-90/140, 74-85.
58 Worker Affidavits of Debt, 10 April 1893 to 13 April 1893, Leong Dong Bankruptcy File, NSWSR 13655-10/22844-6266, 9-24.
59 Charles Wing Schedule, 6 November 1901, Charles Wing Insolvency File, PROV 765/P/0-319-90/3845, 8.
60 This pertains to adult journeymen. See 'The Furniture Trade', *SMH*, 30 October 1886; 'The Furniture Trade', *SMH*, 15 November 1886; William Holman Testimony, 433; 'Cabinetmakers' Wage Dispute', *Leader*, 30 December 1871; 'Blessings of Protection', *Evening News (EN)*, 15 July 1879; 'The Labour Market', *Illustrated Australian News*, 13 June 1883; VIC FSA Report 1887, 16.
61 Mok Leong Shing Affidavit of Debt, 12 December 1883, Kum Leong Insolvency File, NSWSR 13654-2/10028-18374, 12.

higher wages. This was partly an outcome of their industrial action, to be discussed later in this chapter. Factory wages were also driven up by a shrinking labour pool, caused by Chinese immigration restrictions after 1888.[62] In addition, the *Factories and Shops Acts* facilitated formal minimum wages in Victoria in 1897 and New South Wales in 1904, which placed upward pressure on earnings.[63] Chinese woodworkers' pay still seems to have trailed non-Chinese woodworkers' earnings, however, even though all furniture factory employees were supposed to receive the same pay under the *Factories and Shops Acts* and the related determinations by special wages boards. In Sydney, six woodworkers at Henry Louey's establishment in 1910, and six from Charles Lum's in 1914, reported that they were paid the legally mandated minimum wages for the industry: £2/16/- weekly in 1910 and £3 in 1914.[64] In Melbourne, six woodworkers at Lim Juen's factory and nineteen at Sue Gay's – all in the mid-1920s – reported being paid the minimum wage or more at bankruptcy hearings. Yet, almost 100 other wage-earning Chinese woodworkers across fifty-six factories reported being underpaid.[65] This contradicts information collected by factory inspectors, particularly in Melbourne where inspectors' data (based on

---

62   William Holman Testimony, 433.
63   *VIC FSA 1896*, 15, 16; Judgement, 5 December 1904, United Furniture Trade Society of New South Wales v. Anthony Hordern and Sons, NSWSR 2/5714-11/12-1904, 611. See further Andrew Seltzer and Jeff Borland, 'The Impact of the 1896 Factory and Shops Act on Victorian Labour Markets', IZA Discussion Paper, 10388 (2016), 1–43; Joe Isaac, 'The Economic Consequences of Harvester', *Australian Economic History Review*, 48:3 (2008), 280–300.
64   Worker Affidavits of Debt, 9 March 1910 to 14 March 1910, Henry Louey Bankruptcy File, 77–89; Worker Affidavits of Debt, 6 November 1914, Charles Lum Bankruptcy File, NSWSR 13655-10/23741-20077, 56–71.
65   Worker Affidavits of Debt, 16 December to 30 December 1926, Lim Juen Insolvency File, 9–14, 29–39. Worker Affidavits of Debt, 20 September 1927 to 5 October 1927, George Sue Gay Insolvency File, PROV 10246/P/0-124-15/2216, 215–224.

3 Workers

Chinese employers' figures) shows that the minimum wage was *always* paid in the Chinese sector.[66]

Some Chinese woodworkers stated that their bosses paid them piece rates. In 1889, while most of the thirteen woodworkers at Quong Lee's factory in Melbourne identified as wage earners, two of these, Kee Loon (宋基倫 Song Jilun) and Ah Mon (亞文 Ya Wen), identified themselves as pieceworkers.[67] Similarly, Ying Sing, previously a partner in the unsuccessful Sun Hap On and Co. establishment in Sydney, testified of his situation in 1896: 'I am doing piecework at Wing Sing's'.[68] Additionally, at George Suey's Sydney factory in 1911, six woodworkers recorded that they were employed on piece rates and two specified that they received weekly wages.[69]

Earnings on piece rates as reported by the Chinese woodworkers sometimes surpassed non-Chinese workers' pay, although typically led to underpayment by these standards as well. Piece rates mirrored trends in weekly wages, rising over time, and could be higher than wages, especially during the early twentieth century. Louey Fook, the highest-paid pieceworker at George Suey's factory in 1911, reported that he had made two toilet pairs (a dressing chest and a washstand), two hallstands and a wardrobe over an eighteen-day period and was owed £7/10/- for these items.[70] This was nearly £3 every week, more than the minimum of £2/16/- in 1911.[71] In most cases, however, pieceworkers recorded receiving markedly less than these minimum

---

66 *VIC FSA Report 1897–1930*. It was difficult for inspectors to establish contraventions of the minimum wage. See *VIC FSA Report 1908*, 37.
67 Kee Loon and Ah Mon Affidavits of Debt, 25 May 1889, Quong Lee Insolvency File, 40–42, 48–52.
68 Ying Sing Testimony, 5 March 1896, Sun Bankruptcy File, NSWSR 13655-10/23079-10554, 29.
69 Worker Affidavits of Debt, 7 October 1911, George Suey Bankruptcy File, NSWSR 13655-10/23646-18951, 25–40.
70 Louie Fook Affidavit of Debt, 7 October 1911, George Suey Bankruptcy File, 32.
71 'Furniture Trades Award', *SMH*, 10 September 1909.

rates. Some reported exploitation. Hing Pound, a manufacturer who went bankrupt and then went to work for Lee Fee in Sydney in 1909, was one example. 'I am making toilet tables. I get £1/7/- for each table. I can make one table a week if I work hard', he despaired.[72] Hing Pound may have exaggerated his poverty in bankruptcy court in 1909 in an effort to hide any assets. Regardless, piecework, while beneficial to fast woodworkers, still disadvantaged slow ones. According to Ding On from the Sun Kwong Loong and Co. furniture factory in Sydney, pieceworkers all had 'little books' where they kept a record of the items that they had made, affording them some measure of protection.[73] These 'little books' were the bases for Chinese pieceworkers' claims for back earnings when employers went bankrupt.

White-collar furniture factory workers and cooks always reported that they received weekly earnings, and these were normally better than industry minimums. In 1883, Ah Hing, who was 'a sort of clerk' at Loon Cheong and Co's Sydney factory, said that he was paid £3 a week. This was more than most Chinese and many non-Chinese woodworkers in Sydney.[74] Hoong Nam, manager for Khan Meng in Melbourne, received only half this amount in 1894, but his weekly wage was coupled with an attractive share (ten per cent) of the factory profits. This was a strong incentive, although perhaps not in the context of the early 1890s depression that ruined Australian economies.[75] Yit Yung, cook at the Sun Kwong Loong and Co. factory, reported that he was paid £3/3/- a week in 1915, which was more than the £3 minimum wage for cabinetmakers that year.[76] Such employees, unlike some woodworkers, could not be deemed 'cheap' by any measure.

---

72 Hing Pound Testimony, 17 March 1909, Hing Pound Bankruptcy File, NSWSR 13655-10/23578-18024, 45.
73 Ding On Testimony, 151.
74 Ah Hing Testimony, 14.
75 Hoong Nam Contract, 154.
76 Yit Yung Testimony, 165.

3 Workers

The majority of Chinese Australian furniture factory workers must have been aware that their bosses were breaking the law by paying them less than the mandated minimums. Australia's Chinese-language newspapers were normally silent on these legal entitlements, but were occasionally hostile. In 1913, Sydney's *Tung Wah Times* (東華報 *Donghuabao*) condemned the minimum wage due to its 'punishing employers' (罰家主 *fa jiazhu*) through 'adding to their burdens' (給殖過重 *gei zhi guozhong*) and also 'causing workers likewise to lose their lifeblood' (爲工者亦同失其利椿血已 *wei gong zhe yi tong shi qi li chun xue yi*).[77] This was not mere spin, since several Chinese furniture manufacturers operating in Sydney blamed high wages for their bankruptcies around this time.[78] In contrast to such attitudes, non-Chinese furniture trade unionists and government factory inspectors set out to inform Chinese workers that they should receive the minimum wage. The 1906 New South Wales Court of Arbitration case against Ah Wong was launched by the United Furniture Trade Society following its own effort to publicise these rates of pay in Sydney's Chinese furniture sector, and there were other campaigns.[79] The fact that ethnic Europeans often also worked in the Chinese factories – and sometimes as foremen like George Holland at Lim Juen's factory – also made it unlikely that Chinese workers were unaware of their entitlements.

Many furniture workers were obliged to repay the cost of their passage to Australia, which could have made them reluctant to push for higher earnings, at least in the short term. Although the 'credit-ticket

---

77 'Qudi Huaqiao mu ye zhi ke li' [Banning Chinese overseas wood industry severe cases], *TWT*, 13 December 1913.
78 Hing Pound Testimony, 47; Charles Lum Testimony, 26 October 1914, Charles Lum Bankruptcy File, 4.
79 *NSW FSA Report 1897*, 24; *NSW FSA Report 1898*, 23; *VIC FSA Report 1897*, 10–13; 'Furniture Trade', *SMH*, 9 January 1906; 'Factories and Shops Act', *CAH*, 16 July 1910.

system' of the gold-rush period – where Chinese mining magnates sponsored migration and controlled their workers through debt – was not normally used in the furniture industry due to manufacturers' modest financial resources, workers were often still indebted to others in Australia and China.[80] Wong Loong Yin, who worked in an unnamed Melbourne factory, testified in 1901 of his relationship with his sponsor, the 'businessman' Wong Dew Duck. 'He comes from the same village [Fong Lucy Loong, Xinning (新寧), Siyi (四邑)] as I do … there are three or four families in the village … Wong Dew Duck paid my passage to Australia', he said.[81] Wong Loong Yin was thus under pressure to stay working and paying Wong Dew Duck. Otherwise, he risked difficulties for himself and his family in Fong Lucy Loong.

Even though most were underpaid by European Australian working standards, Chinese factory workers' pay in Australia was higher than their potential earnings in China. Sun Sing Loong pointed out in 1891 that most of the workers in Sydney Chinese factories could not have earned 'enough to keep themselves in food' in China.[82] Not only were they feeding themselves in Australia but their remittances were also lifelines for families in the Pearl River Delta counties. Several factory employees discussed the importance of their pay in this latter respect. Ah Wah, cook at Sun Hap On and Co.'s factory in Sydney, said in 1896 that he sent money to his father 'to do business with' in China.[83] Ding On stated that he sent '£214 odd' in savings and 'winnings' (gambling) to his wife in 1915 when he heard from the 'Viceroy of Canton and the

---

80 Paul Macgregor has argued that this system had ceased to exist in Australia by 1880. See Paul Macgregor, 'Chinese Political Values in Colonial Victoria: Lowe Kong Meng and the Legacy of the July 1880 Election', in Sophie Couchman and Kate Bagnall, eds., *Chinese Australians: Politics, Engagement and Resistance* (Leiden: Brill, 2015), 89.
81 Wong Loong Yin Testimony, 28 October 1901, The King v. Shing Duck, Supreme Court of Victoria, PROV 30/P/0-1270-529, 25–26.
82 Sun Sing Loong Testimony, 389.
83 Ah Wah Testimony, 20 March 1896, Sun Bankruptcy File, 5–6.

3 Workers

Chinese Chamber of Commerce' of floods in his hometown.[84] Earnings in Australia were also enough for numerous workers to return to China regularly. As mentioned earlier, many reported having done so in their applications for CEDTs. Workers were sometimes targeted by thieves on such trips due to their relative wealth. Melbourne cabinetmaker and cook Yeong Yick Chick (楊奕赤 Yang Yichi) wrote to the Collector of Customs from China in 1924 for permission to re-enter Australia. He explained that he had been kidnapped from his village by bandits in the turmoil of the 1911 revolution, that his pay from Australia had been stolen and that he had been held for ransom for years. Only a gunboat attack on the kidnappers' river encampment had allowed him to escape, recuperate and raise money for his passage back to Australia.[85] Factory workers' earnings made comfortable retirement in China a possibility as well. Sun Sing Loong stated in 1891 that he had been saving to retire there: 'I would like to get £200 … I would buy rice fields, and get the rents from them'.[86]

Furniture factory accommodation and meals supplemented Chinese workers' pay. Many revealed that they lived in the factories. Those working at Man Sing's Sydney factory reported living there in 1890.[87] Hing Pound similarly said, in 1909: 'I live at the factory'.[88] As discussed in the previous chapter, factory living included meals prepared with staples of Cantonese cuisine – Cantonese sausage, fish, rice, noodles, tofu, lychee nuts, black fungus, bamboo shoots, lotus root – and workers also had access to special items like shark fins,

---

84   Ding On Testimony, 155. See also Yow Cheun Hoe, *Guangdong and Chinese Diaspora: The Changing Landscape of Qiaoxiang* (London: Routledge, 2013), 28–29.
85   Yeong Yick Chick to the Collector of Customs, 17 April 1924, Yeong Yick Chick CEDT Application, Yeong Yick Chick File, NAA Melbourne B13-1924/10206, 5.
86   Sun Sing Loong Testimony, 390. On returns like this, see Michael Williams, *Returning Home with Glory: Chinese Villagers around the Pacific, 1849–1949* (Hong Kong: Hong Kong University Press, 2018), 120–143.
87   Worker Affidavits of Debt, Man Sing Bankruptcy File, 33–57.
88   Hing Pound Testimony, 44.

birds' nests, lobsters and abalone.[89] A number of factories did not ask their employees to pay for these arrangements, and simply paid them less, although higher-paid workers were charged. 'Ten shillings a week was deducted for my food', testified Ding On regarding his wages and living arrangements at the Sun Kwong Loong and Co. factory in 1915.[90] For most people, food and rent cost more than £1 each week in late nineteenth- and early twentieth-century Australian cities, so factory dormitories and food were desirable in terms of saving money.[91] Factory living offered companionship and safety as well.[92] In most instances, it also allowed workers to live centrally in the city. Yet, overcrowding and the risk of fire were ever-present, so the furniture factories were unsuitable for workers with partners and families in Australia. Such workers tended to rent their own residences nearby.[93]

Several Chinese furniture manufacturers told the 1891 Royal Commission in Sydney that a full factory working week left their employees with minimal free time. Sun War Hop said that his employees needed to work 'six o'clock in the morning to half-past five

---

89 Chow Kum Statement, 30 June 1890, Chow Kum Bankruptcy File, NSWSR 13655-10/22648-2524, 19–34; Joe Sing Statement, 2 October 1914, Joe Sing Hong Bankruptcy File, NSWSR 13655-10/23741-20068, 30–35; Lim Juen Statement, 6 December 1926, Lim Juen Insolvency File, 20–22, 112; Kwong Sing Loong and Co. Ledger, 16 February 1889 to 5 December 1889, Ah How Bankruptcy File, NSWSR 13655-10/22653-2602, 2.
90 Ding On Testimony, 152.
91 'The Rent Problem', *SMH*, 19 March 1912; 'Cost of Living', *SMH*, 2 March 1915.
92 In 1910, for example, Ah Sun and Ah Sick, from Wah Fung's factory, were rescued from an attack near Melbourne 'Chinatown' by 'calling out to their countrymen', who rushed to the scene in large numbers. Refer to Ah Sun Testimony and Ah Sick Testimony, 1 August 1910, The King v. William McCasker, Supreme Court of Victoria, PROV 30/P/0-1552-370, 35, 36.
93 One example is William Yee Sing, who lived near his furniture factory workplace, unhappily it would seem, with his wife Alice. Refer to 'Murder and Suicide', *EN*, 15 November 1920. See also Ga Meng Testimony, 7 November 1895, The Queen v. Ah Loy, Supreme Court of Victoria, PROV 30/P/0-1038-479, 21.

o'clock at night', six days per week, which amounted to almost seventy hours weekly.[94] Sydney's Chow Kum (周錦 Zhou Jin) similarly stated that his employees worked 'daylight till dark', six days a week.[95] According to Chow, this schedule was the 'same as in China', so workers might not have been phased, but most non-Chinese furniture workers baulked at these hours, since they worked markedly less – close to forty-eight hours per week – in 1891, according to cabinetmaker William Holman.[96] Chinese manufacturers and workers also revealed through their descriptions of breakfast, lunch and dinner at the factories that cooks were required to work even longer hours than other employees.[97]

Several workers described shorter full-time working weeks in the twentieth century. In 1906, Willie Wing said that he worked six days a week in Ah Wong's factory. Most days, he testified, were 'nine till five', with half a day's work on Saturday.[98] Ah Fat (亞發 Ya Fa), manager of Ah Wong's operation, explained that he worked the same days, but that his hours were irregular, changing with the establishment's workload. 'Sometimes I go eight o'clock, sometimes nine o'clock … sometimes ten o'clock … cannot say what days, any day', he said in relation to his starting times.[99] As earnings increased, working hours appear to have decreased over time due to a mix of industrial action, immigration restrictions and industrial legislation. Chinese-language newspapers also insisted that workers never work at night, nor on Sundays, after implementation of the *Factories and Shops Acts*. Warnings were published repeatedly, in contrast to the relative silence on minimum wages.[100] Kuo has noted that the initiative by Australia's Chinese

---

94 Sun War Hop Testimony, 396.
95 Chow Kum Testimony, 394.
96 William Holman Testimony, 434.
97 Sun War Hop Testimony, 398; Chow Kum Testimony, 394.
98 Willie Wing Testimony, 175.
99 Ah Fat Testimony, 152.

newspapers to persuade Chinese migrants to observe the eight-hour day was to mitigate 'anti-Chinese labour sentiment'.[101] Warnings to avoid working on Sundays were perhaps also an attempt to satisfy Australia's majority Christian population, including Christians within its Chinese communities.

Several workers also stated that they worked one or two days per week in the factories. Lay Jong (鹿童 Lu Tong), who was hired by Sun War Hop after he went bankrupt in 1893, stated that he worked 'one or two days a week' at 'eight shillings a day'.[102] Sing Leng, too, pointed out that he worked 'sometimes' in a 'cabinetmaker's shop' in 1895. Jan Way (威象 Wei Xiang), testifying in 1915 as a partner in the failed Sun Kwong Loong and Co. factory, also said that he was working 'sometimes one day a week, sometimes two days' as a cabinetmaker in Hang Jan and Co.'s factory in Sydney.[103]

Social class

There was a considerable degree of social mobility within the Chinese furniture sector. Bankruptcies saw a number of furniture manufacturers become ordinary factory workers. Bong Shue, Chan King, Sidney Jack, Sing Leng, Hing Pound, Lay Jong and Jan Way were all workers who had previously been bosses. Similarly, some Chinese manufacturers had been workers before becoming bosses. 'I worked three years for wages, and the balance of the time I have been an employer', stated Lay Jong

---

100 'Mugong xuzhi' [Woodworker notice], *TWT*, 30 September 1899; 'Mugong yi shen' [Woodworkers should exercise caution], *TWT*, 30 June 1906; 'Huaren mu hang zhuyi' [Chinese wood industry take notice], *TWT*, 30 June 1906.
101 Kuo, 'Confucian Heritage, Public Narratives and Community Politics of Chinese Australians', 145.
102 Lay Jong Testimony, 27 July 1893, Lay Jong Bankruptcy File, NSWSR 13655-10/22864-6597, 47–48.
103 Jan Way Testimony, 7 September 1915, Jan Way Bankruptcy File, 213.

in 1891 of his activities in Sydney after his arrival in 1876.[104] This social mobility was a result of the modest capital investments needed for entry into the furniture industry – less than a few hundred pounds in the overwhelming majority of cases – which placed proprietorship within workers' reach. 'If I had any money, I would look out for a business for myself', stated Yit Yung the cook, of his ambition in this respect.[105] Going from employee to employer was part of the 'idealised life cycle' of migrants in the 'Cantonese Pacific', as noted by Henry Yu.[106] Ethnic European workers became manufacturers as well, but they did not have the same opportunities due to the increasing influence of 'big business' in their furniture sector, especially in the twentieth century. Running their own businesses too, may have been more familiar to Chinese workers. Historians like Yow Cheun Hoe and Seung-joon Lee have noted the pervasiveness of commercial culture, even among workers, around the Pearl River Delta in this era.[107]

Some in the factories also spoke of unclear distinctions between bosses and workers in daily factory life. Ying Sing said he was one of five partners in the Sun Hap On and Co. establishment in Sydney in the 1890s, and that he also worked there as a 'sandpaper man'.[108] Low Wing, partner in Sun Tong War and Co's Sydney factory, described a similar situation. 'I was a cook ... I also used to measure and cut up the timber', he said in 1901.[109] This kind of close proximity between

---

104 Lay Jong Testimony, 1891, 393; Yee Wye Testimony, 8 July 1889, Yee Wye Insolvency File, 10; Charles Lum Testimony, 26 October 1914, Charles Lum Bankruptcy File, 4; Sun Sing Loong Testimony, 388.
105 Yit Yung Testimony, 163.
106 Henry Yu, 'Unbound Space: Migration, Aspiration, and the Making of Time in the Cantonese Pacific', in Warwick Anderson, Miranda Johnson and Barbara Brookes, eds., *Pacific Futures: Past and Present* (Honolulu: University of Hawai'i Press, 2018), 185.
107 Yow, *Guangdong and Chinese Diaspora*, 20, 68; Seung-joon Lee, *Gourmets in the Land of Famine: The Culture and Politics of Rice in Modern Canton* (Stanford: Stanford University Press, 2011), 24, 42.
108 Ying Sing Testimony, 28.

workers and bosses was different from historian Wellington Chan's observation of the 'Chinese Confucian benevolent authoritarianism' that typified the operation of the Shanghai department stores – the 'Four Great Companies' – run by Chinese Australians in the early twentieth century.[110] It also differed from the 'well-defined chain of command' observed of Chinese gold-mining operations in some parts of Australia by historian Barry McGowan, more closely resembling the 'egalitarian' labour relations described within Chinese mining operations by Mae Ngai.[111]

Native place loyalties further discouraged broad divisions in class lines across the Chinese furniture sector, since workers from different places frequently harboured animosity towards each other. Workers such as Wong Loong Yin from Xinning, Siyi, and Bong Shue from 'Hoi Ping District' (Kaiping [開平]), Siyi, for instance, often fought with Xiangshan workers.[112] Historian Mei-fen Kuo has described one such conflict, a 1907 riot in Melbourne caused by an assault on a group of Siyi men by two Xiangshan men. The melee, as Kuo has noted, stymied the efforts of the pan-Pearl River Delta 'workers' guild' (西家行 *xi jia hang*) to mobilise workers in protest against the 1907 parliamentary bill to harden the Victorian *Factories and Shops Act*.[113] There were several

---

109 Low Wing Testimony, 3 November 1901, Tin Yow and Low Wing Bankruptcy File, NSWSR 13655-10/23338-14814, 69–70.
110 Wellington Chan, 'Personal Styles, Cultural Values and Management: The Sincere and Wing On Companies in Shanghai and Hong Kong, 1900–41', *Business History Review*, 70:2 (1996), 141–166. Refer additionally to Andrew Godley and Haiming Hang, 'Collective financing among Chinese entrepreneurs and department store retailing in China', *Business History*, 58:3 (2016), 9.
111 Barry McGowan, 'The economics and organisation of Chinese mining in Colonial Australia', *Australian Economic History Review*, 45:2 (2005), 119–138; Mae M. Ngai, 'Chinese Gold Miners and the "Chinese Question" in Nineteenth-Century California and Victoria', *Journal of American History*, 101 (2015), 1091–1092.
112 Bong Shue CEDT Application, 9–11.

3 Workers

similar incidents, including one in Sydney immediately after the 1891 Royal Commission, which galvanised workers on the basis of native place, irrespective of their common class identity.[114]

Kinship was a further consideration that probably superseded class in certain cases. As discussed in the last chapter, proprietors sometimes used family ties for recruitment, meaning that employees and employers occasionally owed each other family allegiance. Some workers even suggested that kinship was their default reference point in trying times. In 1894, Ah Tye, who was engaged at an unnamed factory, testified against another worker, Ah Sin, for stealing from a market gardener, Ah Tew. 'I belong to the same family tribe as Ah Tew', he said. 'Ah Sin does not belong to the same tribe.'[115]

In the early twentieth century, Chinese nationalism both enhanced and detracted from the idea of a 'working class' among Chinese Australian furniture workers. A central concern of the nationalist movement that toppled China's Qing Dynasty in 1911 was workers' rights, so nationalism held substantial appeal for Chinese factory employees. As Kuo has mentioned, at least ten workers cut their queues – symbols of their subservience to the Qing authorities – in 1909 as an endorsement of Chinese revolutionary nationalism.[116] Most, however, did not. Perhaps other workers were more directly influenced by how Chinese nationalism was used to promote unity between all Chinese migrants, as well as to encourage antipathy between Chinese and non-Chinese workers. Indeed, newspaper reports appealed for Chinese cohesion amid racism and discouraged worker solidarity using

---

113 Mei-fen Kuo, 'Reframing Chinese Labour Rights: Chinese Unionists, Pro-Labour Societies and the Nationalist Movement in Melbourne, 1900–10', *Labour History*, 113 (2017), 148–149.
114 Kuo, *Making Chinese Australia*, 29–35.
115 Ah Tye Testimony, 22 June 1894, The Queen v. Ah Sin, Supreme Court of Victoria, PROV 30/P/0-982-342, 22. See also Finnane, 'Law as Politics, 117–136.
116 Kuo, 'Reframing Chinese Labour Rights', 150.

racialised language comparable to that of 'white labour' advocates.¹¹⁷ As the Chinese nationalist movement aligned with communism in the 1920s, Chinese furniture workers in Australia were not involved in ways that attracted much notice.¹¹⁸ Factory workforces were shrinking and not being replaced with new migrants from China because of immigration restrictions. Workers' pay had already increased considerably by this period as well. Both of these factors may have prevented greater nationalist and/or communist activism among them.

Yet, in spite of the impediments to doing so, Chinese Australian furniture workers participated in regular, united industrial action as part of furniture industry workers' guilds. In Melbourne, they went out on strike in 1885, 1893, 1897 and 1903.¹¹⁹ In Sydney, the same was seen, but less often, with evidence of only one strike called by the guild there in 1908.¹²⁰ Sydney's *Chinese Australian Herald* (廣益華報 *Guangyihuabao*) scolded workers for their industrial action in 1908, claiming they were 'imitating [foreigners'] disruptive strikes and being influenced by foreigners' laws' (則以罷工抵制亦倣洋人法 *ze yi bagong zhi zhi yi xiao yangren fa*).¹²¹ In both cities, Chinese guilds

---

117 Kuo, *Making Chinese Australia*, 215–256.
118 I have found no evidence of communist furniture workers. On the small number of Chinese Australian communists, see 'Expelled from Chinese Nationalist Party', *SMH*, 25 January 1928 (twelve people altogether).
119 'A Novel Trade Dispute', *Age*, 15 September 1885; 'The Chinese Strike', *Age*, 16 September 1885; 'A Chinese Strike', *Age*, 10 January 1893; 'The Chinese Strike', *Herald*, 24 January 1893; 'The Factories Act', *Argus*, 11 August 1897; 'Duji huaren mujiang' [Jealousy of Chinese woodworkers], *Chinese Times (CT)*, 3 October 1903; 'Dongjia mu hang xin gao' [Employer association wood industry update], *CT*, 7 October 1903; 14 October 1903; 21 October 1903; 'Mu hang si ji' [Wood industry fourth account], *CT*, 21 October 1903.
120 'Chinese Strike', *SMH*, 8 April 1908; 'The Chinese Strike', *EN*, 9 April 1908; 'The Ranks of Labour', *EN*, 8 July 1908; 'Bagong er ji' [Strike second account], *TWT*, 21 March 1908; 'Mujiang bagong hou ye' [Industry after woodworkers' strike], *CAH*, 27 June 1908.
121 'Mujiang bagong fuye' [Woodworker strike resumption of work], *CAH*, 27 June 1908.

3 Workers

attempted to affiliate with European Australian trade unions, indicating they may have subscribed to the idea of a single Australian working class. However, the main furniture trade unions were unsympathetic, even derisive.[122] It is clear, nevertheless, that these workers' guilds were compromised by serious native place rivalries. The Sydney and Melbourne guilds were operated separately, and some Sydney factory workers went south to replace striking Melbourne workers in 1903, more than likely because they owed no native place loyalty to Siyi leaders including Harry Louey Pang (雷鵬 Lei Peng) who dominated the Melbourne body.[123] Gao/yaoming workers also seem to have been marginalised within the Sydney guild, holding their own strike independently of it in 1911.[124] While Chinese strike action may have been deemed novel by European Australian commentators during this period, there were international precedents. Him Mark Lai and Russell Jeung have described employers' and employees' guilds in southern China, and among Chinese migrants in the United States.[125]

---

122 Andrew Markus, 'Divided We Fall: The Chinese and the Melbourne Furniture Trade Union, 1870–1900', *Labour History*, 26 (1974), 1–10.
123 'The Chinese Strike', *Leader*, 21 November 1903; Kuo, 'Reframing Chinese Labour Rights', 141; Mei-fen Kuo, *Unlocking the History of the Australasian Kuo Min Tang 1911–2013* (North Melbourne: Australian Scholarly Publishing, 2013), 12–13.
124 'Gaoyao mujiang tinggong lei jia gong jia' [Gaoyao woodworkers stop work to force increased wages], *CAH*, 21 January 1911.
125 Him Mark Lai and Russell Jeung, 'Guilds, Unions, and Garment Factories: Notes on Chinese in the Apparel Industry', *Chinese America: History and Perspectives*, 21 (2008), 2. See also Walter Fong, 'Chinese Labour Unions in America', *Chinese America: History and Perspectives*, 19 (2008), 13–16; David Pong, 'Government Enterprises & Industrial Relations in Late Qing China', *Australian Journal of Politics and History*, 47:1 (2001), 4–23; Xue, 'Guangshi mudiao yishu jiqi zai jianzhu he shinei zhuangshi zhong de yingyong yanjiu', 37–39.

Conclusion

Chinese furniture factory employees in Sydney and Melbourne identified strongly with the Pearl River Delta counties of Guangdong. Many related to traditional conceptions of skill as 'carpenters' or *mujiang*, beneficiaries of the artisanal legacy of Lu Ban. Most factory workers who reported their earnings as weekly wage earners and pieceworkers were also underpaid by European Australian standards, and many worked relatively long hours. They often appear to have been willing to accept such conditions owing to family commitments in China. Living in factories and eating Cantonese meals prepared by cooks also offset 'low' earnings. Chinese furniture workers further suggested that social mobility, egalitarianism, native place and kinship were central to factory life, and that Chinese nationalism also influenced them, complicating understanding of a 'working class' in the Chinese sector. Surprisingly, workers did not seek to obscure aspects of their activities that were sensitive in Australia, least of all their pay, despite agitation by 'white labour' advocates.

Chinese factory employees also shared, and often conformed to, certain practices of European Australian workers. From the late nineteenth century, woodworkers began to use European furniture trade terminology widely, abandoning the term 'carpenter' in favour of standard terms like 'cabinetmaker', 'French polisher' and 'turner'. Some furniture workers also reported high earnings, higher in some cases than among skilled workers more broadly. Even the comparatively poorly paid majority reported increases in remuneration over time, the result of their strike action, enhanced bargaining power due to immigration restrictions and minimum wage legislation exerting upward pressure on earnings. Their working hours also gradually decreased as earnings rose, becoming similar to those outside the Chinese sector by the twentieth century. Further, Chinese workers revealed their belief in

Chinese–European worker solidarity with strikes and appeals for support from the wider Australian labour movement.

Furniture workers' descriptions and records of their own activities are indicative of a vital, distinctive and dynamic Chinese Australian factory work culture. This was centred on Guangdong's Pearl River Delta counties, since workers appear to have been guided in their activities mainly by circumstances there. Nonetheless, this work culture also incorporated central elements of the Australian labour movement's struggle to improve workers' rights. These nuances show that controversies and racialised restrictions relating to 'cheap labour' and 'coolies' did not have a particularly strong impact on Chinese workers, and did not even cause them to be guarded over highly controversial issues like their pay. This work culture further suggests that Chinese workers frequently made use of, and sought to benefit from, work principles espoused by their ethnic European counterparts, even though such workers regularly premised their ideas on a belief in 'white labour' as superior labour.

4
In the Marketplace

Tack Lee and Yee Lee (義利 Yi Li) ran one of the largest furniture factories in Sydney between the 1870s and 1890s.[1] They sold a variety of products to myriad customers. Among their most important clients were major Sydney retailers David Jones and Co., Lasseter and Co. and W. W. Campbell and Co., and prominent furniture manufacturers Laycock, Son and Nettleton. The partners also sold items to small retailers, and individuals, particularly through metropolitan auction houses.[2] In most instances, Tack Lee and Yee Lee competed directly with manufacturers outside the Chinese furniture sector, and with other Chinese manufacturers. They promoted their products energetically to attract their customers. Yee Lee travelled around Sydney doing this personally. As he pointed out in 1893, he was 'nearly always out of the shop' on such business.[3] The two partners placed

---

1 Tack Lee Testimony, 18 November 1890, Tack Lee Bankruptcy File, New South Wales State Records (NSWSR) 13655-10/22672-02959, 19; Yee Lee Testimony, 11 April 1892, Yee Lee Bankruptcy File, NSWSR 13655-10/22771-4833, 304.
2 Yee Lee and Co. Ledger, 1 January 1890 to 26 January 1892, Yee Lee Bankruptcy File, 7–280.

advertisements in English-language newspapers, too, and they contributed to charity, performing a public good and also boosting the profile of their business.[4] Gaining and securing a broad customer base using effective promotional strategies was crucial for them. At slightly under three per cent, or seven pence in the pound, their profit margin was thin – thin in order to be competitive, and thinner than in most industries – so they could not afford to do otherwise.[5]

This chapter investigates how manufacturers across the Chinese furniture sector sold their products. It first looks at the scope of their sales, that is, to whom they sold products and what types of items they sold. It then examines the promotional strategies that manufacturers employed to reach their customers. Lastly, it discusses the margins of profit involved in Chinese furniture production. We will see in this chapter that manufacturers did not limit their sales to safe, sparsely occupied markets in order to avoid competition in difficult circumstances, that they were bolder and more competitive than we might suppose.

Furniture sales

Chinese factories produced a range of different furniture items. 'I made all sorts of furniture', Sydney's Yuen Gar (蔡元加 Cai Yuanjia) stated in 1914.[6] Sidney Jack recorded a similarly wide range of furniture in his ledger in Sydney during the early twentieth century, that is, bedroom suites, wardrobes, bookcases, hallstands, office tables, dining tables,

---

3   Tack Lee Testimony, 309.
4   'Notice', *Sydney Morning Herald* (*SMH*), 25 August 1886; 'Public Notices', *SMH*, 31 December 1887. Regarding donations, see 'Sydney Hospital', *SMH*, 4 January 1883; 'Sydney Hospital', *SMH*, 1 February 1888.
5   Yee Lee and Co. Ledger, 7–280.
6   Yuen Gar Testimony, 18 November 1914, Yuen Gar Bankruptcy File, NSWSR 13655-10/23743-20093, 41.

cupboards, sideboards, storage boxes, medicine chests and toilet pairs (dressing tables and washstands).[7] Comparable records from Chinese factories in Melbourne reveal an identical picture there. During the 1880s, Quong Lee's factory on Little Bourke Street, for instance, manufactured chests of drawers, wardrobes, bookcases, chiffoniers, sideboards, tables, storage boxes and kitchen safes.[8] Normally missing from such lists in both Sydney and Melbourne, however, were chairs and lounges. Chinese manufacturers regularly reported purchasing chairs from non-Chinese factories and combining them with tables that they made themselves to form sets.[9] Other than avoiding chairs and lounges, there was little specialisation, either within individual Chinese establishments or across the Chinese sector more generally. Melbourne's Inspector Ellis reported in 1900 that there was a high degree of specialisation in Chinese factories, but it is hard to reconcile this with the records of Chinese manufacturers.[10] Ethnic European furniture manufacturers – consistent with their higher degrees of mechanisation – specialised more in any case. Sydney's Co-operative Cabinet Manufacturing Co. for one specialised in chairs, with nothing of the same

---

7   Sidney Jack Ledger, 18 January 1907 to 18 December 1908, Jack Lem Bankruptcy File, NSWSR 13655-10/23574-17992, 4–64. See further Chew Kee and Co. Ledger, 7 August 1875 to 27 November 1875, Chow Young Insolvency File, NSWSR 13654-2/9598-12761, 17–66; Lay Jong Statement, 30 June 1893, Lay Jong Bankruptcy File, NSWSR 13655-10/22864-6597, 78–79.
8   Quong Lee Schedule, 28 May 1889, Quong Lee Insolvency File, Public Record Office of Victoria (PROV) 762/P/0-338-71/5816, 49–55. See also Ernest Lin Schedule, 5 July 1907, Ernest Lin Insolvency File, PROV 765/P/0-399-90/5033, 140–142; Lim Gin Schedule, 22 May 1914, Lim Gin Insolvency File, PROV 766/P/0-113-2681, 9–11; Rupert Yon Statement, 17 September 1925, Rupert Yon Insolvency File, PROV 766-186-A4224, 88–89.
9   Ack Chow Schedule, 29 August 1883, Ack Chow Insolvency File, NSWSR 13654-2/9993-17928, 85–86; Woo Lung Ledger, 8 April 1872 to 29 March 1873, Woo Lung Insolvency File, NSWSR 13654-2/9488-11460, 35, 40–41; Yuen Gar Ledger, 1 October 1912 to 24 August 1914, Yuen Gar Bankruptcy File, 12–17.
10 *Report of the Chief Inspector of Factories, Workrooms, and Shops* (*VIC FSA Report*) *1900*, 20.

order seen in the Chinese sector.[11] Even so, manufacturing a wide array of items predominated throughout the furniture industry.[12]

Most furniture sold by Chinese manufacturers was made to order for non-Chinese metropolitan retailers. Sydney factory operators Chow Kum (周錦 Zhou Jin) and Sun War Hop told the 1891 Royal Commission that one of their best clients was the city's foremost retailer, Anthony Hordern and Sons' department store.[13] Chinese manufacturers also had close relationships with Campbell Brothers, Marcus Clark and Co., A. Hall and Co., Morley Johnson, Murray Brothers, R. H. Gordon and Co. and Farmer and Co., some of the city's other leading retailers.[14] Much the same was seen in Melbourne. Ah Yet recorded during the

---

11 William Holman Testimony, 17 December 1891, *Report of the Royal Commission on Alleged Chinese Gambling and Immorality and Charges of Bribery against Members of the Police Force* (*NSWRC*) (Sydney: Government Printer, 1892), 434.
12 Refer to Kevin Fahy and Andrew Simpson, *Australian Furniture: Pictorial History and Dictionary, 1788–1938* (Sydney: Casuarina Press, 1998), 18–138.
13 Chow Kum Testimony, 12 December 1891, *NSWRC*, 395; Sun War Hop Testimony, 12 December 1891, *NSWRC*, 396.
14 [Campbell Bros.] Chow Kum Testimony, 395; Man Sing Ledger, 27 January 1890 to 31 October 1890, Man Sing Bankruptcy File, NSWSR 13655-10/22675-3020, 8–29; Henry Louey Ledger, 15 January 1909 to 24 January 1910, Henry Louey Bankruptcy File, NSWSR 13655-10/23603-18391, 4–47; Joe Sing Ledger, 16 May 1914 to 24 September 1914, Joe Sing Hong Bankruptcy File, NSWSR 13655-10/23741-20068, 7–12; [Marcus Clark and Co.] Harry Kow Testimony, 18 February 1908, Harry Kow Bankruptcy File, NSWSR 13655-10/23541-17604, 46; Henry Louey Ledger, 4–47; Lee Chun Testimony, 10 August 1915, Jan Way Bankruptcy File, NSWSR 13655-10/23778-20439, 185; [A. Hall and Co.] Joe Sing Ledger, 7–12; Chow Kum Testimony, 395; [Morley Johnson] Hing Pound Testimony, 17 March 1909, Hing Pound Bankruptcy File, NSWSR 13655-10/23578-18024, 44; Henry Louey Ledger, 4–47; [R. H. Gordon and Co.] Charles Lum Ledger, 12 September 1912 to 17 September 1914, Charles Lum Bankruptcy File, NSWSR 13655-10/23741-20077, 11–50; [Farmer and Co.] Ah Nim Ledger, 28 October 1882 to 28 April 1883, Sun Ying Tiy Insolvency File, NSWSR 13654-2/9994-17931, 1–27; Lay Jong Testimony, 12 December 1891, *NSWRC*, 392; Chow Kum Statement, 30 June 1890, Chow Kum Bankruptcy File, NSWSR 13655-10/22648-2524, 36; Henry Louey Ledger, 4–47.

1880s that his most important clients were Samuel Nathan, Robertson and Moffatt, Wallach and Co. and Newing and Co., who all had impressive stores in the city centre.[15] Rupert Yon of Yon Brothers and Co., too, recorded that much of their furniture went to Sidney and Elcon Myer – proprietors of the Myer Emporium in Melbourne – in the 1920s.[16] Ethnic European factories also sold most of their furniture to these same retailer customers. Marie Olsen, who owned a furniture factory on King Street in Melbourne during the 1880s, for example, sold to the retailers Samuel Nathan, Robertson and Moffatt and Wallach and Co. just like Ah Yet.[17] Orders were frequently placed via contracts put out to tender by retailers, for which manufacturers needed to compete. Lee Chun of the Sun Kwong Loong and Co. factory in Sydney mentioned in 1915 that the firm had bid successfully for one such contract, 'a big contract for Marcus Clark and Sons'.[18]

For the most part, factory operators used popular European furniture designs supplied by city retailers. These clients normally ordered furniture manufactured in the latest London and Paris styles, and designs were constantly updated to mirror these styles.[19] 'They are all

---

15 Ah Yet Schedule, 22 December 1882, Ah Yet Insolvency File, PROV 762/P/0-193-71/4046, 15. See also Man Sing Schedule, 19 July 1883, Man Sing Insolvency File, PROV 762/P/0-206-71/4259, 12; Ah Chee Schedule, 19 January 1891, Ah Chee Insolvency File, PROV 765/P/0-12-90/140, 13.
16 Rupert Yon Testimony, 10 June 1925, 20.
17 Marie Olsen Schedule, 12 September 1883, Marie Olsen Insolvency File, PROV 762/P/0-210-4309, 17. See also Alfred Garner and George Boulton Schedule, 24 April 1884, Alfred Garner Insolvency File, NSWSR 13654-2/10058-18713, 3; Charles Servante Schedule, 21 July 1891, Charles Servante Insolvency File, PROV 765/P/0-36-90/399, 25; Henry Ricketts Schedule, 11 July 1912, Henry Ricketts Bankruptcy File, NSWSR 13655-10/23669-19241, 22; Arthur Hunt Schedule, 20 April 1916, Arthur Hunt Insolvency File, PROV 766/P/0-118-A2800, 6–19; Albert Attwells Testimony, 14 May 1919, Albert Attwells Bankruptcy File, NSWSR 13655-10/23911-21726, 9.
18 Lee Chun Testimony, 185.
19 On styles, see, for instance, 'Farmer and Company', *SMH*, 27 July 1900; 'Marcus Clark and Co', *SMH*, 30 June 1906; 'Wallach's', *Melbourne Punch*, 26 January

ordered goods", said Chow Kum in 1891 of the furniture that he produced for Anthony Hordern and Sons and other major retailers, revealing his role as the manufacturer, not the designer, of these products.[20] While no Chinese manufacturers appear to have described how furniture designs were communicated to them on the record, Edgar Cutler of the United Furniture Trade Society in Sydney provided an account in the New South Wales Court of Arbitration in 1904. A 'European piece of work', he explained, was supplied to Chinese factories to 'copy from', and 'in some cases they [retailers] send the article to the Chinese factories'.[21] Cutler implied that this was unique to the Chinese sector, but it occurred across the industry.[22] Major retailers dictated designs to factories and it was in retailers' interests to have multiple manufacturers able to supply the same furniture to maximise competition between them and keep prices low.[23] This was the key reason why the compulsory stamping of furniture was demanded by labour activists such as Cutler and William Holman, that is, to combat retailers' 'deception' regarding the provenance of furniture products.[24] Although to whom they sold it is unknown, a dressing table made by Wing Lee Brothers, now held in Bendigo's Golden Dragon

---

1893; 'Robertson and Moffat', *Leader*, 22 December 1888; 'A. Hall and Company', *Evening News* (*EN*), 20 June 1900; 'Farmer and Company', *SMH*, 27 July 1900; 'Marcus Clark and Co', *SMH*, 30 June 1906; 'Morley Johnson, Ltd', *EN*, 9 January 1909; 'Bargains in Furniture at Myer's', *Herald*, 19 May 1923. Refer also to Kevin Fahy, Andrew Simpson and Christina Simpson, *Nineteenth Century Australian Furniture* (Sydney: David Ell Press, 1985), 38–53.

20   Chow Kum Testimony, 394.
21   Edgar Cutler Testimony, 5 November 1904, United Furniture Trade Society of New South Wales v. Anthony Hordern and Sons, NSWSR 5340-2/5714, 46.
22   Albert Benness Testimony, 25 September 1901, *Evidence Taken by the Royal Commission Appointed to Investigate and Report On the Operation of the Factories and Shops Law of Victoria* (Melbourne: Government Printer, 1903), 466; *VIC FSA Report 1902*, 22.
23   Historian Peter Scott has observed the same in London. See Peter Scott, 'Mr Drage, Mr Everyman, and the creation of a mass market for domestic furniture in interwar Britain', *Economic History Review*, 62:4 (2009), 814.
24   William Holman Testimony, 434.

Museum, is shown in Figure 4.1. It and most other surviving pieces from Chinese factories, such as those catalogued by John Leckey and Kevin Chamberlain, bears no outward indication of traditional Chinese designs like the ones described in the gold rush-era chair from Chapter One.[25]

Chinese establishments also sold furniture to non-Chinese retailers in regional locales. The records of Man Sing and Ah Chee in Melbourne reveal that they sold to regional retailers throughout Victoria in the 1880s.[26] Likewise, Charles Lum's ledger shows that he despatched furniture from Sydney to European Australian shopkeepers around New South Wales, including distant farming communities like Cowra, Gunnedah, Mudgee and Tamworth, in the 1910s.[27] Certain factories, including that of War Hing in Sydney, focused on such customers. According to the partners, the War Hing factory's trade was 'principally a country one'.[28] In most instances, however, selling to country stores was a sideline to fulfilling orders from metropolitan retailers. Non-Chinese manufacturers did the same as their Chinese equivalents, that is, selling regionally while making city clients their top priority.[29] Regional storekeepers do not appear to have communicated furniture designs to factories like city retailers did, probably because they were content to purchase items in styles consistent with those seen in Sydney and Melbourne department stores.[30] More extensive sales

---

25   John Leckey, 'Low, Degraded Broots? Industry and Entrepreneurialism in Melbourne's Little Lon, 1860–1950' (PhD Thesis: University of Melbourne, 2003), 322, 324; Kevin Chamberlain, 'Chinese Furniture Makers in Melbourne', *The Tool Chest*, 61 (2001), 45–55.
26   Man Sing Schedule, 12; Ah Chee Schedule, 13.
27   Charles Lum Ledger, 11–50.
28   Appendix, *NSWRC*, 481.
29   Yong Ching Fatt, *The New Gold Mountain: The Chinese in Australia, 1901–1921* (Richmond: Raphael Arts, 1977), 43.
30   The furniture ranges of regional retailers typically mirrored those available in the city. See, for example, 'Carolin and Co.', *Riverine Herald*, 21 December 1880; 'C. Dyring', *Wagga Wagga Advertiser*, 8 September 1883; 'Bennett's Furniture Mart', *Bathurst Free Press and Mining Journal*, 24 December 1892; '5

by Chinese manufacturers outside cities were hindered by Australia's inadequate intracolonial/state freight services, which constrained all late nineteenth- and early twentieth-century Australian industrialists. Limited intercolonial/state transportation options also discouraged sales between colonies/states.[31]

Factories sold their products to a smaller number of Chinese retailers. Sydney's Kwong Song (廣崇 Guang Chong) and Ah Sun (亞新 Ya Xin) sold mainly to Gangton Brothers, who ran a furniture retail store in Sydney in the 1920s. Soo Gangton's records indicate that this furniture was then purchased by European Australian customers from diverse socioeconomic backgrounds – journalist Robert Kent, clerk John Ireland, engineer David Cubis, confectionery packer Amelia Martin, and bootmaker's assistant Florence Wormleaton – illustrating that it was not simply 'cheap' furniture.[32] Kwong Song and Ah Sun were supplied with furniture designs by Gangton Brothers that reflected popular European styles, some of which appear in a Gangton Brothers advertisement in Figure 4.2.[33] Sales to Chinese metropolitan furniture stores were uncommon, however, due to the scarcity of these businesses. It was more usual for factories – although this was still a

---

'Things to Remember about Furniture', *Northern Star*, 18 July 1903; 'Henderson & Goodisson', *Advocate*, 16 May 1908; 'Fry Bros.' Furniture Warehouse', *Maitland Weekly Mercury*, 20 December 1913.

31 Diane Hutchinson, 'Manufacturing', in Simon Ville and Glenn Withers, eds., *The Cambridge Economic History of Australia* (Melbourne: Cambridge University Press, 2015), 290. One exception was the Kum Leong firm in Sydney, which sent furniture to Victoria. See Wat A. Che Schedule, 22 November 1883, Kum Leong Insolvency File, NSWSR 13654-2/10028-18374, 56.

32 Soo Gangton Ledger, 1 April 1921 to 1 April 1923, Soo Gangton Bankruptcy File, NSWSR 13655-10/24030-23307, 3–63; Soo Gangton Statement, 9 April 1923, Soo Gangton Bankruptcy File, 211–219.

33 On similar furniture designs in Sydney, see Furniture by Grace Brothers, 1923, Caroline Simpson Library and Research Collection, TCQ 749.20492 GRA; Furniture by Grace Brothers, c. 1927, Caroline Simpson Library and Research Collection, TCQ 749.20492 GRA/3. I thank Michael Lech for help with these catalogues.

4 In the Marketplace

Figure 4.1 Wing Lee Brothers Dressing Table, Melbourne, c. 1900s.

GANGTON BROS., Liverpool Street

This Splendid Exhibit fairly represents all that is New and Good in Beautiful Furniture. Highly Seasoned and Sweet-Smelling Woods. Choice and Novel Designs by Artists. Made by Skilled Craftsmen.

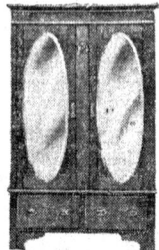

Pedestal Washstand
Marble Top, Tiled Back,
1 Cupboard

Wardrobe
4ft. 6in., 2 Large Oval Glass
Doors, 2 Drawers.

Dressing Table
1 Large Oval Glass,
4 Drawers.

Figure 4.2 Gangton Brothers, *Evening News*, 17 April 1922.

small fraction of sales – to sell to Chinese general stores in regional locales. Charles Lum in Sydney sold to several of them, such as Sam Kee and Co. and Wing Hing Long in the New South Wales town of Tingha, during the early 1910s.[34] Non-Chinese furniture manufacturers also sold to Chinese retailers, including Gangton Brothers.[35]

In addition to selling wholesale to a mix of retailer clients, furniture sales extended to the general public. 'We sell retail in the shop', pointed out Sun War Hop at the 1891 Royal Commission in Sydney.[36] 'I would sell to you or anybody else', quipped Ah Toy when questioned by Commissioner John Stuart Hawthorne about his retail trade.[37] Several Chinese furniture manufacturers' financial records also show extensive retail sales. Those of Sidney Jack in Sydney, for instance, reveal many

---

34 Charles Lum Ledger, 11–50. See further Woo Lung Ledger, 15–45; Ah Nim Ledger, 1–27; Man Sing Ledger, 8–29; Yee Lee and Co. Ledger, 7–280.
35 Soo Gangton Ledger, 3–63. See also Edward Hallshaw Statement, 16 March 1928, Edward Hallshaw Bankruptcy File, NSWSR 13655-10/24345-27163, 27.
36 Sun War Hop Testimony, 396.
37 Ah Toy Testimony, 10 September 1891, *NSWRC*, 41.

sales to unnamed individuals during the 1900s.[38] The extensive range of products that factories sold, along with their varied prices, indicates a tendency towards wide retail customer bases. This furniture was, nevertheless, largely excess stock, or stock made up alongside batches of made-to-order furniture destined for wholesale clients. A few articles were custom-made for homes, according to Ah Toy.[39] Others were made for businesses, including a 'fan-tan table' that Chun Chong of Sun Hap On and Co. factory in Sydney made for the 'fan-tan shops' of the War Hing Tiy (永興泰 Yongxingtai) firm.[40] Selling to retail customers directly from factories was widespread in the Australian furniture industry. Frederick Povey in Melbourne, to take a non-Chinese example, enjoyed a bustling retail trade on his factory floor while also fulfilling orders from city retailers in the 1890s.[41]

Chinese factories regularly had areas to store finished furniture, noted in Chapter Two, and these often doubled as showrooms where customers could view and select their furniture. In 1883, Ah Hing from Sydney's Loon Cheong and Co. factory discussed guiding customers through the factory storerooms to choose their desired items.[42] Ah Toy had 'a store next door' to his factory for retail customers.[43] Chinese

38 Sidney Jack Ledger, 4–64. See further Woo Lung Ledger, 15–45; Ah Nim Ledger, 1–27; Yee Wye Schedule, 13 May 1889, Yee Wye Insolvency File, PROV 762/P/0-335-5786, 36; Ernest Lin Schedule, 26; Yuen Gar Ledger, 12–17; Charles Lum Ledger, 11–50; Toong Hing Ledger, 12 March 1921 to 10 February 1923, Toong Hing Bankruptcy File, NSWSR 13655-10/24025-23254, 4–90.
39 Ah Toy Testimony, 37.
40 Chun Chong Testimony, 20 March 1896, Sun Bankruptcy File, NSWSR 13655-10/23079-10554, 20. Furniture was also imported from China for such venues. See 'An Interesting Exotic', *Sunday Times*, 28 September 1919. I thank Mei-fen Kuo for this article.
41 Frederick Povey Ledger, 2 August 1898 to 20 December 1898, Frederick Povey Insolvency File, PROV 765/P/0-274-90/3274, 50–56. See also Isadore Henry Solomon Schedule, 17 August 1886, Isadore Henry Solomon Insolvency File, PROV 762/P/0-268-71/5065, 12–30.
42 Ah Hing Testimony, 28 May 1883, Ack Chow Insolvency File, 174.

manufacturers rarely aimed to try to match the luxurious show spaces of metropolitan department stores, as they were more interested in the efficient use of industrial space. A special case was the Simpson's (錦順 Jin Shun) firm, which devoted considerable effort to its own furniture retail outlet in Sydney in the 1910s. However, soon after, in 1921, the firm began to move away from manufacturing in Australia, choosing instead to import furniture from China.[44]

Manufacturers sold furniture through metropolitan auction houses as well. 'We used to sell furniture by auction at Bradley's', explained Leong Tong, one partner in the Sun Tong War and Co. establishment in Sydney, when he went bankrupt in 1901.[45] Likewise, Shung Yem (常炎 Chang Yan), who operated a furniture factory in Melbourne in the 1890s, explained in court in 1902 that he regularly sold goods 'by auction at Beauchamp Brothers'.[46] Auction houses were important institutions in this era – comparable to major retail outlets – and auctioneers were often successful and influential. This is perhaps most apparent with Tack Lee's and Yee Lee's auctioneer, wealthy Sydney merchant and parliamentarian Charles Moore.[47] Even so, like some wholesale and most retail sales, auction sales tended to supplement

---

43 Ah Toy Testimony, 37–38.
44 'Jin Shun hao wanquan jia si tai yi shengyi guanggao' [Simpson's complete home furniture firm advertisement], *Tung Wah Times* (*TWT*), 12 April 1919. See also 'H. L. & S. Simpson & Company Limited', *TWT*, 1 October 1921.
45 Leong Tong Testimony, 14 October 1901, Tin Yow and Low Wing Bankruptcy File, NSWSR 13655-10/23338-14814, 65. See further Wong Sum Ling Testimony, 3 May 1889, Wong Sum Ling Bankruptcy File, NSWSR 13655-10/22559-1039, 32; Yee Lee Testimony, 304.
46 Shung Yem Testimony, 9 February 1903, Shung Yem Insolvency File, PROV 766/P/0-36-A819, 60. See also Quong Lee Schedule, 26.
47 Yee Lee Testimony, 306; Mark Lyons, 'Moore, Charles (1820–1895)', *Australian Dictionary of Biography*, accessed 1 June 2018, http://adb.anu.edu.au/biography/moore-charles-4228. Several auctions were also held in factories, including that of Chung War in Melbourne in 1915. See 'Sales by Auction', *Age*, 6 May 1915.

manufacturers' incomes, especially in times of economic uncertainty. Furniture auctions drew a wide variety of potential buyers, particularly 'country people' in Chow Kum's opinion.[48] They also involved furniture of all different types and price ranges, although there seems to have been an emphasis on selling cheaper articles through auction houses. Sun Sing Loong in Sydney explained in 1891 that he and some other Gaoyao/ming operators made up their furniture 'in a hurry' and 'sent [it] to auction to bring what it will'.[49] Yee Lee also described 'selling cheap furniture at auction' in the lead-up to his bankruptcy in 1893.[50] Furniture manufactured in non-Chinese factories appeared alongside Chinese items at auctions, including those from Melbourne's Frederick Povey, who, like Shung Yem, sold through Beauchamp Brothers.[51]

Some manufacturers expanded their sales even further by selling goods to non-Chinese furniture factories. As noted in Chapter Two, Ah Yet in Melbourne sourced timber and table legs from the Cohen Brothers and Co. furniture factory on Lonsdale Street in the 1880s. At the same time, however, Ah Yet was selling them his own products. He sold at least £450 worth in 1882, making Cohen Brothers and Co. almost as crucial to his own operation in terms of sales as the city retailers to whom he sold most items.[52] Quong Lee in Melbourne was doing this as well, but on a smaller scale.[53] Chinese operators in Sydney regularly sold products to Laycock, Son and Nettleton, who operated a large furniture factory. Tack Lee and Yee Lee, Hing Pound, Henry Louey, Charles Lum and Joe Sing all made sales to this establishment.[54] Chinese factories sold various pieces to such clients, which were

---

48 Chow Kum Testimony, 396.
49 Sun Sing Loong Testimony, 11 December 1891, NSWRC, 389–391.
50 Yee Lee Testimony, 5.
51 Frederick Povey Ledger, 50–56. See, furthermore, Percy Board Statement, 12 April 1900, Percy Board Bankruptcy File, NSWSR 13655-10/23285-14011, 6–12.
52 Ah Yet Schedule, 16.
53 Quong Lee Schedule, 21, 26.

incorporated into sets, since it was often more profitable for other manufacturers to ask Chinese factories to supply certain items than to make the furniture in question themselves. Chinese factories also sold components and design-less furniture 'carcasses' or 'husks' to their non-Chinese equivalents, which were used in, or constituted the basis for, finished pieces marketed as the products of 'white labour'.[55]

Occasionally, Chinese furniture and components were sold according to subcontracting agreements with non-Chinese factories to fulfil some of the most lucrative furniture orders. In fact, Chinese articles were placed in Australian government buildings owing to these arrangements.[56] Even the Military College in the new capital of Australia, Canberra, appears to have been furnished partly by Chinese manufacturers working in concert with ethnic European firms in 1911.[57] These sales raised grave concerns within the Australian labour movement, even though, ironically, when Chinese factories were selling their manufactures to non-Chinese factories, there was less competition between them.[58] Competition for such business was far from absent, however, as numerous factories competed against one another to supply the largest furniture manufacturers like Laycock, Son and Nettleton.[59]

---

54   Yee Lee and Co. Ledger, 7–280; Hing Pound Testimony, 44; Henry Louey Ledger, 4–47; Charles Lum Ledger, 10–50; Joe Sing Ledger, 7–12.
55   Lay Jong Statement, 78–79; Henry Louey Ledger, 4–47; Charles Lum Ledger, 10–50; Joe Sing Ledger, 7–12; Gordon Marwood Testimony, 11 November 1904, United Furniture Trade Society of New South Wales v. Anthony Hordern and Sons, 243.
56   'Chinese-Made Furniture', *EN*, 31 December 1900; 'Chinese-Made Furniture', *SMH*, 15 February 1901; 'Chinese Furniture', *Age*, 6 December 1905; 'Chinese Furniture', *Age*, 31 July 1907.
57   'Furniture Contract', *SMH*, 2 June 1911.
58   Gordon Marwood Testimony, 243.
59   Marie Olsen Schedule, 17; Isadore Henry Solomon Schedule, 7–29; Charles Servante Schedule, 25; Frederick Povey Ledger, 50–56; Arthur Henning Ledger, 22 August 1924 to 27 January 1925, Arthur Henning Bankruptcy File, NSWSR 13655-10/24142-24639, 17–36.

Chinese manufacturers also sold other Chinese factory operators finished furniture and furniture parts. In Melbourne, Shung Yem stated: 'I sold chests of drawers to Wah Fung' (another manufacturer). Shung Yem also purchased furniture articles from other operators: a variety of products from Gooey Choon.[60] Similarly, in Sydney during the early 1910s, Fook Hing and Co. sold Charles Lum finished furniture, and Bow War sold him table legs.[61] Non-Chinese furniture manufacturers also sold their Chinese counterparts a mix of products, machine-made components in particular, as seen when Cohen Brothers and Co. supplied table legs to Ah Yet.[62]

Along with selling various furniture products to several different kinds of customers, furniture makers frequently offered delivery with furniture sales. Ah Yet maintained a horse and cart, which he used to collect his supplies and make deliveries.[63] Ah Toy delivered as well, that is, 'up to six o'clock … sometimes half-past six' in the evening, he said.[64] Unlike Ah Yet, he engaged ethnic European 'van men' to deliver furniture on his behalf, a practice which was most prevalent across the Chinese sector.[65] Shipments beyond the city went by train or coastal steamer.[66] Furniture repair services accompanied delivery in many cases, including from Ah Toy, who sent men to people's homes

---

60 Shung Yem Testimony, 53, 57. See further Lim Gin Schedule, 9–11.
61 Charles Lum Ledger, 12, 16. See also Woo Lung Ledger, 18–45; Man Sing Ledger, 8–28; Yuen Gar Ledger, 12–17.
62 Ah Yet Schedule, 14, 105. See also Yee Wye Schedule, 29; Lee Gow and Man Hing Schedule, 13 January 1902, Lee Gow Insolvency File, PROV 765/P/ 0-321-90/3865, 10, 46–53.
63 Ah Yet Schedule, 14, 55.
64 Ah Toy Testimony, 38.
65 Nora Ah Toy Testimony, 31 December 1891, *NSWRC*, 464. See also Man Sing Ledger, 17; Lay Jong Testimony, 27 July 1893, Lay Jong Bankruptcy File, 50; Yee Lee Testimony, 306; Sidney Jack Testimony, 18 March 1909, Jack Lem Bankruptcy File, 102–103.
66 Woo Lung Ledger, 18–45; Man Sing Ledger, 8–28; Charles Lum Ledger, 11–50.

for this purpose as needed.⁶⁷ These services were standard across the furniture industry.⁶⁸

Promotions

Commercial travelling was the most widespread method of sales promotion used among Chinese manufacturers, targeting major city retailers. Factory proprietors and managers discussed calling on these potential city customers in person to drum up business. Sydney's Yee Lee was 'nearly always out of the shop' on this work.⁶⁹ Ah Fat (亞發 Ya Fa), manager of Ah Wong's (王金鐘 Wang Jinzhong) Sydney factory, also described doing so in 1906. 'Sometimes [I] do not go to the shop [factory] at all', he stated, 'sometimes [I] go 'round and get orders and sell furniture'.⁷⁰ Hoong Nam (洪南 Hong Nan), the manager for Khan Meng (恳明 Ken Ming) in Melbourne, similarly spoke of 'selling goods and furniture at warehouses' in 1896.⁷¹ In a smaller number of instances, furniture factory operators and their salespeople travelled around beyond the cities. In 1893, Lay Jong (鹿童 Lu Tong) noted visiting retailers in Sydney to secure orders, and 'transacting business two or three times a year' in the New South Wales regional centre of Newcastle.⁷² This promotional work was done on foot, by tram and

---

67 Ah Toy Testimony, 38.
68 See, for example, 'Furniture, Fittings, &c', *Age*, 6 August 1885; 'Furniture', *SMH*, 3 August 1887; 'Furniture, Etc', *SMH*, 3 August 1900; 'Furniture, Pianos, &c', *Age*, 29 April 1901; 'Furniture, Etc', *SMH*, 29 December 1914; 'Furniture, Pianos, &c', *Age*, 16 April 1918; 'Furniture, Etc', *SMH*, 20 April 1922.
69 Tack Lee Testimony, 309.
70 Ah Fat Testimony, 9 March 1906, Furniture Trade Union v. Ah Wong, NSWSR 5340-2/74-18, 152. See also Hing Pound Testimony, 44; Charlie Young Testimony, 172.
71 Hoong Nam Testimony, 1 July 1896, Hoong Nam Insolvency File, PROV 765/P/0-229-90/2610, 201.

with horse and cart in the cities, while trains and steamships allowed access to regional areas.[73] In later years, company cars such as that described by Quong Wing from the Rising and Co. factory in 1926 were driven.[74] Commercial travelling was the key means of marketing across a broad range of industries in the late nineteenth and early twentieth centuries, especially before professional advertising centred on print media developed in the 1920s.[75] 'Face-to-face intimacy' was critical for doing business around the Pearl River Delta as well, historian Seung-joon Lee has noted, so this was perhaps one of the most familiar promotional methods to new Chinese migrants in Australia.[76]

Customised stationery was a common accessory for commercial travelling, into which factory proprietors invested significant time, effort and expense. Chow Kum recorded having thousands of red business cards – red for good fortune – printed for him during the 1890s.[77] Yee War Hie in Melbourne also had business cards made in the 1910s, but these cards were plain white.[78] Along with business cards, furniture

---

72   Lay Jong Testimony, 1893, 44–45. See also Tin Yow Testimony, 12 September 1901, Tin Yow Bankruptcy File, NSWSR 13655-10/23335-14768, 125; Hing Pound Testimony, 44.
73   Lay Jong Testimony, 1893, 44–45; Tin Yow Testimony, 125.
74   Quong Wing Testimony, 19 October 1926, Pennell v. Quong Wing, trading as W. Rising and Co., Supreme Court of New South Wales, NSWSR 2713-6/1309, 33.
75   Robert Crawford, *But Wait, There's More…: A History of Australian Advertising, 1900–2000* (Carlton: Melbourne University Press, 2008), 6–32; Michael French, 'Commercials, careers, and culture: travelling salesmen in Britain, 1890s–1930s', *Economic History Review*, 58:2 (2005), 352–377; Sophie Loy-Wilson, 'The Smiling Professions: Salesmanship and Promotional Culture in Australia and China, 1920–1939' (PhD Thesis: University of Sydney, 2012), 257–308.
76   Seung-joon Lee, *Gourmets in the Land of Famine: The Culture and Politics of Rice in Modern Canton* (Stanford: Stanford University Press, 2011), 43.
77   Chow Kum Ledger, 16 December 1889 to 3 March 1890, Chow Kum Bankruptcy File, 19–34.
78   Bong Shue Certificate Exempting from Dictation Test Application, Bong Shue File, National Archives of Australia Melbourne B13-1915/11306, 4.

manufacturers or their managers were normally equipped with factory invoice pads.[79] Such stationery did not invoke orientalist stereotypes via distinctive lettering and illustrations. Historian Anne Soon Choi has detailed how this approach was used by Asian food businesses to target niche markets in the United States.[80] Indeed, it is clear that Chinese Australian furniture manufacturers sought a wider appeal. Most other Chinese Australian salespeople, the majority of whom sold vegetables, rarely seem to have carried these accoutrements.[81] However, non-Chinese travellers did.[82] Hence, Chinese furniture manufacturers needed to match or outdo them, and each other.

Chinese operators invested in English for commercial travelling as well. Yee Wye in Melbourne, for instance, testified in 1889 that he needed to be able to 'speak a little English' in order to handle the 'buying and selling' for his establishment.[83] Likewise, Hoong Nam, Khan Meng's manager in Melbourne, mentioned speaking 'a little English' for this reason.[84] Reading and writing in English were also

---

79 Lim Gin Schedule, 10. See also Rupert Yon Statement, 126–129. According to William Holman, Chinese factory travellers often brought gifts to prospective clients as well. See William Holman Testimony, 434.
80 Anne Soon Choi, '"La Choy Chinese Food Swings American": Korean Immigrant Entrepreneurship and American Orientalism Before WWII', *Cultural and Social History*, 13:4 (2016), 528.
81 On Chinese Australian hawkers, see James Hayes, '"Good Morning Mrs. Thompson!": A Chinese–English word-book from 19th century Sydney', in Paul Macgregor, ed., *Histories of the Chinese in Australasia and the South Pacific* (Melbourne: Museum of Chinese Australian History, 1995), 113–126; Kate Bagnall, 'Across the Threshold: White Women and Chinese Hawkers in the White Colonial Imaginary', *Hecate*, 28:2 (2002), 9–32; Joanna Boileau, 'Chinese Market Gardening in Australia and New Zealand, 1860s–1960s: A Study in Technological Transfer' (PhD Thesis: University of New England, 2014), 199–206.
82 See, for instance, Ah Yet Schedule, 14, 105; Yee Wye Schedule, 29; Lee Gow and Man Hing Schedule, 10, 46–53.
83 Yee Wye Testimony, 8 July 1889, Yee Wye Insolvency File, 6, 9.

necessary on many occasions, that is, for reading information like potential client addresses and writing invoices.[85]

Along with commercial travelling, Chinese furniture factories utilised print media, targeting retailers and retail customers through English-language newspaper advertisements. Ah Toy informed 'country storekeepers' and 'furniture dealers' of his increased capacity (thanks to his new steam boiler) in Sydney's *Evening News* in 1878.[86] Loon Cheong and Co. similarly encouraged 'the general public' to visit their furniture establishment and view their 'large and superior stock of furniture' in the *Sydney Morning Herald* in 1880.[87] Chow Kum, too, advised people of their 'chance to furnish cheaply' in Sydney's *Evening News* in 1904.[88] All Chinese migrant groups were represented in English-language newspaper advertisements, but Chinese manufacturers in Melbourne advertised less than in Sydney, perhaps due to the harsher political climate there, which will be discussed in Chapter Five.[89] Nevertheless, Chinese furniture factory advertisements were always sporadic and low-key, normally with only a few lines of text and no pictures.[90] This

---

84 Hoong Nam Testimony, 201. See also Yee Lee Testimony, 304; Loon Moon Testimony, 3 October 1913, Loon Moon Bankruptcy File, NSWSR 13655-10/23707-19673, 6.
85 Phrasebooks aided furniture factory salespeople, but were intended primarily for use by vegetable hawkers. See James Hayes, '"Good Morning Mrs. Thompson!"', 113-126.
86 'Ah Toy', *EN*, 26 March 1878; 'Notice', *SMH*, 16 March 1877.
87 'Important Sale of Furniture', *SMH*, 15 December 1880; 'Selling Off', *SMH*, 25 December 1880.
88 'A Chance to Furnish Cheaply', *EN*, 13 January 1904. On other manufacturers, see 'Notice', *EN*, 18 June 1881; 'Tack Luung', *SMH*, 10 October 1884; 'Sun Kwong Loong', *SMH*, 2 December 1884; 'Go Bo Bros.', *Freeman's Journal*, 8 April 1915; 15 April 1915.
89 Yee War Hie for one advertised his retirement in 1927. See 'Furniture Manufacturer Retiring from Business', *Age*, 7 October 1927. I thank Julia Martínez for this article.
90 Rising and Co. had article-length advertisements in English-language newspapers in the late 1920s and 1930s. See 'Gifts of Furniture', *Farmer and Settler*, 27 September 1930; 'From Factory to the Buyer', *Truth*, 29 March 1931.

was not unusual, however. Most firms in Australia, especially before professionalised advertising, did not advertise.[91] The fact that some Chinese manufacturers did – and even promised prices that could 'defy competition', as in the case of Ah Toy, and 'enormous reductions' in furniture prices, as in Chow Kum's advertisement – suggests that they approached advertising competitively.

A number of Chinese manufacturers also advertised in Chinese-language newspapers, appealing to Chinese customers and asking for referrals to non-Chinese customers. John Hoe (冼俊豪 Xian Junhao) placed regular advertisements in Sydney's *Tung Wah Times* (東華報 *Donghuabao*) from the early 1900s onwards, addressing 'honoured customers' (貴客 *guike*) 'no matter near or far' (不拘遠景 *buju yuanjing*).[92] Usually appearing above John Hoe's, James Kwong Sing's (廣盛 Guang Sheng) furniture factory advertisements, in contrast, appear to have targeted metropolitan customers, neglecting customers outside the city.[93] In Melbourne, too, War Fung and Co. and Lim Wing War and Co. both advertised in the *Chinese Times* (愛國報 *Aiguobao*) in the late 1910s and early 1920s. They appealed to all potential buyers, all 'patrons' (光顧著 *guangguzhe*) whose custom was 'warmly welcomed' (大加歡迎 *dajia huanying*), to quote Lim Wing War and Co.[94] Such advertisements were

---

Although it began to focus its efforts away from manufacturing and towards importing and retailing in the 1920s, Simpson's also placed large advertisements in the *Sun* in Sydney. See 'H. L. & S. Simpson & Coy. Ltd.', *Sun*, 3 January 1923; 3 September 1923; 17 December 1923; 1 January 1924.

91 Robert Crawford, '*Emptor Australis*: the Australian consumer in early twentieth century advertising literature', *Australian Economic History Review*, 45:3 (2005), 224.

92 'Junhao hao mu chang guanggao' [John Hoe wood factory advertisement], *TWT*, 16 February 1918; 8 February 1919; 2 August 1919; 21 February 1920; 2 July 1921; 23 July 1921; 28 January 1922; 28 July 1922; 17 February 1923; 9 February 1924.

93 'Guang Sheng hao jiqi zao mu dian' [Kwong Sing machine–driven wood shop], *TWT*, 16 February 1918.

regular, albeit more so in Sydney than Melbourne, and were placed by manufacturers with diverse backgrounds. Even so, like those placed in English-language newspapers, most of these advertisements were small and plain. Non-Chinese furniture manufacturers like Nettleton, Son and Co. also advertised in Australia's Chinese-language newspapers, but far less frequently.[95]

Simpson's furniture firm placed a particularly noteworthy advertisement in Sydney's *Tung Wah Times* in 1919 (Figure 4.3). It filled half a page and had pictures of the firm's factory and showroom, a newlywed couple, and a new home being built. It thanked 'honourable hometown companions' (Chinese migrants) (貴梓友 *gui zi you*) for recommending their 'Western friends' (西人朋友 *Xiren pengyou*) and encouraged recommendations to 'Chinese or Western men and women getting married and building a new marital home' (中西男女結婚及新建屋宇 *Zhong Xi nan nv jiehun ji xinjian wu zi*).[96] The extravagance and

---

94 'War Fung & Co', *Chinese Times* (*CT*), 24 January 1920; 'Lim Wing War and Co', *CT*, 24 January 1920.
95 'Nettleton, Son & Co', *Chinese Australian Herald* (*CAH*), 16 May 1914 to 10 July 1920. See also 'Craftsman Furniture', *CAH*, 19 February 1921.
96 'Jin Shun hao wanquan jia si tai yi shengyi guanggao' [Simpson's complete home furniture firm advertisement], *TWT*, 12 April 1919. [Author's translation] [Title] 'Simpson firm complete home furnishing business advertisement'; [Main text] 'My dearest Chinese overseas gentlemen, I am eternally grateful. You, my honourable hometown companions, have recommended to Western friends that they visit my humble shop to transact business, and it is fitting that I express my gratitude. Gentlemen, wealth has flown into my family and into my home, and I can never hope to repay you. I wish, therefore, to declare my heartfelt appreciation in this special message. I also have a favour to ask of you, my large circle of dear compatriots. Gentlemen, if you should hear of any Chinese or Western men and women getting married and building their new marital home, please introduce them to my humble store. If you could consider granting me this favour, I would be especially grateful. The merchandise in my little shop is available for inspection. It is elegant and tasteful and the prices are very reasonable indeed. On payment, goods will be despatched far and wide in an attentive and considerate manner. I respectfully hope that you will keep this in mind.'

Figure 4.3 Simpson's, *Tung Wah Times*, 12 April 1919.

the presentation of a desirable domestic ideal indicates that Simpson's was subscribing to the new doctrine of highly visible and evocative newspaper advertising that began to emerge in Australia and around the world at this time.[97]

A significant proportion of Chinese furniture factory proprietors were also listed in commercial directories, which reached a large audience. Furniture historians Kevin Fahy, Christina Simpson and Andrew Simpson have compiled summaries of nineteenth-century business directories, which, when compared with factory inspectors' reports, indicate that thirty per cent of Chinese factories were listed.[98]

Sincerely wishing you good fortune, shopkeeper Li.'; [Address, provided in Chinese and English] [Illustrations, top to bottom then right to left] 'Note the man and woman getting married'; 'Note the construction of their new marital home'; 'Furniture factory'; 'Complete home furnishing showrooms'.

97 Crawford, *But Wait, There's More...*, 44–64. This was also occurring in Hong Kong and the counties of the Pearl River Delta. Refer to Lee, *Gourmets in the Land of Famine*, 76.

4 In the Marketplace

This was similar over the twentieth century. In 1913, for instance, at their recorded maximum in Sydney, twenty-three out of sixty-nine Chinese factories (thirty-three per cent) were listed in the *Sands' Directory*, the pre-eminent commercial directory of this period.[99] Ethnic European manufacturers, on the other hand, were listed in these commercial directories far more frequently.[100] Smaller Chinese factories were rarely listed in directories, which in Sydney meant that Gao/yaoming (高/要明) establishments were the least visible.

Signs on factories guided customers drawn by other means and targeted passers-by. These consisted of factory operators' names and 'cabinetmaker', 'furniture manufacturer' or 'furniture factory'. Signs often included brief outlines of manufacturers' goods and services, as with the 'all kinds of furniture repairs' phrase on War Sing and Co.'s building in Sydney, shown in Figure 4.4.[101] Signs on factories were not normally painted in Chinese characters: manufacturers did not have Chinese customers first in mind. Chinese and non-Chinese furniture factories were almost identical in relation to signage. Exceptions were the small number of factory signs that contained phrases pertaining to 'White Australia'.[102]

Charity was yet another promotional strategy used by Chinese furniture factories, intended to create goodwill and increase general awareness of their businesses. City hospitals were the most popular charitable causes, with many factory proprietors becoming involved in fundraising drives. Chow Kum regularly contributed to Sydney

---

98 Fahy, Simpson and Simpson, *Nineteenth Century Australian Furniture*, 530–613; *VIC FSA Report 1886–1900*; *Report on the Working of the Factories and Shops Act* (*NSW FSA Report*) *1897–1900*.
99 *Sands' Sydney & Suburban Directory 1913*, 1731–1732, 1796–1797; *NSW FSA Report 1913*, 46.
100 *Sands Commercial Directory 1880–1930*; *Sands & McDougall's Directory*, *1880–1930*.
101 City of Sydney Archives, NSCA CRS 51/166.
102 Fahy, Simpson and Simpson, *Nineteenth Century Australian Furniture*, 57.

Figure 4.4 War Sing and Co., Sydney, c. 1902.

hospitals in these initiatives, as listed in the *Evening News* and the *Sun*.[103] Quong Wing's Rising and Co. also made a generous donation of £225 in furniture to Sydney's Royal Hospital for Women in 1929, leading to a full-page report in the *Sunday Times*.[104] Manufacturers donated to other causes, too, like orphanages, benevolent asylums and, in 1904, victims of the Russo-Japanese war.[105] They often dazzled

---

103 'Royal Prince Alfred Hospital', *EN*, 4 July 1906; 'Public Notices', *Sun*, 4 April 1914; 'Public Notices', *Sun*, 5 March 1918. Refer also to 'Nan Xueli yiyuan zhixie juanzhu zhi gao yi' [South Sydney Hospital expresses gratitude for offering of friendship], *TWT*, 13 August 1921.
104 'Rising and Co.', *Sunday Times*, 15 September 1929; 'Help for Hospital', *EN*, 6 December 1929.
105 'The Orphan's Fair', *EN*, 19 September 1902; 'The Chinese Village and Monster Carnival', *Sunday Sun*, 18 December 1904. Chinese manufacturers'

4 In the Marketplace

people with spectacle to draw attention to these causes, and to factories. This was seen when Long Tuck led his team of Chinese furniture workers to victory over Chinese market gardeners in a tug-of-war match for the Melbourne Benevolent Asylum in 1905.[106] All Chinese migrant groups in Sydney and Melbourne contributed generously to charity. Other manufacturers did as well, but Chinese manufacturers appear to have been more committed to this activity. Perhaps this was because charity helped them counter racism while at the same time proving effective in terms of promotion. Charity as a form of advertising was also common among entrepreneurs in Hong Kong and the Pearl River Delta counties, so it is likely that this further influenced Chinese Australian manufacturers.[107]

Chinese factories occasionally participated in trade and industry exhibitions, one more element in their broad spectrum of promotional approaches. The Loon Cheong and Co. partners were participants in the International Exhibition in Sydney in 1879, and Weh Sack won a prize for his cedar wardrobe at the International Exhibition in Melbourne in 1880.[108] Chinese involvement in these events continued well into the early twentieth century. In 1931, Rising and Co. exhibited in the Hall of Industries at the Royal Easter Show. According to the *Sun* newspaper, their stall was 'outstanding', 'bathed in a subdued flow of electric light' and topped with a flashing sign and the firm slogan,

---

involvement in anti-opium campaigns also worked to their advantage in terms of publicity. See Mei-fen Kuo, *Making Chinese Australia: Urban Elites, Newspapers and the Formation of Chinese-Australian Identity, 1892–1912* (Clayton: Monash University Publishing, 2013), 136.

106 'Charity Carnival', *Leader*, 24 June 1905. See also 'The Orphan's Fair', *EN*, 19 September 1902.
107 Lee, *Gourmets in the Land of Famine*, 64–70. Hospitals could have been preferred owing to the success of Chinese merchants in Hong Kong in relation to the Tung Wah Hospital. See Elizabeth Sinn, *Power and Charity: A Chinese Merchant Elite in Colonial Hong Kong* (Hong Kong: Hong Kong University Press, 2005).
108 Fahy, Simpson and Simpson, *Nineteenth Century Australian Furniture*, 73, 193.

'Rising is Rising'.[109] While these efforts were significant in terms of marketing, ethnic European operators dominated trade and industry exhibitions, which indicates that they deemed participation in such events to be more valuable than their Chinese counterparts did.[110]

Smaller establishments selling chiefly through auction sales relied on auction houses to promote their goods. Sun Sing Loong in Sydney, who sent most of his furniture to auction 'to bring what it will', as he mentioned, had no need of newspaper advertisements and other promotional methods himself.[111] He did, however, require auctioneers to publicise auctions and attract potential buyers of his furniture.

Profit margins

Chinese furniture operations in Australia normally involved slim profit margins. Tack Lee and Yee Lee, who had one of the largest and longest-running furniture factories in Sydney, earned a gross income of £8220 and a net income of £294 over the two years between 1890 to 1892.[112] This meant a profit margin of just under three per cent, below standards in most other industries.[113] Man Sing in Sydney ran his factory with a similarly thin margin, that is, slightly less than three per cent (£1151 gross income and £32 net income) in 1890.[114] The

109 'Like Hive', *Sun*, 7 April 1931. See also 'Kwong Sing's Furniture', *Glen Innes Examiner*, 13 March 1930.
110 Fahy, Simpson and Simpson, *Nineteenth Century Australian Furniture*, 73, 193.
111 Sun Sing Loong Testimony, 389–391.
112 Yee Lee and Co. Ledger, 7–280.
113 'Furniture Factories', *Australian Star*, 23 October 1889; [Shirt manufacturers] VIC FSA Report 1892, 18; [Bakers] *Evidence Taken by the Royal Commission Appointed to Investigate and Report on the Operation of the Factories and Shops Law of Victoria* (Melbourne: Government Printer, 1903), 599; [Chinese market gardeners] Boileau, 'Chinese Market Gardening in Australia and New Zealand, 1860s–1960s', 192–199.
114 Man Sing Ledger, 8–29.

depression that started in the 1890s could have had an impact on these profits, although such slim margins were common up through the twentieth century as well. Manufacturer and industry representative Harry Louey Pang (雷鵬 Lei Peng) wrote to Melbourne's *Chinese Times* in 1909 describing the margins on the two most profitable articles to make, as he judged them: dressing tables, at eight per cent profit, and washstands, at five per cent.[115] Overall, however, factories could expect much thinner margins. Sydney's Joe Sing for one carried on business during the first part of 1914 with a profit margin of slightly over two per cent (£1355 gross and £29 net income).[116] High margins were not often seen in European Australian furniture factories, either. Melbourne's Inspector Ellis reported in 1899 that cutthroat competition across the furniture industry (encouraged by metropolitan retailers) had driven prices down so far that 'little left in the shape of profit' remained in any factory.[117] In 1904, Edgar Cutler of Sydney's United Furniture Trade Society further explained that of all furniture manufacturing: 'margin of profit on any particular line is very fine, and it is perhaps a very small increase in the cost which will turn now a small margin of profit into a loss'.[118]

Some establishments saw profit, generating only enough income for workers' and proprietors' modest weekly pay. Sun Sing Loong told the Sydney Royal Commission that his 'business done during the year represents a turnover of £100', which allowed him to pay himself and a worker '10s a week', but which otherwise involved no profit.[119] This was also the situation in factories run by Henry Louey, Yuen Gar (蔡元加 Cai Yuanjia) and Charles Lum in Sydney during the 1900s and

---

115 'Aozhou shi' [Australian matters], *CT*, 24 April 1909.
116 Joe Sing Ledger, 7–12.
117 *VIC FSA Report 1899*, 14. See also *VIC FSA Report 1902*, 22.
118 Edgar Cutler Testimony, 61–62. See also Arthur Henning Ledger, 17–36.
119 Sun Sing Loong Testimony, 388.

1910s. These manufacturers' financial records reveal only the payment of bills and what were typically listed as 'wages' with the money that they received from their sales.[120] No profit is evident in these records, but it is possible that the manufacturers simply took their firms' net income as their 'wages', although these barely exceeded the wages of managers and clerks.

Other factories operated with negative profit margins. Sydney's Woo Lung ran his at negative 0.2 per cent during the early 1870s (£6071 gross and negative £10 net income).[121] Sidney Jack also ran his factory at a loss between 1907 and 1909, but his margin was lower, at negative six per cent or minus thirteen pence for every pound (£4266 gross and negative £242 net).[122] Toong Hing carried on his business similarly in Sydney over the early 1920s, with a profit margin of minus three per cent (£11,465 gross and negative £344 net income).[123]

Furniture manufacturers were particularly sensitive to market downturns given their profit margins. Even minor downturns in market conditions could cause otherwise successful or borderline enterprises to fail, a likelihood made all the more probable by the fact that so few Chinese furniture manufacturers had substantial reserves of capital on which to fall back.[124]

In spite of the apparent absence of high profit margins, however, Chinese operators regularly enjoyed success. With thin margins, it was still possible for factories to make profits as long as sales volumes were high. This was indeed the situation for Tack Lee and Yee Lee, whose factory carried on for over a decade, ensuring that they had sufficient personal wealth to live comfortable lives in Australia and still produce

---

120 Henry Louey Ledger, 4–47; Yuen Gar Ledger, 12–17; Charles Lum Ledger, 11–50.
121 Woo Lung Ledger, 15–45.
122 Sidney Jack Ledger, 4–64.
123 Toong Hing Ledger, 4–90.
124 *VIC FSA Report 1902*, 22.

a respectable net profit for the firm.[125] Slim profit margins and fewer sales also enabled certain manufacturers and their employees to earn at least modest personal incomes. Even when furniture factories carried on at a loss, and although they often failed, operators and workers still received money over long periods, with their creditors usually bearing the brunt of losses. In the context of Cantonese migration during the late nineteenth and early twentieth centuries, this was still useful, since it enabled remittances to families and successful returns to the Pearl River Delta.

Conclusion

Chinese Australian furniture manufacturers generally sold products in a competitive manner. They tended to have extensive customer bases – retailers, retail customers, auction attendees, and furniture manufacturers – to whom they provided a wide variety of furniture products, along with delivery and repair services. In almost all instances, their customers and their goods and services were similar to those of European Australian furniture manufacturers, against whom they competed. Chinese factory operators promoted their enterprises using mixed strategies, namely through commercial travelling and associated promotional material, print media, factory signage, charity, and trade and industry exhibitions. Chinese furniture factories also tended to involve narrow, no or negative profit margins: the standard for their industry in the late nineteenth and early twentieth centuries, and revelatory of its cutthroat competition.

Chinese manufacturers often focused on certain furniture markets. Most preferred major metropolitan retailers, while others concentrated on regional retailers or selling furniture through auction houses.

---

125 On Yee Lee's reputed wealth, refer to Appendix, *NSWRC*, 480.

Factory proprietors also showed a preference for some promotional strategies over others, sometimes with specific markets in mind, as when they advertised in newspapers with small readerships or favoured charity events over trade and industry exhibitions.

Yet, there is minimal indication that Chinese factory proprietors concentrated on unoccupied, safe markets. Making furniture to order for major city retailers like Sydney's David Jones and Co. and Melbourne's Myer Emporium was intensely competitive, as was selling furniture via auction houses. Even when operators sold design-less 'carcasses' or 'husks' to non-Chinese factories and one another, competition for these sales, even though less intense, was far from absent. Further, emphases by some manufacturers on certain promotional methods over others did not reflect a targeted, subtle approach to marketing, because these strategies were always deployed in conjunction with other methods for maximum reach. In addition, the profit margins of Chinese Australian furniture manufacturing suggest that manufacturers felt constant pressure to keep their prices low in order to match and outdo their competitors. When taken together, this marketplace behaviour indicates that Chinese factory proprietors did not sell furniture in a manner that suggests that they were fearful of possible conflict with European Australian manufacturers and labour agitators, or among themselves. It also shows that European Australians – even in the furniture factories that decried Chinese 'cheap labour' – were receptive to Chinese-made wares.

5
Restriction and Resistance

In the early twentieth century, Wing Lee Brothers of Melbourne placed a 'Chinese labour' stamp on a newly made dressing table. As well as the words 'Chinese labour', the stamp specified the firm's name, the nature of its business and its address, with the lettering in indelible ink and arranged in a distinctive triangular configuration. The stamp slowly faded, but was digitally restored by the staff at the Golden Dragon Museum in Bendigo (Figure 5.1) where the dressing table is now on display. This particular stamp, judging by the information contained and its triangular shape, was compulsory under Victoria's *Factories and Shops Act* from 1900.[1] This was one in a series of racialised stamps required on furniture produced in late nineteenth- and early twentieth-century Australia. These were a key part of a broader push to contain the 'threat' of Chinese furniture factories to Australian industry and labour.

This last chapter examines efforts made to restrict Chinese furniture manufacturing, along with how Chinese furniture industry participants and their allies resisted these efforts. The chapter's first

---

1   Victorian *Factories and Shops Act (VIC FSA) 1900*, 43–44.

Figure 5.1 'Chinese labour' stamp, Melbourne, early 20th century.

section addresses labour campaigning between the 1860s and the 1880s that led to the first anti-Chinese industrial laws in Melbourne. The next section explores ongoing labour movement agitation that found support through two public inquiries into Chinese Australian furniture production, the outcome of which was new anti-Chinese restrictions via Victoria's *Factories and Shops Act* of 1896 and its 1900 amendment. In the third section of the chapter, we will look at how laws against Chinese factories were strengthened and enacted around Australia from 1904 owing to an upsurge in 'white' nationalism after Australia's six British colonies had made the transition into a single, federated nation in 1901. Finally, we will consider the political opportunism of the 1920s that led to the piece of legislation targeting Chinese factories in Sydney: New South Wales' *Factories and Shops (Amendment) Act, 1927*. We will see here how the 'White Australia' vision had different implications across different places and time periods in terms of how Chinese furniture industry participants were met with anti-Chinese sentiment and restrictions, and how they resisted.

Labour agitation and the first laws, 1860–89

As Chinese people were entering the Australian furniture industry after the gold rushes, ethnic Europeans in Australian urban centres were at a critical point in the struggle for workers' rights.[2] Trade unions, including cabinetmakers' unions, had been organised in Australia as early as the 1830s.[3] However, it was not until the 1850s and 1860s that they began to take co-ordinated strike action. In 1856, the stonemasons of Melbourne successfully went on strike for an eight-hour working day, encouraging action in other industries over the following years for this and similar goals.[4] Cabinetmakers like Melbourne's William Murphy played key roles in these early campaigns.[5]

---

2 Bradley Bowden, 'The Rise and Decline of Australian Unionism: A History of Industrial Labour from the 1820s to 2010', *Labour History*, 100 (2011), 53.
3 Timothy A. Coghlan, *Labour and Industry in Australia* (Oxford: Oxford University Press, 1918), 212–213, 427; Godfrey J. R. Linge, *Industrial Awakening: A Geography of Australian Manufacturing, 1788 to 1890* (Canberra: ANU Press, 1979), 490.
4 Coghlan, *Labour and Industry in Australia*, 727–728, 736–737.
5 William Murphy, *History of the Eight Hours' Movement* (Melbourne: Spectator, 1896). See also Lynn Beaton, *Part of the Furniture: Moments in the History of the Federated Furnishing Trades Society of Victoria* (Melbourne: Melbourne University Publishing, 2007), 2–3. See further 'The Cabinetmakers' Wage Dispute', *Age*, 28 December 1871; 'Cabinetmakers' Strike', *Weekly Times*, 20 January 1872.

Labour activism in the 1850s and 1860s contributed to the enactment of the first major law applicable to industrial manufacturing in Australia, the *Supervision of Workrooms and Factories Statute* of Victoria in 1873. This law dealt primarily with workplace sanitation, although there was also a clause limiting the employment of women workers to eight hours.[6] Legislation like this was not passed by parliaments in other Australian colonies at the time due to their rejection of what they saw as economic protectionism.[7]

Despite the sometimes violent anti-Chinese activities associated with the gold rushes, and earlier agitation against Chinese indentured labour, there is little evidence of overt racialisation of early urban labour activism. The very few Chinese people in urban industry in this period presented no significant challenge to ethnic Europeans. The Chinese furniture manufacturers who established operations in the 1860s had mostly entered the industry from the goldfields. As a result, they could have been seen by other furniture makers as a fleeting presence, only passing through the industry on their way back to China.

The first signs of anti-Chinese sentiment in the expanding urban labour movement were seen in the mid-1870s, when alarm was raised over the 'Chinese labour problem' in California. Australian newspapers sympathetic to 'European labour', most notably the *Newcastle Morning Herald and Miners' Advocate* in New South Wales, warned of the 'threat' from Chinese workers in California and linked this to Australia's furniture industry.[8] The *Advocate* further reported on the 'union label'

---

6   *Supervision of Workrooms and Factories Statute 1873*, 4–5.
7   Coghlan, *Labour and Industry in Australia*, 700–703, 903–905, 1137–1139.
8   'Chinese v. European Labor', *Newcastle Morning Herald and Miners' Advocate (NMHMA)*, 16 October 1876; 'Chinese Labour', *Sydney Mail and New South Wales Advertiser (SMNSWA)*, 20 May 1876; 'The Chinese Question', *Argus*, 25 May 1876; 'The Question of Chinese Labour', *Evening News (EN)*, 9 October 1877.

developed by the Cigarmakers' Union in San Francisco. This label, featuring the phrase 'made by white men', was developed in 1874 in an attempt to oppose Chinese manufacturers in the cigar industry.[9] It was more than likely the first inspiration for a racialised furniture stamp in Australia.[10] Yet, 'white men's furniture' was not stamped at this time, probably because the nascent state of furniture trade unions prevented them from organising this unilaterally.

In late 1878, non-Chinese workers in the Australian Steamship Navigation Company (ASN Company) went on strike over its employment of Chinese seamen, and the strike was strongly supported in the furniture industry. In Sydney, when the strike was declared in November, cabinetmakers such as Ninian Melville rallied around the striking workers, stoking anti-Chinese feeling.[11] Melville's father, a Scottish convict, ran a furniture factory which had allegedly been ruined by competition from foreign imports during the 1860s.[12] There was strong support for the ASN strikers from ethnic European

---

9   'Chinese Immigration', *NMHMA*, 20 January 1877.
10 Andrew Markus, *Fear and Hatred: Purifying Australia and California, 1850–1901* (Sydney: Hale & Iremonger, 1979), 124–125; Marilyn Lake and Henry Reynolds, *Drawing the Global Colour Line: White Men's Countries and the Question of Racial Equality* (Melbourne: Melbourne University Press, 2008), 1–12; Marilyn Lake, 'Challenging the "Slave-Driving Employers": Understanding Victoria's 1896 Minimum Wage through a World-History Approach', *Australian Historical Studies*, 45:1 (2014), 97–99. It is also highly likely that controversies over trade marks provided inspiration for a racialised furniture stamp. Refer to 'Counterfeiting Trade Marks', *Argus*, 15 November 1876; '110 years of trade marks', IP Australia, accessed 26 January 2018, https://www.ipaustralia.gov.au/about-us/news-and-community/news/110-years-trade-marks. On the earliest furniture maker's mark in Australia (1830s), see Kevin Fahy, Christina Simpson and Andrew Simpson, *Nineteenth Century Australian Furniture* (Sydney: David Ell Press, 1985), 49.
11 Ann Curthoys, 'Conflict and Consensus: The Seamen's Strike of 1878', in Ann Curthoys and Andrew Markus, eds., *Who Are Our Enemies? Racism and the Australian Working Class* (Sydney: Hale and Iremonger, 1978), 54; Phil Griffiths, '"This is a British Colony": The Ruling-Class Politics of the Seafarers' Strike, 1878–79', *Labour History*, 105 (2013), 133.

furniture workers in Melbourne as well. William Murphy pledged his help from the Melbourne Trades Hall, where he was then Secretary.[13] A number of furniture industry identities, including Murphy, also supported the strike by helping to establish Victoria's Anti-Chinese League in 1878.[14] Similar agitation took place in other locations, especially Brisbane, but on a smaller scale.[15] The strikers and their advocates warned that 'replacement' by Chinese workers within the ASN Company was a harbinger of things to come in all industries. The response to this warning was dramatic. Many anti-Chinese meetings were held.[16] One such gathering of 10,000 torch-wielding protesters in Hyde Park in Sydney in 1878 precipitated a riot outside Ah Toy's furniture factory and its attempted destruction by arson.[17] This would have sent a powerful message to Chinese participants and would-be entrants to reconsider their position in the industry, although Ah Toy himself remained in business for many years thereafter.

In answer to the agitation of 1878–79, Melbourne Chinese leaders Lowe Kong Meng (劉光明 Liu Guangming), Cheong Cheok Hong (張卓雄 Zhang Zhuoxiong) and the former woodworker from Penang Louis Ah Mouy (雷亞妹 Lei Yamo) jointly published a booklet, *The Chinese Question in Australia, 1878–79*. They argued that Chinese workers' earnings 'will soon rise to the European level'. Similar events had occurred, they pointed out, among the 'Irishmen in this colony

---

12 Bruce E. Mansfield, 'Melville, Ninian (1843–1897)', *Australian Dictionary of Biography*, accessed 21 September 2018, http://adb.anu.edu.au/biography/melville-ninian-4184/text6725.
13 'The Chinese Labour Question', *Argus*, 4 December 1878.
14 Victorian Anti-Chinese League, *Minute Book*, Melbourne Trades Hall Files, Mitchell Library MSS 308/8, 31–32.
15 Curthoys, 'Conflict and Consensus', 60.
16 'Anti-Chinese Meeting', *EN*, 19 August 1878; 'Attack on the Chinese', *EN*, 27 August 1878; 'Meeting at Maryborough', *Queenslander*, 14 December 1878; 'Anti-Chinese Meeting', *Sydney Morning Herald (SMH)*, 16 December 1878.
17 'Alarming Raid on Chinese', *EN*, 5 December 1878.

who have known what it was to work for four or five shillings a week in the island they came from'. The Chinese authors discussed San Francisco as well, describing how deleterious racialised measures such as the 'union label' had been for both Chinese migrants and indeed the state of California more broadly in terms of lost business.[18] Other campaigning in the form of petitions to parliaments and letters to newspaper editors was seen among Chinese people in Sydney in 1878 and 1879.[19] Chinese activism generally involved co-operation among activists with different Pearl River Delta origins, and aid from non-Chinese supporters.

Agitation against Chinese factories intensified in Melbourne in 1880. As historians Andrew Markus and John Leckey have detailed, Chinese manufacturers bid for the contract to make 6,000 chairs needed for the 1880 International Exhibition in Melbourne. In response, European Australian factory proprietors and employees banded together and successfully prevented the awarding of the contract to Chinese factories. They insisted, as in 1878, that Chinese 'cheap labour' posed a serious threat, not only to them, but across all industries.[20] This move was not violent like the riot outside Ah Toy's furniture factory in Sydney. Yet, perhaps even more menacingly, it was calculated, co-ordinated and officially sanctioned.

---

18 Lowe Kong Meng, Cheong Cheok Hong and Louis Ah Mouy, *The Chinese Question in Australia, 1878-79* (Melbourne: Bailliere, 1879), 20-22.
19 'A Chinese View of the Chinese Question', *Maitland Mercury and Hunter River General Advertiser*, 17 September 1878; 'The Chinese Question', *SMNSWA*, 22 February 1879; Jack Brook, *From Canton with Courage: Parramatta and Beyond—Chinese Arrivals, 1800-1900* (Sydney: Blacktown District Historical Society, 2010), 25.
20 Andrew Markus, 'Divided We Fall: The Chinese and the Melbourne Furniture Trade Union, 1870-1900', *Labour History*, 26 (1974), 1; John Leckey, 'Low, Degraded Broots? Industry and Entrepreneurialism in Melbourne's Little Lon, 1860-1950' (PhD Thesis: University of Melbourne, 2003), 310.

Elections in Victoria and New South Wales in 1880 led to legislation that restricted Chinese migration to both colonies in 1881. Paul Macgregor has pointed out how there was little debate over this issue in Victoria in 1880. There was consensus among politicians that Chinese migration needed to be discouraged.[21] The political situation was much the same in New South Wales, and the anti-Chinese lobby received a strong boost with Ninian Melville's election to the Legislative Assembly in 1880.[22] In both colonies, new restrictions limiting Chinese arrivals, based on gold rush-era legislation, were proposed and enacted in 1881. These restricted the number of Chinese migrants permitted on ships and required a £10 tax for each migrant. Similar legislation was enacted in South Australia in 1881, even though Chinese workers there were few, and Queensland had already passed a law in 1877 to limit Chinese arrivals for the Palmer River gold rush.[23] The United States did not create its own *Chinese Exclusion Act* until 1882.[24] Indeed, Australia was now leading in the struggle against the so-called 'Chinese labour problem', in spite of the fact that its entire Chinese population at this time (around 38,000) only just exceeded that of San Francisco alone (around 30,000).[25] As well as discouraging Chinese migration

---

21 Paul Macgregor, 'Chinese Political Values in Colonial Victoria: Lowe Kong Meng and the Legacy of the July 1880 Election', in Sophie Couchman and Kate Bagnall, eds., *Chinese Australians: Politics, Engagement and Resistance* (Leiden: Brill, 2015), 54.
22 Mansfield, 'Melville, Ninian (1843–1897)'.
23 Joseph Lee, 'Anti-Chinese Legislation in Australasia', *Quarterly Journal of Economics*, 3:2 (1889), 219–222.
24 Mae M. Ngai, 'Chinese Gold Miners and the "Chinese Question" in Nineteenth-Century California and Victoria', *Journal of American History*, 101:4 (2015), 1102; Adam McKeown, *Melancholy Order: Asian Migration and the Globalization of Borders* (New York: Columbia University Press, 2012), 121–148.
25 Choi Chingyan, *Chinese Migration and Settlement in Australia* (Sydney: Sydney University Press, 1975), 22; Yong Chen, *Chinese San Francisco: A Trans-Pacific Community, 1850–1943* (Stanford: Stanford University Press, 2000), 59.

and limiting the supply of labour, these laws diverted capital – £10 for every newly arrived migrant – away from Chinese Australian economic activity, including furniture manufacturing.

The first law intended to give ethnic European furniture factories an edge over their Chinese counterparts was enacted in Melbourne in 1885. Buoyed by their many successes, labour agitators demanded far more comprehensive industrial legislation than the Victorian *Supervision of Workshops and Factories Statute* of 1873. In 1884, as historian Lynn Beaton has described, the United Furniture Trade Society in Melbourne petitioned the Victorian parliament to require that all pertinent furniture be legally stamped 'European labour only'.[26] Thus, a provision for the stamping of furniture was included in the 1885 *Factories and Shops Act*, along with more general clauses for factory inspection, registration, sanitation and safety.[27] Laws like this were not seen elsewhere in Australia at the time, mainly because the idea of supporting 'local' industries held particular appeal for economic protectionists in Victoria, who, uniquely, held sway over the parliament there.[28]

According to Melbourne's *Age* newspaper, an 1885 strike by Melbourne Chinese furniture workers successfully harnessed the broader wave of militant labour agitation and compelled employers to introduce a piecework system of payment. Chinese furniture workers had a labour union, known as the 'workers' guild' (西家行 Xijiahang), which represented all Pearl River Delta county groupings and was probably established around this time. There was also the pan-Pearl River Delta factory proprietors' association, the 'employers' guild' (東家行 Dongjiahang).[29] European Australian trade unionists were

---

26 Beaton, *Part of the Furniture*, 44. See also 'The Chinese Brand', *Australasian*, 21 November 1885; 'The Factories Bill and the Furniture Trade', *Age*, 14 December 1885.
27 *VIC FSA 1885*, 59.
28 Allan Martin, 'Free trade and protectionist parties in New South Wales', *Historical Studies: Australia and New Zealand*, 6:23 (1954), 315–323.

unsupportive of the Chinese furniture workers' strike, denying them participation in the broader labour movement.[30]

The law of 1885 was a dead letter from the outset, so it was amended in 1887. The United Furniture Trade Society had insisted on a racialised furniture stamp, although the Victorian Legislative Council resolved that it was 'invidious to make distinctions'. As such, the racist phrase was dropped, and indeed there were no such clauses in the 1885 version.[31] The form of the stamp was not clearly specified either, and there was no penalty laid down for non-compliance.[32] There were further attempts to racialise furniture stamping and set a monetary penalty for non-compliance with the stamping clause via an 1887 amendment, although these attempts failed as well.[33] Nevertheless, significantly, the amendment stipulated that any place where more than one Chinese person was involved 'in any handicraft or in preparing or manufacturing articles' was to be considered a 'factory', whereas six or more non-Chinese people thusly engaged were required to meet this definition.[34] This meant that smaller Chinese furniture factories were made subject to more regulation than their non-Chinese equivalents. The law was applied haphazardly, however, due chiefly to the immense work of registering all the factories.[35] Even so, the extra requirements

---

29 On names for these groups, see 'Duji huaren mujiang' [Jealousy of Chinese woodworkers], *Chinese Times (CT)*, 3 October 1903. See further Mei-fen Kuo, 'Reframing Chinese Labour Rights: Chinese Unionists, Pro-Labour Societies and the Nationalist Movement in Melbourne, 1900–10', *Labour History*, 113 (2017), 133–155.
30 'A Novel Trade Dispute', *Age*, 15 September 1885; 'The Chinese Strike', *Age*, 16 September 1885.
31 'The Factories Bill and the Furniture Trade', *Age*, 14 December 1885; VIC FSA 1885.
32 VIC FSA 1885, 59.
33 'Stamping Colonial Furniture', *Argus*, 10 December 1886; 'The Chinese and the Furniture Trade', *Age*, 18 May 1887.
34 VIC FSA 1887, 3; VIC FSA 1885, 3.
35 *Report of the Chief Inspector of Factories, Workrooms, and Shops (VIC FSA Report) 1887*, 3.

for Chinese furniture manufacturers and workers, even if these meant little in practical terms, could have caused some to focus on other, less controversial, industries like agriculture.

The end of the 1880s saw further anti-Chinese agitation around Australia, leading to more stringent immigration restrictions in all the colonies in 1888. As Marilyn Lake has suggested, this was due to the perceived threat of China's rapid development over this period.[36] In 1888, the arrival of the *Afghan* and several other ships that were transporting Chinese passengers to Melbourne and Sydney caused widespread consternation. As a consequence, there was an emergency intercolonial government conference and discriminatory immigration laws were reinforced – with the £10 poll tax increased to £100 – to effectively stop Chinese inbound migration.[37] These measures also seriously obstructed the flow of Chinese investment into Australian industries, contributing to the limited capital situation in the Chinese furniture sector.

Furniture makers were once more at the centre of the anti-Chinese agitation of 1888, amid which the first clear calls for racialised furniture industry regulations were made outside Victoria. Furniture makers were members of deputations, including Anti-Chinese Leagues in Melbourne and Sydney, that demanded the governments of Victoria and New South Wales turn away the *Afghan* and other vessels carrying Chinese passengers.[38] Both of the Leagues, in addition, lobbied for legally mandated furniture stamps to identify Chinese-made items.[39]

---

36 Marilyn Lake, 'The Chinese Empire Encounters the British Empire and Its "Colonial Dependencies": Melbourne, 1887', in Sophie Couchman and Kate Bagnall, eds., *Chinese Australians: Politics, Engagement and Resistance* (Leiden: Brill, 2015), 98–116.
37 Lee, 'Anti-Chinese Legislation in Australasia', 222–224.
38 Markus, *Fear and Hatred*, 134–136; Ian Welch, 'Alien Son: The Life and Times of Cheok Hong Cheong, 1851–1928' (PhD Thesis: Australian National University, 2003), 231, 240, 250.
39 Markus, *Fear and Hatred*, 136, 149.

Ninian Melville, who was still a Member of the Legislative Assembly, led the campaign for a New South Wales furniture stamp, with support from both manufacturers and workers in the furniture industry.[40] In Brisbane, there were parallel calls for anti-Chinese furniture stamps, and an excise duty on Chinese-made items.[41] Historian Mei-fen Kuo has described how the 1888 immigration restrictions differed from those of a decade earlier as they emerged from an 'exclusionary national vision'.[42] The intercolonial agitation for new furniture industry laws was part of that vision.

As the events of the late 1880s unfolded, Chinese community leaders in Melbourne published another booklet, *Chinese Remonstrance to the Parliament and People of Victoria*, in 1888. As in 1879, Cheong and the book's other contributors contested claims made against Chinese factory workers. Workers did not, they argued, 'live in the most wretched hovels and upon the scantiest fare', and did not 'need to be told that they ought to live comfortably': they were not 'cheap labour'.[43] There were other initiatives by the leaders and supporters of Chinese communities around Australia during the late 1880s. Some of these also defended Chinese furniture industry participants.[44] Such campaigns were ineffective in terms of the 1888 immigration restrictions, but might have prevented more onerous industrial legislation.

Chinese migrants in Australia also looked expectantly towards China for assistance. In 1887, Sydney and Melbourne Chinese communities were instrumental in facilitating an official visit by two

---

40 'Deputations', *SMH*, 31 May 1889; Linge, *Industrial Awakening*, 498.
41 'Chinese Furniture', *Telegraph*, 26 October 1888.
42 Mei-fen Kuo, *Making Chinese Australia: Urban Elites, Newspapers and the Formation of Chinese-Australian Identity, 1892–1912* (Clayton: Monash University Publishing, 2013), 24.
43 Cheong Cheok Hong et al, *Chinese Remonstrance to the Parliament and People of Victoria* (Melbourne: William Marshall & Co., 1888), 31.
44 'Chinese Protest', *SMNSWA*, 23 June 1888; 'The Chinese Protest', *Australian Star*, 28 June 1888.

5 Restriction and Resistance

Chinese Imperial Commissioners, Wong Yung Ho and U Tsing, to the Australian colonies. As Lake has detailed, their mission was to investigate and report on the treatment of Chinese subjects in South-East Asia and Australia, and they criticised Australia's racialised laws after close consultation with Chinese migrants.[45] This visit reflected a China that had become increasingly assertive on the global stage following its several decades of modernisation and militarisation after the Opium Wars, a resurgent China on which many Chinese Australians pinned their hopes for redress.[46]

Official inquiries and the new laws, 1890–1900

The start of the 1890s saw the onset of a serious economic depression in Australia caused by protracted drought and the collapse of urban property markets.[47] Industrial manufacturing was devastated. Hundreds of factories shut and thousands were forced into unemployment. Furniture production declined rapidly. Melbourne's furniture industry almost halved in size compared with its late 1880s level.[48] In Sydney, the furniture industry was also impacted, although less severely than in Melbourne.[49]

---

45 Lake, 'The Chinese Empire Encounters the British Empire and Its "Colonial Dependencies"', 98–116.
46 On militarisation, see Michael Williams, '"Would This Not Help Your Federation?"', in Sophie Couchman, John Fitzgerald and Paul Macgregor, eds., *After the Rush: Regulation, Participation and Chinese Communities in Australia, 1860–1940* (Fitzroy: Otherland Literary Journal, 2004), 35.
47 Rod Maddock, 'Capital markets', in Simon Ville and Glenn Withers, *The Cambridge Economic History of Australia* (Melbourne: Cambridge University Press, 2015), 267–286.
48 *VIC FSA Report 1889*, 8, 13, 16; *VIC FSA Report 1895*, 8, 24.
49 *Census of New South Wales 1891*, 612, 718; 'Industrial Census Returns', *SMH*, 24 March 1892; 'The Furniture Trade', *NMHMA*, 31 August 1894. New South Wales industry was protected by emergency tariffs. See 'Effect of the Tariff on the Furniture Trade', *Australian Star (AS)*, 13 April 1893.

The depression triggered the largest industrial dispute seen in the Australian colonies, which involved, among others, furniture factory workers. This dispute began, as historian Timothy Coghlan wrote in 1918, with anger over the employment of Chinese and non-union shearers on sheep stations in the late 1880s. The discontent spread rapidly to wharf workers and seamen, who were expected to load and transport non-union wool, and a strike was declared in 1890.[50] It expanded to include thousands of workers across many industries and became known as the 'Great Strike'.[51] Furniture trade unionists supported the strikers, donating money to workers' relief funds.[52] The strike failed for the most part owing to the willingness of unemployed workers to stand in for strikers, which prompted labour activists to engage more with the legal systems of their respective colonies.[53]

Chinese furniture workers in Melbourne initiated their own industrial action in 1893. Like non-Chinese workers, they were affected by the economic instability of the depression. Chinese employers attempted to save money by curtailing their employees' working hours, which employees resisted.[54] Unlike ethnic European workers, however, Chinese workers did not face the same prospect of immediate replacement by the unemployed. Laws limiting Chinese migration to Australia had all but frozen the Chinese labour pool, thereby bolstering workers' bargaining power.[55] Hence, they were able to reach an arrangement with employers; that is, a measured reduction in their pay while the depression lasted.[56] European Australian trade unionists were

---

50 Coghlan, *Labour and Industry in Australia*, 1591–1594; 'The Shearers' Dispute', *Queenslander*, 18 April 1891.
51 'The Great Strike', *SMNSWA*, 13 September 1890.
52 'Furniture Trades', *AS*, 6 January 1891; 'Furniture Trades', *AS*, 4 August 1891.
53 William Spence, *Australia's Awakening: Thirty Years in the Life of an Australian Agitator* (Sydney and Melbourne: Worker Trustees, 1909), 111.
54 'A Chinese Strike', *Age*, 10 January 1893.
55 'Industrial Census Returns', *SMH*, 24 March 1892.
56 'The Chinese Strike', *Herald*, 24 January 1893.

5 Restriction and Resistance

again unsupportive, refusing to include Chinese furniture workers in the broader struggle for workers' rights.[57]

Amid the economic and the industrial strife of the early 1890s, labour movement calls for tougher laws against Chinese factories were renewed. In Melbourne, there were drives to racialise furniture stamping via changes to the *Factories and Shops Act* in 1890 and 1893.[58] In Sydney, the new New South Wales Labor Electoral League – forerunner to the current-day Labor Party – also committed to a law for an anti-Chinese furniture stamp. The relevant plank of the League's founding platform sat alongside much more progressive, universalist planks, including an eight-hour work day and a 'living' wage for all workers.[59]

In early 1890s Melbourne, a parliamentary inquiry recommended stricter rules for furniture manufacturers there. The inquiry was appointed in 1893 to explore the effectiveness of the *Factories and Shops Act*. Labour agitators, including cabinetmaker Archibald Dobson, exerted pressure on the Victorian parliament for workers' excessive hours and low wages – one result of the depression – to be controlled. The inquiry hence probed into this 'sweating'. It also investigated methods for limiting Chinese furniture production. A key determination was that furniture should be stamped with the words 'European' or 'Chinese', as well as the names and addresses of manufacturers, and that penalties should apply for non-compliance. The inquiry also advised that any place in which even one Chinese person was involved in manufacturing be considered a 'factory' and made subject to the Act, that furniture factory working hours and sanitation be much more tightly regulated, and that government contracts ought not be awarded to Chinese manufacturers.[60]

---

57 Markus, 'Divided We Fall', 10.
58 'The Chinese Question', *Age*, 12 August 1892.
59 'Labor Electoral League', *AS*, 1 April 1891; 'Chinese Furniture', *SMH*, 30 April 1892; 'Chinese Furniture', *SMNSWA*, 7 May 1892.

In 1896, following the parliamentary inquiry in Victoria, the *Factories and Shops Act* was amended to enable world-first protection of workers' wages, working hours and safety; however, it simultaneously brought additional discrimination to bear on Chinese people. The *Factories and Shops Act* of 1896 fixed the minimum wage for all factory employees at £2/6/- each week and provided for industry wages boards to regularly review the minimum and set rates for pieceworkers.[61] Such provisions were revolutionary for this period. Even so, any place where even one Chinese person was engaged in manufacturing was indeed made a 'factory', and sleeping in factories was prohibited with a view to eliminating this common Chinese practice.[62] Chinese representatives were excluded from the wages board for the furniture industry, and all furniture factories were assigned special hours of operation, intended to handicap Chinese establishments.[63] Racialised furniture stamps were introduced as well, with penalties for non-compliance.[64] The stamps needed to specify manufacturers' names and addresses and one of three fixed phrases. Dependent on ethnicity, these were 'European labour only', 'Chinese labour' and 'European and other labour'.[65]

In 1891, New South Wales initiated its own inquiry, a Royal Commission in Sydney, which, like its parliamentary counterpart in Victoria, endorsed racialised furniture stamping. The Commission was appointed to inquire into the affairs of Sydney's Chinese community, focusing on allegations of 'gambling', 'immorality' and 'bribery' of police, although it also looked closely at the furniture industry. Two cabinetmakers and trade union representatives, Edgar Cutler and

---

60 *Factories Act Inquiry Board, Second Progress Report* (Melbourne: Government Printer, 1894), 15–18.
61 *VIC FSA 1896*, 15, 16.
62 *VIC FSA 1896*, 3 (1a), 90.
63 *VIC FSA 1896*, 23; *VIC FSA Report 1897*, 5, 10–12.
64 *VIC FSA 1896*, 58.
65 *VIC FSA 1896*, 56, 57.

5 Restriction and Resistance

William Holman, appeared before the Royal Commission and argued that Chinese-made colonial furniture needed to be identified. This was required, the men stated, because most city department stores sold this furniture surreptitiously, such that customers were not able to identify and buy furniture that supported European Australian industry.⁶⁶ The commissioners recommended that Chinese furniture be stamped to reduce this 'deception' and to 'protect' manufacturers, workers and the general public.⁶⁷ Chinese furniture industry representatives, including Ah Toy, were called before the Commission to describe their work. While they stood accused of unethical practices, they were at least heard by the Commission, and questioned by Commissioner Quong Tart (梅光達 Mei Guangda). This contrasted with Victoria's parliamentary inquiry, which did not involve any Chinese people.

Perhaps surprisingly, an endorsement for furniture stamping came from the Sydney Chinese-language press in 1894. The *Chinese Australian Herald* (廣益華報 *Guangyihuabao*) reported that the depression had prompted certain Chinese manufacturers to save on costs by reducing the quality of their furniture. The practice, the newspaper criticised, was having a negative impact on the reputation of Chinese factories, which had led some to use a 'label' (招牌 *zhaopai*) on their furniture as an assurance of quality. The *Chinese Australian Herald* noted the findings of the inquiries in Sydney and Melbourne in the same report and cautioned Chinese operators to take the issue more seriously.⁶⁸ It was also as a mark of its quality that many Chinese

---

66   Edgar Cutler Testimony, 6 December 1891, *Report of the Royal Commission on Alleged Chinese Gambling and Immorality and Charges of Bribery against Members of the Police Force (NSWRC)* (Sydney: Government Printer, 1892), 429; William Holman Testimony, 17 December 1891, *NSWRC*, 433.
67   *NSWRC*, 27.
68   'Mujiang xin yi' [Woodworker news], *Chinese Australian Herald (CAH)*, 15 September 1894. Makers' marks were subject to national regulation in China with the Qing government's 1902 trademark law. See Zuo Xuchu (左

manufacturers elected to stamp their furniture regardless of industrial legislation. Non-Chinese manufacturers often did the same.[69]

New South Wales enacted its first *Factories and Shops Act* in 1896, but this was less comprehensive than the legislation in Victoria. The Act did, in the same spirit as that in Victoria, define a 'factory' as a place where 'Chinese' were involved in manufacturing, whereas 'four or more [non-Chinese] persons' engaged accordingly were to be considered a 'factory'.[70] The Act's clauses with regard to sanitation and safety were also comparable, and factory inspectors were appointed as well.[71] However, unlike in the Victorian case, a minimum wage, prohibition on sleeping in factories, minimum wage boards, special operating hours for furniture factories, and furniture stamping were all noticeably absent. Clauses in the 1896 Victorian legislation were certainly advocated by the labour movement in New South Wales, but labour activists failed in having these included because of the stronger sympathy for the principles of free trade over protectionism in the New South Wales parliament.[72] It is likely, too, that the Chinese furniture industry figures who spoke before the Royal Commission defended their activities with a degree of success.

South Australia and Queensland enacted similar legislation to New South Wales in 1894 and 1896 respectively. The Queensland legislation mirrored that of New South Wales.[73] The South Australian *Factories Act* also had several parallels with the New South Wales law, although it did not have any racialised provisions.[74] The small scale of industrial

---

旭初), 'Zhongguo shangbiao falv zhidu de lishi huigu' [Historical review of China's trademark legal system], *Zhonghua shangbiao* [China trademark], 11 (2012), 19–21.
69 Kevin Fahy and Andrew Simpson, *Australian Furniture: Pictorial History and Dictionary, 1788–1938* (Sydney: Casuarina Press, 1998), 18–138.
70 New South Wales *Factories and Shops Act (NSW FSA) 1896*, 2 (a), (b), (c).
71 *NSW FSA 1896*, III, IV, V.
72 Martin, 'Free trade and protectionist parties in New South Wales', 315–323.
73 Queensland *Factories and Shops Act (QLD FSA) 1896*.

manufacturing in these other colonies, and the relatively weak representation of furniture workers in their labour organisations, prevented more wide-ranging, Victorian-style industrial legislation. Nevertheless, that the laws were even implemented at all, with so few Chinese factories operating in these colonies, suggests the influence of the 'White Australia' principle.

There were objections from European Australian manufacturers to the new rules. Most criticisms came from Victoria in relation to the minimum wage. Stamping of furniture was another source of complaint for industrialists in Melbourne. Some alleged that stamping was encouraging large retailers to make their own furniture rather than sell articles stamped with the details of other businesses, resulting in hardship for established factories.[75] Complaints were also made by many manufacturers in New South Wales in relation to its *Factories and Shops Act*, even though they had far less with which to take issue.[76]

There was resistance among Chinese furniture manufacturers and workers to the laws as well. According to the well-known barrister William Ah Ket, who was at the time working as a court interpreter and as a spokesperson for the Melbourne Chinese furniture workers' guild, Chinese employers were disgruntled as they were under pressure to pay the minimum wage. Previously, he pointed out, 'they had paid just what they liked'. Employers dismissed their older and slower employees in a bid to be able to comply with the *Factories and Shops Act*. This caused another furniture workers' strike in Melbourne in 1897, bringing the sector to a standstill. Ah Ket described how, while numerous Chinese workers insisted on the new wage, they did not approve of their co-workers having been let go.[77] Work was resumed only when sacked

---

74 South Australian *Factories Act (SA FA) 1894*.
75 *VIC FSA Report 1897*, 10–13.
76 *Report on the Working of the Factories and Shops Act during the year (NSW FSA Report) 1897*, 5.
77 'The Factories Act', *Argus*, 11 August 1897.

employees were re-employed on piecework, without the minimum wage (despite the minimum wage regulations).[78]

Chinese-language newspapers in Australia expressed more general, moral grievances with industrial law over the late 1890s. The *Chinese Australian Herald* and *Tung Wah News* (東華新報 *Donghuaxinbao*) in Sydney published reports criticising the discrimination of the *Factories and Shops Acts*.[79] The newspapers also disputed claims made by ethnic European furniture trade unionists against Chinese workers, but at the same time urged them to follow 'Western' practice – especially to avoid working on the 'rest day' (安息日 *anxiri*), Sunday – in an effort to guard against the strengthening of New South Wales industrial law to match Victoria's.[80]

Chinese migrants in Australia could not turn to China with much expectation of help in this period. Its international position was weakened substantially following defeat in the First Sino-Japanese War (1894–95). In addition, Qing authorities were reluctant to support Chinese migrants in Australia. There was sympathy among their community leaders for the Reform Movement in China, an initiative that sprang up out of the military defeat by Japan and worked towards the overhaul of numerous aspects of Chinese governance and society. Although encouraging initially, Qing authorities quickly outlawed the Movement, deeming it a threat to the continued survival of the Qing Dynasty.[81]

Serious practical limitations to the policing of the 1896 *Factories and Shops Acts* in Victoria and New South Wales were noted by factory inspectors and labour agitators in the first years of operation. One of

---

78 *VIC FSA Report 1897*, 10; Yong Ching Fatt, *The New Gold Mountain: The Chinese in Australia, 1901–1921* (Richmond: Raphael Arts, 1977), 43.
79 'Jian lun mugong' [Comparing woodworkers], *Tung Wah News (TWN)*, 'Dou mu geng gui' [Fight more wood regulations], *TWN*, 31 August 1898; 'Shi you shi pian' [Continued worries], *CAH*, 6 May 1899.
80 'Mugong xuzhi' [Woodworker notice], *TWN*, 30 September 1899.
81 Kuo, *Making Chinese Australia*, 83–86.

the most significant problems was inspectors' staffing levels, with small teams expected to cover thousands of factories and tens of thousands of workers.[82] This hampered policing of the minimum wage, working hours and stamping in Victoria.[83] Beaton has described how the modest capacity of factory inspectors to monitor night work led ethnic European furniture workers in Melbourne to conduct intimidatory night patrols past Chinese factories.[84] Communication difficulties also hampered the enforcement of the *Factories and Shops Acts* within the Chinese furniture sector. In Sydney and Melbourne, factory inspectors reported difficulty entering Chinese factories, and additional frustrations once admitted, due to their inability to communicate in Chinese.[85] A specific criticism of the Victorian 'Chinese labour' stamp was its substantial advertising value to Chinese operators. Racialised furniture stamping was intended chiefly to dissuade customers from purchasing Chinese-made furniture items. Yet, factory inspectors reported that the stamp had enabled some customers to seek out Chinese manufacturers personally and buy furniture from them directly, cutting out retailers and saving money, which was a boon to the Chinese factories.[86] In order to attempt to make furniture stamping more effective, a modification was made through a 1900 amendment to the 1896 *Factories and Shops Act*, with more detailed specifications (including a triangle shape for the 'Chinese labour' stamp), but their advertising value was not addressed.[87]

---

82 *VIC FSA Report 1897–1899*; *NSW FSA Report 1897–1899*.
83 Historians Andrew Seltzer and Jeff Borland have shown that inspectors were moderately successful in raising Melbourne workers' wages under the Victorian *Factories and Shops Act*. See Andrew Seltzer and Jeff Borland, 'The Impact of the 1896 Factory and Shops Act on Victorian Labour Markets', IZA Discussion Paper, 10388 (2016), 1–43.
84 Beaton, *Part of the Furniture*, 43.
85 *VIC FSA Report 1898*, 16; *NSW FSA Report 1898*, 23.
86 *VIC FSA Report 1898*, 13.

In spite of its limitations, anti-Chinese industrial legislation would have made the process of recovering from the depression that started in the early 1890s more difficult for Chinese furniture industry participants. Indeed, in combination with immigration restrictions, these laws would have hindered investment in the Chinese sector. Pressure for higher pay in Melbourne owing to the institution of the minimum wage, even though the minimum wage itself was widely rejected by Chinese workers, would have also reduced the feasibility of Chinese furniture production.

Furniture for 'White Australia', 1901–20

With the formal unification of the colonies into a federated nation in 1901, the discriminatory *Immigration Restriction Act* was instituted in accordance with the 'White Australia' vision. Australia, as labour movement rhetoric often held, would become a haven for 'white labour'. This notion was also lauded by conservative politicians, to court working-class voters.[88] Australia was further imagined as an economic powerhouse. An Anglo-Australian economy with a large manufacturing base was seen as one remedy to the new nation's isolation from Europe on the doorstep of Asia.[89]

A key figure in the struggle for a new China, Liang Qichao (梁啟超), was present at Australia's birth as a nation, and offered new hope to Chinese migrants with his message of Chinese nationalism and a strong China to protect them. Travelling in exile following his

---

87 *VIC FSA 1900*, 43–44; *VIC FSA Report 1900*, 25; *VIC FSA Report 1901*, 42–43; *VIC FSA Report 1901*, 43.
88 Gwenda Tavan, *The Long, Slow Death of White Australia* (Melbourne: Scribe, 2005), 7–29.
89 Diane Hutchinson, 'Manufacturing', in Simon Ville and Glenn Withers, eds., *The Cambridge Economic History of Australia* (Melbourne: Cambridge University Press, 2015), 287–308.

attempted arrest in China for his central role in the Reform Movement, he met with many Chinese Australians, including those in the furniture industry, and attended the Federation celebrations in Sydney. As Kuo has noted, however, he was unable to raise substantial funds, suggesting that migrants did not regard his message as a practical means of opposition to the racialised legislation underpinning Australian Federation.[90] The disastrous Boxer Rebellion (1899–1901), which saw foreign forces capture Beijing, probably made the idea of a strong China seem remote.

Inspired by the idea of 'White Australian' industrial advancement, another inquiry – this time a Victorian Royal Commission in Melbourne – was launched into manufacturing, including furniture production. Its focus was to consider the amendment of the Victorian *Factories and Shops Act* and it collected more than 900 pages of evidence from witnesses.[91] In their report of 1902–03, the commissioners recommended the licensing of furniture factories that engaged 'persons of Asiatic race', and that a maximum of twenty licences be allowed.[92] They also advised that the phrases stamped on furniture be modified to 'European make' and 'Asiatic make' (an effort to resolve ambiguities and guard against entry of 'Syrians' into the furniture industry), that registration numbers be used instead of factory names and addresses (to remove the advertising value of stamps), and that retailers – not only manufacturers – be penalised for selling unstamped furniture.[93] The commissioners suggested other measures unrelated to Chinese furniture, yet many of these were similarly concerned with uplifting 'white labour'.[94]

---

90 Kuo, *Making Chinese Australia*, 96–100, 190.
91 None were Chinese.
92 *Report of the Royal Commission Appointed to Investigate and Report on the Operation of the Factories and Shops Law of Victoria (VICRC)* (Melbourne: Government Printer, 1903), 73.
93 *VICRC*, 74.
94 *VICRC*, 69–78.

Furniture stamping was also raised again in Sydney to coincide with the Royal Commission in Melbourne. Edgar Cutler from the United Furniture Trade Society demanded that furniture sold to the government be stamped to prevent Chinese furniture being used in state buildings like Government House.[95]

The challenge of responding to the Royal Commission's determinations divided the Chinese community in Melbourne along class lines, precipitating yet another strike in 1903. The larger Chinese factories formed an alliance against the smaller ones in anticipation of only twenty being permitted registration. Workers reacted by going on strike, intent on disrupting what they saw as collaboration with racist authorities.[96] As Kuo has described, however, appeals to Chinese nationalism by prominent figures like Harry Louey Pang (雷鵬 Lei Peng) and the *Chinese Times* (愛國報 *Aiguobao*) in Melbourne helped reunite the divided community, dissolving the alliance and settling the strike.[97]

There were strenuous efforts to adopt the Royal Commission's findings in Melbourne in 1904 and 1905, but these failed. Historian John Leckey has detailed how bills to amend the *Factories and Shops Act* in line with its advice were presented to the parliament in both years. Dobson, the cabinetmaker who campaigned for the 1893 parliamentary inquiry, and who had become President of the Melbourne Trades Hall Council, was one of the bills' foremost proponents. Both bills were

---

95   'Chinese Made Furniture', *AS*, 15 February 1901; 'The Furniture Trade', *SMH*, 10 January 1903.
96   'Duji huaren mujiang' [Jealousy of Chinese woodworkers], *CT*, 3 October 1903; 'Dongjia mu hang xin gao' [Employer association's wood industry update], *CT*, 7 October 1903; 14 October 1903; 21 October 1903; 'Mu hang si ji' [Wood industry fourth account], *CT*, 21 October 1903.
97   Kuo, 'Reframing Chinese Labour Rights', 133–155. Louey Pang was also convicted of indecent assault on two separate occasions. Refer to The King v. Louey Pang, Supreme Court of Victoria, Public Record Office of Victoria 30/P/0-1613-191.

rejected by a majority of parliamentarians due to the perceived contravention of so-called 'British fair play'.[98]

In 1905, Victoria's industrial law was modified slightly, and one new furniture stamp was included. For the most part, the 1905 *Factories and Shops Act* was a consolidation of amendments to the legislation since 1896. A new furniture stamp phrase was to specify whether pieces were 'partly prepared by' the manufacturers whose details were specified, which was an effort to restrict the use of Chinese components in non-Chinese furniture.[99] Further, according to one of the recommendations of the Royal Commission in Melbourne, manufacturers and retailers were both made liable for selling unstamped furniture.[100] Inspectors reported that this clause had increased the amount of furniture being stamped.[101] Two additional bills to amend the *Factories and Shops Act* to reflect the Royal Commission's recommendations more closely were put before Victorian parliamentarians in 1906 and 1907, but these failed, too, like earlier bills.[102] Indeed, while the Royal Commission in Melbourne promoted much harsher anti-Chinese measures, this had minimal bearing on the Victorian legislation that was enacted.

Campaigns by Melbourne's Chinese community probably ensured the failure of efforts to harden industrial legislation in Victoria. Cheong Cheok Hong, co-author of the 1879 and 1888 remonstrances, was an influential campaigner. He penned letters, organised public meetings and arranged for petitions to the Legislative Council of Victoria, often with the assistance of non-Chinese friends and associates, solicitor William Calder in particular.[103] William Ah Ket, formerly a court interpreter but a barrister by this time, was another key

---

98 Leckey, 'Low, Degraded Broots?', 346–349.
99 *VIC FSA 1905*, 69 (1).
100 *VIC FSA 1905*, 73.
101 *VIC FSA 1905*, 69 (1).
102 Leckey, 'Low, Degraded Broots?', 351.

campaigner. In 1906, he wrote *A Paper on the Chinese and the Factories Acts*, where he contested the reasons that 'white labour' activists gave to justify further handicaps on Chinese factories.[104] Melbourne's Chinese manufacturers also published a booklet entitled *The Chinese Case against the Chinese Employment Bill*, authored by solicitor J. L. Clarke. This disputed claims about furniture workers' rates of pay and conduct in Australia, and the bill of 1907.[105] Again, these initiatives involved a high degree of pan-Pearl River Delta co-operation, as well as co-ordination with European Australian supporters.

It is also possible that the Qing government's decision to appoint a Consul-General to Australia and New Zealand in 1905, at the request of Chinese Australians, prevented harsher industrial law. Although a federated nation, Australia remained a part of the British Empire, which supported the Qing government under the Boxer Protocol of 1901. Therefore, this diplomatic appointment may have played some role in the actions of Victorian lawmakers.[106]

While it was mostly rejected as legislation in Victoria, the recommendations of the Victorian Royal Commission were adopted almost in full in Western Australia with the *Factories Act* of 1904. Working hours among 'Asiatic' workers were sharply restricted, existing 'Asiatic' furniture factories needed to be licensed (with no new factories permitted), and the 'Asiatic labour' furniture stamp was implemented.[107] This was despite the fact that there were only around 100 Chinese participants in Perth's furniture industry when the law came into operation, and slightly more non-Chinese participants.[108]

---

103 Cheong Cheok Hong Letter Books, State Library of Victoria, MS9821, 1904–1907.
104 William Ah Ket, *A Paper on the Chinese and the Factories Act* (Melbourne: Arbuckle, Waddell & Fawckner, 1906).
105 J. L. Clarke, *The Chinese Case against the Chinese Employment Bill* (Melbourne: Arbuckle, Waddell & Fawckner, 1907).
106 Kuo, *Making Chinese Australia*, 201.
107 Western Australian *Factories Act (WA FA) 1904*, 15, 23, 46, 47.

5 Restriction and Resistance

Historian Anne Atkinson has noted several Chinese legal challenges to the *Factories Act* in Perth, as has Mark Finnane.[109] Its opponents, however, were unsuccessful in preventing such onerous legislation, as they did in Melbourne, more than likely because Perth's Chinese community was considerably smaller and less influential.

Less stringent legislation was advocated by the labour movement in Sydney in 1904. The Trades and Labour Council launched its own investigation into 'Chinese competition' across several different industries. Its report advised the enactment of a law similar to that already operating in Victoria, with a 'Chinese manufacture' stamp, limited furniture factory operating hours and no sleeping in furniture factories. Licensing, a limit on the number of Chinese establishments and using the term 'Asiatic' were not recommended.[110] The report had little impact beyond the Sydney Trades Hall, due chiefly to conservative control of the New South Wales parliament. In addition, as historian Shirley Fitzgerald has suggested, the Chinese Merchants' Defence Association (保商會 Baoshanghui), founded to oppose the new Anti-Chinese and Anti-Asiatic League in Sydney in 1904–05, limited the impact of the report as well.[111]

The furniture industry in Sydney also formalised its first minimum wage in 1904. Sydney's United Furniture Trade Society took the city's

---

108 'Asiatic Competition in Factories', *Kalgoorlie Miner*, 2 January 1906; 'Asiatic Labor', *Westralian Worker*, 18 May 1906.
109 Anne Atkinson, 'The responses of Chinese capital to social and economic restrictions and exclusions in Western Australia', in Paul Macgregor, ed., *Histories of the Chinese in Australasia and the South Pacific* (Melbourne: Museum of Chinese Australian History, 1995), 29–45; Mark Finnane, 'Law as Politics: Chinese Litigants in Australian Colonial Courts', in Sophie Couchman and Kate Bagnall, eds., *Chinese Australians: Politics, Engagement and Resistance* (Leiden: Brill, 2015), 124–125.
110 'Trades and Labour Council', *EN*, 1 April 1904; 'Chinese Furniture Trade', *Worker*, 1 October 1904.
111 Shirley Fitzgerald, *Red Tape Gold Scissors: The Story of Sydney's Chinese* (Sydney: Halstead, 2008), 121.

largest furniture manufacturer, Anthony Hordern and Sons, to the newly established New South Wales Court of Arbitration seeking a minimum wage and other rights. The court heard non-Chinese unionists such as Edgar Cutler testify that Chinese factories were driving down industry wages and conditions. It ruled that a minimum wage of £2/8/- be adopted – with equivalent pay for pieceworkers – and along with the forty-eight-hour working week.[112] The United Furniture Trade Society took factory boss Ah Wong (王金鐘 Wang Jinzhong) to the Court of Arbitration soon after, in 1906, alleging a breach of the court's ruling on the minimum wage. Society member Phillip Hassett had been placed in Ah Wong's factory, masquerading as a genuine worker, where he had gathered evidence of underpayment. Because of his deception and thus the inadmissibility of evidence, the court ruled in favour of Ah Wong.[113] This was reported in the *Chinese Australian Herald* as a 'win' (勝 *sheng*) for Chinese people in the industry.[114]

Minimum wage developments contributed to strike action among Sydney's Chinese furniture workers in 1908. Workers had achieved pay rises since the minimum wage ruling, so employers tried to increase the price of factory accommodation and food to compensate. Workers went on strike as part of the 300-strong Sydney Chinese furniture workers' guild, which operated independently of the Melbourne guild. Chinese bosses and their association were determined to secure the increase, and locked workers out of the factories. The strikers held out for two months before returning to the factories victorious, without

---

112 Judgement of Court, 5 December 1904, United Furniture Trade Society of New South Wales v. Anthony Hordern and Sons, New South Wales Court of Arbitration, New South Wales State Records (NSWSR), 2/5714-11/12-1904, 611–615.
113 Judgement of Court, Furniture Trade Union v. Ah Wong, New South Wales Court of Arbitration, NSWSR, 5340-2/74-18, 267.
114 'Yangren gongdang konggao huaren mu dian huaren sheng an' [Foreigners' workers' party accuses Chinese woodshop, Chinese win case], *CAH*, 7 April 1906.

5 Restriction and Resistance

the extra expense as well as the right to elect their own foremen: a right that their European Australian counterparts had not yet achieved. From around this time, Chinese manufacturers, including Hing Pound and Charles Lum, started citing high wages as a leading cause of bankruptcies.[115] As in Melbourne, European furniture unionists were unsupportive of, even hostile towards, Chinese industrial action.[116]

The New South Wales *Factories and Shops Act* of 1896 was modified in 1909. Changes relating to workplace sanitation and safety were made, and a forty-eight-hour week was set for furniture factories.[117] The latter clause was to reinforce the Court of Arbitration's earlier ruling and provide fresh impetus for factory inspectors to try to eliminate night work. As a supplement to the new legislation, a furniture industry wages board was set up by the Court of Arbitration in 1909 (but it excluded Chinese people, as in Melbourne). The board reviewed minimum wages regularly and encouraged stricter policing.[118] Lacking staff, however, factory inspectors struggled with the additional burden of monitoring Chinese factories.[119] The *Factories and Shops Act* was amended further in 1912, with a provision to outlaw sleeping in factories, but this too, owing to inspectors' low staffing levels and the clause's vagueness, had limited impact.[120] Sydney Chinese manufacturer Joe Sing testified during

---

115 Hing Pound Testimony, 17 March 1909, Hing Pound Bankruptcy File, NSWSR 13655-10/23578-18024, 47; Charles Lum Testimony, 26 October 1914, Charles Lum Bankruptcy File, NSWSR 13655-10/23478-20077, 4.
116 'Chinese Strike', *SMH*, 8 April 1908; 'The Chinese Strike', *EN*, 9 April 1908; 'The Ranks of Labour', *EN*, 8 July 1908; 'Bagong er ji' [Strike second account], *Tung Wah Times (TWT)*, 21 March 1908; 'Mujiang bagong hou ye' [Industry after woodworkers' strike], *CAH*, 27 June 1908.
117 *NSW FSA 1909*, 16 (42A).
118 'United Furniture Trade', *EN*, 19 May 1909.
119 *NSW FSA Report 1910*, 15–16, 21. Inspectors issued few fines overall, although there were several instances. See, for example, 'Chinese Fined', *EN*, 22 January 1914.
120 *NSW FSA 1912*, 23; *NSW FSA Report 1913*, 21. The South Australian *Factories Act 1907* and the Tasmanian *Factories Act 1910* were comparable to New South Wales legislation, with no furniture stamp. See *SA FA 1907*; *TAS FA 1910*.

his bankruptcy hearing in 1914 that he had never even seen a factory inspector, and that a market downturn associated with World War One had caused his factory to fail.[121]

Some members of the Chinese community in Sydney challenged the drive for the new *Factories and Shops Act*. Factory proprietor John Hoe (冼俊豪 Xian Junhao) participated in a *Sydney Morning Herald* debate on the matter with three opponents in 1908: one anonymous 'sweated cabinetmaker', Tom Madeley of the Furniture Manufacturers' Association and Mayor Thomas Ross of Waterloo municipal council.[122] The *Tung Wah Times* (東華報 *Donghuabao*), in which Hoe had a sizeable interest, also published articles condemning discrimination against Chinese manufacturers and their employees at this time.[123] Even so, the need for resistance in Sydney was less than in Melbourne, so Sydney's Chinese community did not mobilise with the same sense of urgency.

After the initial approval in 1905, a Chinese Consul-General was sent to Australia in 1908, although it became clear that he had little power in relation to the New South Wales industrial law of 1909. According to Kuo, Consul-General Liang Lan-hsun implored the

---

121 Joe Sing Testimony, 17 November 1914, Joe Sing Hong Bankruptcy File, NSWSR 13655-10/23741-2006861, 61. In 1913, when Joe Sing was in business, a mere seven inspectors needed to inspect 4322 factories across all industries in Sydney, including sixty-nine Chinese furniture factories. See *NSW FSA Report 1913*, 17-37.
122 'The Chinese Question', *SMH*, 1 July 1908; 'Chinese in Waterloo', *SMH*, 2 July 1908; 'The Chinese Question', *SMH*, 27 July to 15 August 1908.
123 'Huaren mu hang zhuyi' [Chinese Wood Industry Notice], *TWT*, 30 June 1906; 'Xueli yi jiang xianzhi huaren mugong yi' [Sydney too will restrict Chinese woodworkers], *TWT*, 23 November 1907; 'Jinggao wo mu huang zhujun' [Warning to my wood industry ladies and gentlemen], *TWT*, 30 November 1907; 'Jinggao wo huaren cao mu yezhe' [Warning to my Chinese wood industry participants'], *TWT*, 21 December 1907; 'Huaren mugong zhuyi' [Chinese woodworker notice], *TWT*, 18 January 1908; 'Hateful agitation against Chinese' [Choushi huaren zhi fengchao], *TWT*, 9 May 1908.

Chinese Ambassador in London to request that British authorities overturn this legislation, but, clearly, he was unsuccessful.[124] Chinese diplomatic influence in Australia would soon weaken further with the overthrow of the Qing Dynasty in 1911 and then the disintegration of the country into states controlled by warlords in 1916.

In answer to Australia's purported 'crisis' of 'Asiatic labour' in the furniture industry, Western Australia adopted an especially confronting furniture stamp in 1912. John Scaddan's Labor government, which pursued radical industrial reform as a part of what Scaddan termed 'state socialism', decreed that 'Asiatic labor' be burned into Chinese-made furniture with a branding iron.[125] Even so, while grim, this seems to have been more a visually compelling endorsement of 'White Australia' than a considered answer to a genuine or even a genuinely perceived threat, since Perth's Chinese furniture sector was so small, and in decline by 1912.[126] Significantly, the New South Wales Labor government under Premier William Holman – once a cabinetmaker who advocated furniture stamps at the Royal Commission in Sydney, and who shared Scaddan's views on 'state socialism' – never tried to follow suit.[127]

Queensland changed its own *Factories and Shops Act* to introduce anti-Chinese furniture stamps in 1916. The 1896 legislation, almost identical to its New South Wales counterpart, specified no such requirement. The 1916 amendment included a number of provisions for furniture stamping, similar to those specified in Victoria. However, as in Western Australia in 1912, stamping was most likely a sign of support for the principle of 'White Australia'. Indeed, Brisbane's

---

124 Kuo, *Making Chinese Australia*, 209.
125 'Factories Act', *EN*, 7 March 1912.
126 'Factories Act', *Daily News*, 25 July 1912.
127 Bede Nairn, 'Holman, William Arthur (1871–1934)', *Australian Dictionary of Biography*, accessed 21 September 2018, http://adb.anu.edu.au/biography/holman-william-arthur-6713/text11589.

Chinese furniture sector was smaller than that in Perth, and it was also in decline.[128] These stamps also coincided with campaigns to buy 'Australian' during World War One.[129] Chinese resistance to the legislation was most likely limited, as in Western Australia, by the small size of Brisbane's Chinese community. Yet, its small size also meant lax policing of this law.[130] Not long after the furniture stamps were introduced in Queensland, Western Australia created a 'European labour only' stamp – to use with the 'Asiatic' stamp – through the *Factories and Shops Act* of 1920.[131]

Opportunism and the final legislation, 1921–30

In the 1920s, there was another push to restrict Chinese factories in Sydney. In 1921, furniture industry representatives demanded that the parliament create the stamps advised by the Sydney Trades and Labour Council in 1904.[132] This did not succeed, but there was a further initiative in 1926 led by influential cabinetmaker and unionist Oscar Schreiber.[133] As a result, a parliamentary bill was arranged by Jack Lang's Labor

---

128 There were forty-five Chinese participants in 1910. See 'Chinese Labour', *Telegraph*, 3 March 1910.
129 Robert Crawford, '*Emptor Australis*: the Australian consumer in early twentieth century advertising literature', *Australian Economic History Review*, 45 (2005), 221–243.
130 Queensland *Reports of the Chief Inspector of Factories and Shops* (for) *1917–1920*.
131 *WA FSA 1920*, 94–97.
132 '"Unfair Competition"', *Daily Telegraph*, 25 June 1921; 'Furniture Factories', *SMH*, 28 June 1921.
133 Michael Lech, '"European Labour Only": Stamping/marking of Chinese-Australian furniture, 1880–1930', paper presented to the Chinese Women's Association of Australia, Sydney Mechanics' School of Arts, 14 February 2015; Ray Markey, 'Schreiber, Oscar Ferdinand Gordon (1887–1963)', *Australian Dictionary of Biography*, accessed 21 September 2018, http://adb.anu.edu.au/biography/schreiber-oscar-ferdinand-gordon-11635/

government to limit the operating hours of Chinese factories, ban factory dormitories, empower furniture trade union representatives to both enter and inspect furniture factories, and implement a 'Made by Chinese' furniture stamp.[134] Lang was regarded as a strongman and such a tough stance allowed him to consolidate this reputation.[135]

Sydney's Chinese community vigorously contested the proposed changes. The city's Chinese-language press, particularly the organ of the Australasian Chinese Nationalist Party, the *Chinese Republic News* (民國報 *Minguobao*), rallied opposition from within the Sydney Chinese community.[136] The Chinese Chamber of Commerce, of which the outspoken activist William Liu (劉光福 Liu Guangming) was part, published a booklet, perhaps inspired by the Melbourne Chinese furniture manufacturers' strategy of 1907. The booklet, called *A Chinese Appeal (against the discriminating legislation as embodied in the New South Wales Factories and Shops (Amendment) Bill, 1926)*, criticised the proposal to further restrict the remaining Chinese furniture factories in Sydney.[137] The Chamber also entered into negotiations with European Australian furniture trade unionists.[138]

---

text20783; Oscar Schreiber correspondence, 22 July to 14 December 1926, Noel Butlin Archives, Furnishing T11/17. I thank Julia Martínez for this correspondence.
134 'Must Be Stamped', *EN*, 22 October 1926; 'Chinese Goods', *Sun*, 22 October 1926.
135 John Thomas Lang, *I Remember* (Sydney: Invincible Press, 1956), 36; Bede Nairn, 'Lang, John Thomas (Jack) (1876–1975)', *Australian Dictionary of Biography*, accessed 21 September 2018, http://adb.anu.edu.au/ biography/lang-john-thomas-jack-7027/text12223.
136 'Tan cong mugong' [Talking woodworkers], *Chinese Republic News (CRN)*, 30 May 1925; 'Jiang bu zhun gongren zai mu chang zhusu' [Woodworkers will not be allowed to stay in wood factories], *CRN*, 28 August 1926; 'Mu pu xin li' [Woodshop new regulations], *CRN*, 6 November 1926.
137 Chinese Chamber of Commerce of New South Wales, *A Chinese Appeal (against the discriminating legislation as embodied in the New South Wales Factories and Shops (Amendment) Bill, 1926)* (Sydney: Chinese Chamber of Commerce, 1926).

Sydney's Chinese community had no prospect of redress from China in this period. The Warlord Era (1916–28) had entered its bloodiest phase. In 1926, Nationalist Party forces launched an offensive from their base in Guangdong to reunite the divided country, which, even though largely successful in strategic terms, precipitated a deep rift between left- and right-wing members of the Party. This led to opposing Chinese governments and all-out civil war prior to effective reunification under the right-wing faction in 1928.[139]

In 1927, the *Factories and Shops Act* was amended to include most clauses proposed. Special Chinese-only factory working hours were set, making the law harsher in this regard than any other law in Australia. Factory dormitories were outlawed, too, and trade union officials were indeed granted new powers of entry and inspection. Stamps on all furniture with the name, address and registration number of manufacturers also became mandatory for the first time in New South Wales, although the racialised tone of the stamp was abandoned.[140] The Sydney Chinese Chamber of Commerce's negotiations with furniture trade unionists contributed to this reversal.[141] Nevertheless, little was done to enforce the new regulations. Factory inspectors' reports have remarkably few references to the legislation of 1927, indicating that neither they nor ethnic European trade unionists had much presence in the Chinese sector thereafter, probably because only a small number of Chinese establishments remained by 1927.[142] Growing internationalism within the Australian labour movement at this time, notably evident in its anti-imperialist and anti-racist 'Hands Off China'

---

138 Lech, "'European Labour Only'", 8.
139 H. Owen Chapman, *The Chinese Revolution 1926–27: A Record of the Period under Communist Control as Seen from the Nationalist Capital, Hankow* (London: Constable & Co. Ltd., 1928).
140 *NSW FSA 1927*, 5, 6 (5A).
141 Lech, "'European Labour Only'", 8.
142 *NSW FSA Report 1927–30*.

campaign, perhaps also played a role.[143] Even so, these new restrictions would have further discouraged new investment by Chinese furniture manufacturers and only hastened the sector's decline, which was near-total by 1933.[144]

Conclusion

This chapter has illustrated how the political and legal restraints on Chinese Australian furniture factories were inspired by an overarching belief in the advancement of 'white' industry and labour, but that these restraints also varied considerably with place and time. Where and when anti-Chinese activism was effectual, and resultant legislation was both strict and strictly enforced, Chinese factories needed to operate with significant impediments. This was most pronounced in Melbourne after the 1896 Victorian *Factories and Shops Act*. However, where and when anti-Chinese campaigns did not lead to the desired legislation, or where rules were hard to police, Chinese manufacturers and workers faced fewer difficulties. This was the case in Sydney for most of the period under consideration.

This chapter has also demonstrated how Chinese resistance to anti-Chinese measures in the furniture industry was heavily informed by the contexts in which factories operated. Indeed, resistance had distinctive local and temporal features, with significant differences between Sydney and Melbourne. In Melbourne, Chinese migrants and their descendants resisted more actively and vocally than their comparatively silent Sydney counterparts, reflecting the need to resist stronger anti-Chinese activism and tougher restrictions. Yet, both the Melbourne and Sydney Chinese communities were large and powerful

---

143 'Labour Council', *SMH*, 29 January 1927.
144 *NSW FSA Report 1932*, 17; *VIC FSA Report 1933*, 17.

compared with Chinese communities in other locations where limited furniture manufacturing took place, which made them far more capable of organising opposition. Both communities resisted by mobilising considerable resources to publish booklets and appeal to politicians, and both used Chinese-language newspapers. Resistance most often meant co-operation among the different Pearl River Delta county groups, prominent roles for Australian-born Chinese spokespeople, and, except for workers' strikes, substantial support from European Australian allies.

Conclusion

In 1928, at the age of sixty-eight, wood polisher Poey Fay (配輝 Pei Hui) returned to Melbourne from China after spending six months there in retirement. For nearly thirty-five years, he worked in Melbourne's furniture industry, much of the time at Horp Hing's factory on La Trobe Street. He had saved his earnings and accumulated enough to retire to his hometown in Zhongshan (中山), Guangdong, and had commenced this next phase in his life by late 1927.[1] However, turmoil stemming from civil war in China soon prompted his decision to return to Melbourne and resume his work. Poey Fay's decision meant that he was subject once more to Australia's racialised *Immigration Restriction Act*, which had constrained his movement for many years and meant that he had to negotiate for permission to return, despite his long-term residency.[2] When he arrived back in Melbourne, he also had to comply again with the racist restrictions that had overshadowed his factory work, in the form of Victoria's *Factories and Shops Act*. Once

---

1 Xiangshan was renamed Zhongshan in 1925 in commemoration of Sun Yat-sen (aka Sun Zhongshan).
2 Poey Fay Certificate Exempting from Dictation Test Application, 30 May to 3 August 1928, Poey Fay File, National Archives of Australia (Melbourne), B13-1928/15740, 1-17.

more, as this legislation stated, 'Chinese labour' stamps were required on the furniture that he made.[3]

Poey Fay's is a contradictory story, one of many at the centre of this book. Poey Fay, his Chinese co-workers and his employers were all subject to extensive discrimination from Australian governments and a labour movement that operated largely on the basis of 'race'. Nonetheless, he had sustained himself through furniture factory work, and had helped to support his relatives in China, for close to thirty-five years. If not for the civil war, he would also have been able to realise the ultimate ambition of most Chinese overseas migrants of his era, that is, to return to China and retire in comfort and respectability. Even when it had become apparent to him during his brief stint in Zhongshan that he might never achieve this goal, Melbourne's furniture industry offered him an alternative place where he could spend his autumn years in relative safety and security.

This book has examined Chinese furniture factories in Australia, concentrating on Sydney and Melbourne, over the period between 1880 and 1930. It has aimed to facilitate a fuller appreciation of how Chinese migrants and their descendants participated in industry in late nineteenth- and early twentieth-century Australia. The book has drawn on rich and diverse evidence from untapped archival sources, especially bankruptcy and other court files, with a primary emphasis on manufacturers' and workers' personal statements and records. These materials have enabled an unprecedented insight into the Chinese factories. However, most sources are products of racialising and marginalising systems. In courtrooms especially, even though Chinese manufacturers and workers regularly used the law to their advantage, they may have felt forced to speak and act in certain ways. Their words were often mediated as well. Thus, we should treat the evidence used in this book with caution.

---

3   Victorian *Factories and Shops Act*, 69 (1).

Conclusion

Chinese migrants from Guangdong's Pearl River Delta became established in the Australian furniture industry between 1800 and 1880 for cultural, political and, above all, economic reasons. They were influenced by a long, proud tradition of Chinese woodwork, embodied in the master craftsman and deity Lu Ban (鲁班). They were also prompted by political and economic difficulties within China to seek out better opportunities overseas. On their arrival in Australia, racialised hierarchies constrained their choices of occupation. Modest capital requirements fostered entry into the furniture industry, and word of this opportunity spread. The opening in Australian manufacturing existed due to Australia's burgeoning consumer culture and growing population, especially after the gold rushes of the 1850s. Most importantly, Australia's capacity to manufacture furniture was underdeveloped, with its economy orientated towards pastoralism and supplying raw wool to spinning mills in Britain, not manufacturing. This was the principal reason why Chinese furniture factories were viable in Australia on a substantial scale and never, for example, in North America, where the already advanced furniture industry on the eastern seaboard of the United States was able to meet most demand.

By examining the key role of Australian economic development in shaping the options available to Chinese migrants, we can better appreciate why they undertook certain activities and not others. Hierarchies of 'race' must be recognised as one significant factor influencing Chinese migrants' entry into the Australian furniture industry. Ambitions and experiences in China were also central to migrants' choosing this endeavour. However, the state of economic development within their migration destination was the main reason they became involved in furniture production. Australia developed a European consumer culture and a strong demand for furniture, although neglected the required manufacturing base.

In setting up furniture factories, Chinese entrepreneurs used a mix of approaches. When deciding on proprietors, mobilising firm finance, configuring factory premises and purchasing equipment and supplies, they regularly made use of imported cultural resources. This meant that family proprietorship, collective financing, operating from 'Chinatown' and factory supply networks stretching back to the Pearl River Delta often underpinned ventures. Imported practices were also partly responsible for the large number of sole-trading owner-operators and partnerships defined by friendship and complementary skill sets, along with financing using personal savings, loans from small groups of friends and relatives, other business interests, and generous credit from other Chinese businesses. Firms had to accommodate members' regular journeys to China as well (part of Chinese overseas cultural practice), making for constant change in their proprietorship. At the same time, however, Chinese manufacturers set up their factories in ways that were more specific to Australian industrial environments. Regarding proprietorship, many chose to register their individual interests in businesses or sign contracts in efforts to protect themselves under Australian law. Most of them also used trade credit extended to them by European Australian creditors, often even to the point that it constituted their principal source of financing. Factory premises were typically configured for self-sufficiency, were centrally located and were leased from European Australian landlords. Furthermore, manufacturers sourced most of their tools and machinery, and their materials including timber, nails, glue and glass, from ethnic Europeans. These approaches to business organisation were not present around the Pearl River Delta, having been clear adaptations to new settings.

That furniture manufacturers did not limit themselves to imported cultural resources in setting up their industrial concerns helps us to better understand Chinese overseas business. Chinese furniture manufacturers regularly drew upon these resources, with kinship and native place bonds rooted in China particularly indispensable to Chinese furniture factories. Such organisational approaches could be valuable in negotiating some of the constraints met in an overseas

Conclusion

environment. Even so, setting up Chinese Australian furniture factories also involved other resources adopted within the migration destination, and often even resembled non-Chinese industrial operations to the extent that their 'Chineseness' was unclear. Indeed, Chinese manufacturers regularly used the methods of wider Australian industrial enterprise. Moreover, they sought help in doing so from European Australian individuals and businesses, who were willing to render that assistance, in ignorance or defiance of 'White Australia'.

There was minimal distinction between Chinese bosses and workers in many factories, but furniture workers consistently expressed different views on factory life from manufacturers. Their skill, rates of pay, working hours and interaction with their employers were among their most important everyday considerations. When addressing these matters, workers regularly used Chinese points of reference. This was apparent when they described themselves as 'carpenters', the translation of the Chinese *mujiang/gong* (木匠/工). It was also seen in relation to their social mobility, egalitarianism, native place loyalties, kinship ties and Chinese nationalism. The main issue that alarmed 'white labour' activists was workers' pay and hours of work. These were – according to workers' own records, and their employers' records – generally lower and longer than those outside the Chinese furniture sector. Chinese workers sought to justify this situation with reference to conditions in China. Employer-subsidised lodgings and meals in Australia were another critical mitigating factor, which helped them save their earnings and support their families back in China. While their activities overseas were heavily informed by work and life around the Pearl River Delta, Chinese workers also embraced new conceptions of work for the Australian factories. Over time, many of them adopted European trade terminology to describe their own skill sets, no longer identifying as 'carpenters', but as 'cabinetmakers', 'French polishers' and 'turners'. Many also aspired to earnings and working hours that approached the standards in non-Chinese furniture factories. In spite of their employers' condemnations and their emotional appeals to Chinese nationalism, Chinese furniture workers sometimes even advocated Australian working-class solidarity, calling strikes and seeking the support (albeit unsuccessfully) of their ethnic European counterparts.

The Chinese Australian furniture factory work culture revealed here through workers' reflections and records offers a new perspective on Chinese overseas labour. They were much more than the mere 'coolies' or 'cheap labour' of Australian labour movement rhetoric. However, their work culture centred on the Pearl River Delta, where Australian earnings stretched further than in Australia, so in fact Chinese workers could afford to earn less than other workers. They even reported freely that they did so, suggesting that they felt little pressure to avoid negative characterisations, regardless of efforts by the European Australian labour movement and Australian authorities to restrict 'cheap labour'. This work culture also shows, nevertheless, that Chinese furniture workers were far from hostile to the broader campaigns for workers' rights in Australia. They shared many ideas about work with its ethnic European labour proponents, even though uplifting 'white labour' was often at the forefront of such activists' concerns.

When selling products, Chinese furniture manufacturers competed energetically in the Australian marketplace. Most vied with non-Chinese manufacturers and each other to secure a diverse customer base. They sold chiefly to large, non-Chinese metropolitan retailers via made-to-order arrangements using designs that reflected the latest London and Paris styles, and to smaller non-Chinese and Chinese retailers in cities and rural areas. Chinese operators also welcomed customers into their factories, guiding them through furniture storerooms to peruse and select their desired items. Sales at auction houses were common as well, as were sales of furniture parts and design-less 'husks' or 'carcasses' to both non-Chinese and other Chinese manufacturers. Deliveries and repairs, too, were standard for most Chinese factories. To attract and retain customers, Chinese

Conclusion

factory operators used diverse promotional methods. They or their managers travelled around the cities, and sometimes to country towns, to negotiate furniture contracts, armed with personalised factory stationery and the necessary English-language skills. Chinese manufacturers also took advantage of English- and Chinese-language newspapers, commercial directories and factory signage. Contributing generously and publicly to charity was another promotional strategy, along with participating in trade and industry exhibitions. Factories typically sold with slim profit margins, and even no or negative profit margins, reflecting the perpetual state of cutthroat competition in Australia's furniture industry.

Chinese factories did not sell their furniture meekly in efforts to avoid conflict. Manufacturers competed directly with ethnic European and other Chinese businesspeople, even though it might have been safer to do the opposite in the face of anti-Chinese racism. This demonstrates that they were bold. Their behaviour in the Australian marketplace also reveals that they sold their furniture in an environment that was conducive to such competition, that is, trading conditions that existed irrespective of overarching ideological imperatives. The receptiveness of European Australian consumers to Chinese-made furniture products created those conditions.

Anti-Chinese furniture stamping was one of many means by which 'white labour' activists, business groups and governments sought to curtail Chinese furniture production between 1880 and 1930, but these efforts did not play out uniformly. Anti-Chinese measures varied according to both location and time period. Chinese resistance to discrimination in the furniture industry reflected these variations. In Sydney, racist campaigning and legislation were weak for much of the period under consideration, so resistance there was often muted. In Melbourne, on the other hand, where there was strong and regular anti-Chinese activism and harsh regulation, racism was met with vigorous Chinese protest on numerous occasions. Chinese factory operators and workers, and their allies, resisted by publishing pamphlets, authoring newspaper articles and letters to editors, organising petitions, appealing to the Chinese government and, as seen with Melbourne factory workers, declaring strikes. Opposition also included European Australian advocates.

The anti-Chinese measures and Chinese resistance described in this book deepen our knowledge of 'White Australia'. There were similarities between Australia's two largest cities in terms of how labour agitators and legislators sought to restrict Chinese furniture factories. This aids our understanding of how an exclusionary vision acted as a homogenising force in Australian politics and law. Yet, there were clear differences in this respect, too, in that there was a high degree of political and legislative heterogeneity under the influence of 'White Australia'. In addition, Chinese resistance to discrimination was perhaps more nuanced than we might have thought. There was strong Chinese opposition to racism within the furniture industry, but acquiescence was often preferred or necessary as well.

This book has presented detailed insights into a vital yet previously underexplored Chinese overseas economic activity, as it was described by its participants. Through their own words, we have gained a sense of who furniture manufacturers were and how they ran their factories. Their private lives, their dreams, why they were in Sydney and Melbourne in this industry, how they understood failure, and even how they worded contracts have been discussed here. We know precisely which materials were used for manufacturing, along with the spaces, tools, machines and furniture designs, as well as the sources of these necessities. This book has also shown to whom factories sold their products and how they tried to drum up business, and their profits as recorded in proprietors' own ledgers. Even the private details of Chinese workers' lives, like how much they were paid, where they slept and what they ate – details that have typically eluded historians – have been revealed here through workers' descriptions and records of their experiences.

Conclusion

Chinese furniture manufacturers and workers – and their dealings with Australia's ethnic European population – were part of a complex history. Chinese furniture makers were not mere victims. They were resourceful, negotiating their way to a place at the heart of Australian industrial manufacturing and maintaining that central position over a long period. Relatedly, the obstacles laid down before them were not as effective as had been imagined. 'White Australia' was not the death knell for Chinese factories. While racist restrictions on Chinese migration to Australia took their toll on most Chinese businesses and occupations, anti-Chinese measures designed to limit Chinese Australian furniture production specifically, however objectionable, fell well short of expectations. Chinese migrants and their families, acting in concert with numerous European Australians, did business and worked in the Australian furniture industry anyway.

Bibliography

A. PRIMARY SOURCES
Insolvency and Bankruptcy Files
New South Wales State Records
1873 Woo Lung 13654-2/9488-11460.
1876 Chow Young 13654-2/9598-12761.
1883 Ack Chow 13654-2/9993-17928.
1883 Lee Fee 13654-2/10017-18229.
1883 Kum Leong 13654-2/10028-18374.
1883 Sun Ying Tiy 13654-2/9994-17931.
1884 Ah Kum 13654-2/10087-19025.
1887 Low Wing 13654-2/10351-22105.
1888 Sing Lee 13655-10/2250-00112.
1889 Ah How 13655-10/22653-2602.
1889 Wong Sum Ling 13655-10/22559-1039.
1890 Chow Kum 13655-10/22648-2524.
1890 Man Sing 13655-10/22675-3020.
1890 Tack Lee 13655-10/22672-02959.
1892 Wong King Gee 13655-10/22605-1778.
1893 Lay Jong 13655-10/22864-6597.
1893 Leong Dong 13655-10/22844-6266.
1893 Yee Lee 13655-10/22771-4833.
1895 Sing Leng 13655-10/23072-10431.
1896 Sun 13655-10/23079-10554.
1900 Percy Board 13655-10/23285-14011.
1901 Tin Yow 13655-10/23335-14768.
1901 Tin Yow and Low Wing 13655-10/23338-14814.
1907 Harry Kow 13655-10/23541-17604.

Bibliography

1909 Hing Pound 13655-10/23578-18024.
1909 Jack Lem 13655-10/23574-17992.
1910 Henry Louey 13655-10/23603-18391.
1911 George Suey 13655-10/23646-18951.
1912 Henry Ricketts 13655-10/23660-19241.
1913 Loon Moon 13655-10/23707-19673.
1913 Willie King 13655-10/23691-19488.
1914 Alfred Graham 13655-10/23738-20044.
1914 Charles Lum 13655-10/23741-20077.
1914 Joe Sing Hong 13655-10/23741-20068.
1914 Sam War Lee 13655-10/23744-20102.
1914 Yuen Gar 13655-10/23743-20093.
1915 Jan Way 13655-10/23778-20439.
1916 Charles Ah Chong 13655-10/23795-20654.
1916 Harry Yuen Gar 13655-10/23807-20778.
1917 Ernest Quong 13655-10/23844-21213.
1919 Albert Attwells 13655-10/23911-21726.
1920 Alfred Jarvis 13633-10/24002-22211.
1923 Soo Gangton 13655-10/24030-23307.
1923 Toong Hing 13655-10/24025-23254.
1925 Arthur Henning 13655-10/24142-24639.
1925 Leun Ah Chong 13655-10/24188-25180.
1928 Edward Hallshaw 13655-10/24345-27163.
1870–1930 Others (re numerical data) 13654–13655.

Public Record Office of Victoria
1883 Ah Yet 762/P/0-193-71/4046.
1883 Man Sing 762/P/0-206-71/4259.
1883 Marie Olsen 762/P/0-210-4309.
1884 Alfred Garner 13654-2/10058-18713.
1886 Isadore Henry Solomon 762/P/0-268-71/5065.
1889 Quong Lee 762/P/0-338-71/5816.
1889 Yee Wye 762/P/0-335-5786.
1891 Ah Chee 765/P/0-12-90/140.
1891 Charles Servante 765/P/0-36-90/399.
1894 You Kee Young 765/P/0-187-90/2095.
1896 Hoong Nam 765/P/0-229-90/2610.
1896 John Penman 765/P/0-221-90/2508.
1898 Frederick Povey 765/P/0-274-90/3274.
1901 Charles Wing 765/P/0-319-90/3845.

1902 Lee Gow 765/P/0-321-90/3865.
1903 Shung Yem 766/P/0-36-819.
1907 Bong Shue 765/P/0-402-90/5084.
1907 Ernest Lin 765/P/0-399-90/5033.
1911 Wong Ah Leet 765/P/0-437-90/5527.
1914 Lim Gin 766/P/0-113-2681.
1914 Pon Kee 766/P/0-118-90/2797.
1916 Arthur Hunt 766/P/0-118-A2800.
1923 Francis Edward McCall 10246/P/0-54-15/903.
1924 Ernest Marshall 10246/P/0-77-15/1318.
1925 Rupert Yon 766/P/0-186-A4224.
1926 Lim Juen 10246/P/0-111-15/197049.
1926 Quong Yick 10246/P/0-108-15/1915.
1927 George Sue Gay 10246/P/0-124-15/2216.
1870–1930 Others (re numerical data) 762/P/0–10246/P/0.

National Archives of Australia (Melbourne)
1929 Ah Gan B741-V/7678.

Other Court Records
New South Wales State Records
1883 The Queen v. Johnny Ah Ehing, Supreme Court of New South Wales, 9/6690-83/134.
1904 United Furniture Trade Society of New South Wales v. Anthony Hordern and Sons, New South Wales Court of Arbitration, 2/5714-11/12-1904.
1906 Furniture Trade Union v. Ah Wong, New South Wales Court of Arbitration, 5340-2/74-18.
1926 Pennell v. Quong Wing, trading as W. Rising and Co., Supreme Court of New South Wales, 2713-6/1309.

Public Record Office of Victoria
1885 The Queen v. Ah Toy, Supreme Court of Victoria, 30/P/29-650-9.
1894 The Queen v. Ah Sin, Supreme Court of Victoria, 30/P/0-982-342.
1895 The Queen v. Ah Loy, Supreme Court of Victoria, 30/P/0-1038-479.
1901 The King v. Shing Duck, Supreme Court of Victoria, 30/P/0-1270-529.
1903 The King v. Ah Chuck, Supreme Court of Victoria, 30/P/0-1323-208.
1903 The King v. Wong Dew Duck, Supreme Court of Victoria, 30/P/0-1338-469.
1910 The King v. William McCasker, Supreme Court of Victoria, 30/P/0-1552-370.
1912 The King v. Louey Pang, Supreme Court of Victoria, 30/P/0-1613-191.

Bibliography

Official Inquiries
New South Wales
Report of the Royal Commission on Alleged Chinese Gambling and Immorality and Charges of Bribery against Members of the Police Force (Sydney: Government Printer, 1892).

Victoria
Factories Act Inquiry Board, First Progress Report (Melbourne: Government Printer, 1893).
Factories Act Inquiry Board, Second Progress Report (Melbourne: Government Printer, 1894).
Factories Act Inquiry Board, Minutes of Evidence and Appendices (Melbourne: Government Printer, 1895).
Report of the Royal Commission Appointed to Investigate and Report on the Operation of the Factories and Shops Law of Victoria (Melbourne: Government Printer, 1903) and *Evidence Taken by the Royal Commission Appointed to Investigate and Report On the Operation of the Factories and Shops Law of Victoria* (Melbourne: Government Printer, 1903).

Immigration Records
National Archives of Australia (Sydney)
Ching Yow SP42/1-B1907/2726.
Chun Lit SP42/1-C1939/201.
Ding Larn SP42/1-C1930/247.
George Joy SP42/1-C/1917/208.
Go Chock and Chong Ah Wong SP42/1-C1912/7152.
Tung Wai Hee A1/1925/22539.
Wong Ah Chew SP42/1-C1929/6422.

National Archives of Australia (Melbourne)
Ah Cheong B13-1914/21688.
Bong Shue B13-1915/11306.
Chin Youey B13-1925/27576.
Hong Bow B13-1925/10543.
Hong Sing B13-1924/26848.
Louey Foo B13-1925/10588.
Poey Fay B13-1928/15740.
Quong Chor B13-1927/7411.
Wong Hop B13-1922/22357.
Yeong Yick Chick B13-1924/10206.

Made in Chinatown

Newspapers and Gazettes
Advocate (Melbourne).
Age (Melbourne).
Argus (Melbourne).
Australasian (Melbourne).
Australian Star (Sydney).
Bathurst Free Press and Mining Journal (Bathurst).
Chinese Australian Herald (廣益華報 *Guangyihuabao*) (Sydney).
Chinese Republic News (民國報 *Minguobao*) (Sydney).
Chinese Times (愛國報 *Aiguobao*) (Melbourne).
Chinese Times (大漢日報 *Dahanribao*) (Vancouver).
Chung Sai Yat Po (中西日報 *Zhongxiribao*) (San Francisco).
Daily News (Sydney).
Daily Telegraph (Sydney).
Evening News (Sydney).
Farmer and Settler (Sydney).
Freeman's Journal (Sydney).
Glen Innes Examiner (Glen Innes).
Herald (Melbourne).
Illustrated Australian News (Melbourne).
Kalgoorlie Miner (Kalgoorlie).
Launceston Advertiser (Launceston).
Leader (Melbourne).
Maitland Mercury and Hunter River General Advertiser (Maitland).
Maitland Weekly Mercury (Maitland).
Melbourne Punch (Melbourne).
New South Wales Government Gazette (Sydney).
Newcastle Morning Herald and Miners' Advocate (Newcastle).
Northern Star (Lismore).
Queenslander (Brisbane).
Riverine Herald (Echuca-Moama).
Singleton Argus (Singleton).
Sun (Sydney).
Sunday Times (Sydney).
Sydney Mail and New South Wales Advertiser (Sydney).
Sydney Morning Herald (Sydney).
Telegraph (Brisbane).
Truth (Sydney).
Tung Wah News (東華新報 *Donghuaxinbao*) (Sydney).

Bibliography

Tung Wah Times (東華報 *Donghuabao*) (Sydney).
Wagga Wagga Advertiser (Wagga Wagga).
Weekly Times (Melbourne).
Westralian Worker (Perth).
Worker (Wagga Wagga).

Books, Booklets and Pamphlets
Ah Ket, William. *A Paper on the Chinese and the Factories Act* (Melbourne: Arbuckle, Waddell & Fawckner, 1906).
Cheong Cheok Hong et al. *Chinese Remonstrance to the Parliament and People of Victoria* (Melbourne: William Marshall & Co., 1888).
Chinese Chamber of Commerce of New South Wales, *A Chinese Appeal (against the discriminating legislation as embodied in the New South Wales Factories and Shops (Amendment) Bill, 1926)* (Sydney: Chinese Chamber of Commerce, 1926).
Clarke, J. L. *The Chinese Case against the Chinese Employment Bill* (Melbourne: Arbuckle, Waddell & Fawckner, 1907).
Lowe Kong Meng, Cheong Cheok Hong and Louis Ah Mouy. *The Chinese Question in Australia, 1878–79* (Melbourne: Bailliere, 1879).
Sun Johnson. *The Self Educator* (Sydney: Sun Johnson, c. 1892).

Factory Inspectors' Reports
Reports of the Chief Inspector of Factories, Workrooms, and Shops 1886–1933 (Victoria) (Melbourne: Government Printer, 1887–1934).
Reports of the Chief Inspector of Factories and Shops 1917–1920 (Queensland) (Brisbane: Government Printer, 1918–1921).
Reports on the Working of the Factories and Shops Act 1897–1933 (New South Wales) (Sydney: Government Printer, 1898–1934).
Victorian Factory Registration Notices, 1897–1930, PROV 1399/P/0-1-4.

Legislation
New South Wales
Bankruptcy Act 1887.
Factories and Shops Act 1896.
Factories and Shops Act 1909.
Factories and Shops (Amendment) Act, 1927.

Victoria
Factories and Shops Act 1885.
Factories and Shops Act 1887.

Factories and Shops Act 1896.
Factories and Shops Act 1900.
Factories and Shops Act 1905.
Insolvency Act 1890.
Supervision of Workrooms and Factories Statute 1873.

Queensland
Factories and Shops Act 1896.
Factories and Shops Act 1916.

South Australia
Factories Act 1894.
Factories Act 1907.

Western Australia
Factories Act 1904.
Factories Act 1920.

Tasmania
Factories Act 1910.

Australian Censuses
Australian Historical Population Statistics, Population by sex, state and territories, 31 December, 1788 onwards, Australian Bureau of Statistics, cat. no. 3105.0.65.001 accessed 1 July 2018, http://www.abs.gov.au/ausstats/abs@.nsf/INotes/3105.0.65.0012008Data%20Cubes?opendocument&T.
Census of the Commonwealth of Australia 1911 (Melbourne: Government Printer, 1911).
Census of New South Wales 1856 (Sydney: Government Printer, 1856).
Census of New South Wales 1891 (Sydney: Government Printer, 1891).
Census of Queensland 1881 (Brisbane: Government Printer, 1881).
Census of Victoria 1861 (Melbourne: Government Printer, 1861).
Census of Victoria 1871 (Melbourne: Government Printer, 1871).

Bibliography

Images and Objects
Ah Wong's Factory, City Council Resumptions, 1912–1928, Mitchell Library F981.1S.
'Chinese cabinet-maker, Victoria, Australia, Armchair, c. 1870', Art Gallery of South Australia, 898F11A, accessed 1 September 2018, http://www.artgallery.sa.gov.au/agsa/home/Collection/detail.jsp?accNo=898F11A.
'Chinese labour' stamp, Melbourne, early twentieth century, Golden Dragon Museum.
Chung Lee Furniture Factory, City of Sydney Archives, NSCA CRS 51/99.
War Sing and Co., City of Sydney Archives, NSCA CRS 51/166.
Wing Lee Brothers Dressing Table, Melbourne, c. 1900s, Golden Dragon Museum.

Catalogues and Directories
Furniture by Grace Brothers, 1923, Caroline Simpson Library and Research Collection, TCQ 749.20492 GRA.
Furniture by Grace Brothers, c. 1927, Caroline Simpson Library and Research Collection, TCQ 749.20492 GRA/3.
Sands Commercial Directory 1860–1930 (Sydney).
Sands & McDougall's Directory, 1860–1930 (Melbourne).

Other Primary Sources
Bale, Manfred. *Woodworking Machinery: Its Rise, Progress and Construction with Hints on the Management of Saw Mills and the Economical Conversion of Timber* (London: Crosby, Lockwood and Co., 1880).
Chen, Ta. *Chinese Migrations, with Special Reference to Labor Conditions* (Washington: Government Printing Office, 1923).
Cheong Cheok Hong Letter Books, 1904–07, State Library of Victoria, MS9821.
Documents lodged under Companies Acts, New South Wales State Records, 12951.
Index to New South Wales Colonial Secretary's Papers 1788–1825, New South Wales State Records Indexes, accessed 1 July 2018, https://www.records.nsw.gov.au/archives/collections-and-research/guides-and-indexes/colonial-secretarys-papers.
Lu Ban Jing, in Klaas Ruitenbeek, *Carpentry and Building in Late Imperial China: A Study of the Fifteenth-Century Carpenter's Manual Lu Ban Jing* (Leiden: Brill, 1993).
Melbourne Rate Books, 1870–1930, Ancestry.com, accessed 1 October 2018, https://search.ancestry.com.au/search/db.aspx?dbid=60706.

New South Wales Register of Firms, 1903–22, New South Wales State Records, 12961.
Oscar Schreiber correspondence, 22 July to 14 December 1926, Noel Butlin Archives, Furnishing T11/17.
Register of Miscellaneous Companies, 1853–1959, Public Records Office of Victoria, 8279.
Sydney Assessment Books, 1870–1930, City of Sydney Archives, accessed 1 October 2018, http://photosau.com.au/CosRates/scripts/home.asp.
Tye Shing Factory and Sue Gay Factory, *The Architecture of Arthur Purnell*, Culture Victoria, accessed 15 September 2017, https://cv.vic.gov.au/stories/built-environment/the-architecture-of-arthur-purnell/.
Victorian Anti-Chinese League, *Minute Book*, Melbourne Trades Hall Files, Mitchell Library, MSS 308/8.
Victorian Register of Firms, 1893–1926, Public Records Office of Victoria, 12342.

B. SECONDARY SOURCES
Published Sources
Amatori, Franco and Geoffrey Jones, eds. *Business History around the World* (Cambridge: Cambridge University Press, 2003).
Amatori, Franco and Andrea Colli. *Business History: Complexities and Comparisons* (London: Routledge, 2013).
Atkinson, Anne. 'The responses of Chinese capital to social and economic restrictions and exclusions in Western Australia', in Paul Macgregor, ed., *Histories of the Chinese in Australasia and the South Pacific* (Melbourne: Museum of Chinese Australian History, 1995), 29–45.
Bagnall, Kate. 'Across the Threshold: White Women and Chinese Hawkers in the White Colonial Imaginary', *Hecate*, 28:2 (2002), 9–32.
Barth, Gunther. *Bitter Strength: A History of the Chinese in the United States, 1850–1870* (Massachusetts: Harvard University Press, 1964).
Bates, Elizabeth Bidwell and Jonathan L. Fairbanks. *American Furniture: 1620 to the Present* (New York: Richard Marek Publishers, 1981).
Beaton, Lynn. *Part of the Furniture: Moments in the History of the Federated Furniture Trades Society of Victoria* (Melbourne: Melbourne University Press, 2007).
Boileau, Joanna. *Chinese Market Gardening in Australia and New Zealand: Gardens of Prosperity* (Cham: Palgrave Macmillan, 2017).
Bose, Bijoy Kumar. 'A Bygone Chinese Colony in Bengal', *Bengal Past and Present*, 47:2 (1934), 120–122.
Bowden, Bradley. 'The Rise and Decline of Australian Unionism: A History of Industrial Labour from the 1820s to 2010', *Labour History*, 100 (2011), 51–82.

Bibliography

Boyajian, James. *Portuguese Trade in Asia under the Habsburgs, 1580–1640* (Baltimore: Johns Hopkins University Press, 2008).

Broadbent, James, Suzanne Rickard and Margaret Steven. *India, China, Australia: Trade and Society 1788–1850* (Glebe: Historic Houses Trust of New South Wales, 2003).

Brook, Jack. *From Canton with Courage: Parramatta and Beyond—Chinese Arrivals, 1800–1900* (Sydney: Blacktown District Historical Society, 2010).

Chamberlain, Kevin. 'Chinese Woodworking Tools in Victoria', *The Tool Chest*, 52 (1999), 6–18.

Chamberlain, Kevin. 'Chinese Furniture Makers in Melbourne', *The Tool Chest*, 61 (2001), 45–55.

Chan, Sucheng. *This Bittersweet Soil: Chinese in California Agriculture, 1860–1910* (Berkeley: University of California Press, 1986).

Chan, Wellington. 'Personal Styles, Cultural Values and Management: The Sincere and Wing On Companies in Shanghai and Hong Kong, 1900–41', *Business History Review*, 70:2 (1996), 141–166.

Chapman, H. Owen. *The Chinese Revolution 1926–27: A Record of the Period under Communist Control as Seen from the Nationalist Capital, Hankow* (London: Constable & Co. Ltd., 1928).

Chen, Song-Chuan. *Merchants of War and Peace: British Knowledge of China in the Making of the Opium War* (Hong Kong: Hong Kong University Press, 2017).

Chen, Yong. *Chinese San Francisco: A Trans-Pacific Community, 1850–1943* (Stanford: Stanford University Press, 2000).

Choi, Anne Soon. '"La Choy Chinese Food Swings American": Korean Immigrant Entrepreneurship and American Orientalism Before WWII', *Cultural and Social History*, 13:4 (2016), 521–538.

Choi Chingyan. *Chinese Migration and Settlement in Australia* (Sydney: Sydney University Press, 1975).

Chou, Bon-Wai. 'The sojourning attitude and the economic decline of Chinese society in Victoria, 1860s–1930s', in Paul Macgregor, ed., *Histories of the Chinese in Australasia and the South Pacific* (Melbourne: Museum of Chinese Australian History, 1995), 59–74.

Chung, Sue Fawn. *Chinese in the Woods: Logging and Lumbering in the American West* (Chicago: University of Illinois Press, 2015).

Coghlan, Timothy A. *Labour and Industry in Australia* (Oxford: Oxford University Press, 1918).

Collins, Jock. 'Chinese Entrepreneurs: The Chinese Diaspora in Australia', *International Journal of Entrepreneurial Behaviour & Research*, 8:1/2 (2002), 113–133.

Coolidge, Mary. *Chinese Immigration* (New York: H. Holt and Co., 1909).

Coşgel, Metin and Boğaç Ergene. 'The selection bias in court records: settlement and trial in eighteenth-century Ottoman Kastamonu', *Economic History Review*, 67:2 (2014), 517–534.

Craig, Clifford, Kevin Fahy and E. Graeme Robertson. *Early Colonial Furniture in New South Wales and Van Diemen's Land* (Melbourne: Georgian House, 1972).

Crawford, Robert. '*Emptor Australis*: the Australian consumer in early twentieth century advertising literature', *Australian Economic History Review*, 45 (2005), 221–243.

Crawford, Robert. *But Wait, There's More...: A History of Australian Advertising, 1900-2000* (Carlton: Melbourne University Press, 2008).

Crossman, Carl. *The China Trade: Export Paintings, Furniture, Silver & Other Objects* (Princeton: Pyne Press, 1972).

Curthoys, Ann. 'Conflict and Consensus: The Seamen's Strike of 1878', in Ann Curthoys and Andrew Markus, eds., *Who Are Our Enemies? Racism and the Australian Working Class* (Sydney: Hale and Iremonger, 1978), 48–65.

Curthoys, Ann. 'White, British and European: historicising identity in settler societies', in Jane Carey and Claire McLisky, eds., *Creating White Australia* (Sydney: Sydney University Press, 2009), 3–24.

Dai Yi. *Concise History of the Qing Dynasty* (Singapore: Enrich Professional Publishing, 2012).

Du Xuncheng (杜恂诚). *Minzu zibenzhuyi yu jiu Zhonguo zhengfu, 1840-1937* [National capitalism and the old Chinese government, 1840-1937] (Shanghai: Shanghai Academy of Social Sciences Press, 1991).

Fahey, Charles and André Sammartino. 'Work and Wages at a Melbourne Factory, The Guest Biscuit Works 1870-1921', *Australian Economic History Review*, 53:1 (2013), 22–46.

Fahy, Kevin, Andrew Simpson and Christina Simpson. *Nineteenth Century Australian Furniture* (Sydney: David Ell Press, 1985).

Fahy, Kevin and Andrew Simpson. *Australian Furniture: Pictorial History and Dictionary* (Sydney: Casuarina Press, 1998).

Faure, David. *Emperor and Ancestor: State and Lineage in South China* (Stanford: Stanford University Press, 2007).

Faure, David. 'Beyond Networking: An Institutional View of Chinese Business', in Malik Kudaisya and Ng Chin-keong, eds., *Chinese and Indian Business: Historical Antecedents* (Leiden: Brill, 2009), 31–61.

Finnane, Antonia. 'Chinese Domestic Interiors and "Consumer Constraint" in Qing China: Evidence from Yangzhou', *Journal of the Economic and Social History of the Orient*, 57 (2014), 112–144.

Bibliography

Finnane, Mark. 'Law as Politics: Chinese Litigants in Australian Colonial Courts', in Sophie Couchman and Kate Bagnall, eds., *Chinese Australians: Politics, Engagement and Resistance* (Leiden: Brill, 2015), 117–136.

Fitzgerald, John. *Big White Lie: Chinese Australians in White Australia* (Sydney: University of New South Wales Press, 2007).

Fitzgerald, Shirley. *Red Tape Gold Scissors: The Story of Sydney's Chinese* (Sydney: Halstead, 2008).

Fong, Walter. 'Chinese Labour Unions in America', *Chinese America: History and Perspectives*, 19 (2008), 13–16.

French, Michael. 'Commercials, careers, and culture: travelling salesmen in Britain, 1890s–1930s', *Economic History Review*, 58:2 (2005), 352–377.

Frost, Lionel. 'Urbanisation', in Simon Ville and Glenn Withers, eds., *The Cambridge Economic History of Australia* (Melbourne: Cambridge University Press, 2014), 245–264.

Frost, Warwick. 'Migrants and Technological Transfer: Chinese Farming in Australia, 1850–1920', *Australian Economic History Review*, 42: 2 (2002), 113–131.

Gardella, Robert, Andrea McElderry and Jane K. Leonard, eds. *Chinese Business History: Interpretive Trends and Priorities for the Future* (New York: Routledge, 2017).

Gibson, Peter. 'Australia's Bankrupt Chinese Furniture Manufacturers, 1880–1930', *Australian Economic History Review*, 58:1 (2018), 87–107.

Gibson, Peter. 'Voices of Sydney's Chinese Furniture Factory Workers, 1890–1920', *Labour History*, 112 (2017), 99–117.

Godley, Andrew and Haiming Hang. 'Collective financing among Chinese entrepreneurs and department store retailing in China', *Business History*, 58:3 (2016), 1–14.

Griffiths, Phil. '"This is a British Colony": The Ruling-Class Politics of the Seafarers' Strike, 1878–79', *Labour History*, 105 (2013), 131–152.

Hainsworth, David. 'The New South Wales shipping interest 1800–1821: a study in colonial entrepreneurship', *Australian Economic History Review*, 8:1 (1968), 17–30.

Hayes, James. '"Good Morning Mrs. Thompson!": A Chinese-English word-book from 19th century Sydney', in Paul Macgregor, ed., *Histories of the Chinese in Australasia and the South Pacific* (Melbourne: Museum of Chinese Australian History, 1995), 113–126.

Hilleman, Ulrike. *Asian Empire and British Knowledge: China and the Networks of British Imperial Expansion* (Basingstoke: Palgrave Macmillan, 2009).

Hirst, John. *Freedom on the Fatal Shore: Australia's First Colony* (Melbourne: Black Inc., 2008).

Huang Zisheng (黃滋生) and He Sibing (何思兵), *Feilvbin huaqiao shi* [Philippine overseas Chinese history] (Guangzhou: Guangdong Higher Education Press, 1987).

Hutchinson, Diane. 'Manufacturing', in Simon Ville and Glenn Withers, eds., *The Cambridge Economic History of Australia* (Melbourne: Cambridge University Press, 2015), 287–308.

Isaac, Joe. 'The Economic Consequences of Harvester', *Australian Economic History Review*, 48:3 (2008), 280–300.

Jack, Ian. 'Some Less Familiar Aspects of the Chinese in 19th-Century Australia', in Henry Chan, Ann Curthoys and Nora Chiang, eds., *The Overseas Chinese in Australasia: History, Settlement and Interactions* (Canberra: Centre for the Study of the Chinese Southern Diaspora, 2001), 44–53.

Jacobson, Dawn. *Chinoiserie* (London: Phaidon, 1993).

Jia, Jungying. 'The evolution of the *qiaopi* trade: a case study of the Tianyi firm', in Gregor Benton, Hong Liu and Huimei Zhang, eds., *The Qiaopi Trade and Transnational Networks in the Chinese Diaspora* (London: Routledge, 2018), 110–129.

Joy, Edward T. *The Country Life Book of English Furniture* (London: Country Life, 1964).

Kelly, David St L. *Convict and Free: The Master Furniture-Makers of New South Wales 1788–1851* (North Melbourne: Australian Scholarly Publishing, 2014).

Kent, David. 'Small Businessmen and their Credit Transactions in Early Nineteenth-Century Britain', *Business History*, 36 (1994), 47–64.

Khoo Su Nin. *Streets of George Town, Penang: An Illustrated Guide to Penang's City Streets & Historic Attractions* (Penang: Phoenix Press, 2007).

Kuhn, Philip A. 'Three Cultures of Migration', in Leo Suryadinata, ed., *Migration, Indigenization and Interaction: Chinese Overseas and Globalization* (Singapore: World Scientific, 2014), 39–53.

Kuo, Mei-fen. *Making Chinese Australia: Urban Elites, Newspapers and the Formation of Chinese-Australian Identity* (Clayton: Monash University Publishing, 2013).

Kuo, Mei-fen. 'Confucian Heritage, Public Narratives and Community Politics of Chinese Australians at the Beginning of the 20th Century', in Sophie Couchman and Kate Bagnall, eds., *Chinese Australians: Politics, Engagement and Resistance* (Leiden: Brill, 2015), 137–173.

Kuo, Mei-fen. 'Reframing Chinese Labour Rights: Chinese Unionists, Pro-Labour Societies and the Nationalist Movement in Melbourne, 1900–10', *Labour History*, 113 (2017), 133–155.

Bibliography

Kwok, Jen Tsen. 'Postscript: Beyond "Two Worlds"', in Sophie Couchman and Kate Bagnall, eds., *Chinese Australians: Politics, Engagement and Resistance* (Leiden: Brill, 2015), 290–307.
Lai, Chi-Kong. 'Xiangshan County and the 1911 Revolution', *New Asia Review*, 13 (2012), 162–167.
Lai, Him Mark. 'Chinese Guilds in the Apparel Industry Of San Francisco', *Chinese America: History and Perspectives*, 21 (2008), 17–23.
Lai, Him Mark and Russell Jeung. 'Guilds, Unions, and Garment Factories: Notes on Chinese in the Apparel Industry', *Chinese America: History and Perspectives*, 21 (2008), 1–10.
Lake, Marilyn and Henry Reynolds. *Drawing the Global Colour Line: White Men's Countries and the Question of Racial Equality* (Melbourne: Melbourne University Press, 2008).
Lake, Marilyn. 'Challenging the "Slave-Driving Employers": Understanding Victoria's 1896 Minimum Wage through a World-History Approach', *Australian Historical Studies*, 45:1 (2014), 87–102.
Lake, Marilyn. 'The Chinese Empire Encounters the British Empire and Its "Colonial Dependencies": Melbourne, 1887', in Sophie Couchman and Kate Bagnall, eds., *Chinese Australians: Politics, Engagement and Resistance* (Leiden: Brill, 2015), 98–116.
Lancashire, Rod. 'Blanche Street, Wahgunyah: A Pre-Federation Australian Chinese Community on the Border', in Sophie Couchman, John Fitzgerald and Paul Macgregor, eds., *After the Rush: Regulation, Participation and Chinese Communities in Australia, 1860–1940* (Fitzroy: Otherland Literary Journal, 2004), 191–202.
Lang, John Thomas. *I Remember* (Sydney: Invincible Press, 1956).
Lee, Joseph. 'Anti-Chinese Legislation in Australasia', *Quarterly Journal of Economics*, 3:2 (1889), 218–224.
Lee, Seung-joon. *Gourmets in the Land of Famine: The Culture and Politics of Rice in Modern Canton* (Stanford: Stanford University Press, 2011).
Li Zhen (李浈). *Zhongguo chuantong jianzhu mu zuo gongju* [Chinese traditional construction and woodwork tools] (Shanghai: Tongji University Press, 2004).
Linge, Godfrey J. R. *Industrial Awakening: A Geography of Australian Manufacturing 1788 to 1890* (Canberra: Australian National University Press, 1979).
Loy-Wilson, Sophie. 'Rural Geographies and Chinese Empires: Chinese Shopkeepers and Shop-Life in Australia', *Australian Historical Studies*, 45:3 (2014), 407–424.

Loy-Wilson, Sophie. 'Coolie Alibis: Seizing Gold from Chinese Miners in New South Wales', *International Labor and Working-Class History*, 91 (2017), 28–45.

Macdonald-Taylor, Margaret. *English Furniture from the Middle Ages to Modern Times* (London: Evans Brothers, 1965).

Macgregor, Paul. 'Chinese Political Values in Colonial Victoria: Lowe Kong Meng and the Legacy of the July 1880 Election', in Sophie Couchman and Kate Bagnall, eds., *Chinese Australians: Politics, Engagement and Resistance* (Leiden: Brill, 2015), 53–97.

Maddison, Ben. '"The skilful unskilled labourer": The Decline of Artisanal Discourses of Skill in the NSW Arbitration Court, 1905–15', *Labour History*, 93 (2007), 77–84.

Maddock, Rod. 'Capital markets', in Simon Ville and Glenn Withers, *The Cambridge Economic History of Australia* (Melbourne: Cambridge University Press, 2015), 267–286.

Markus, Andrew. 'Divided We Fall: The Chinese and the Melbourne Furniture Trade Union, 1870–1900', *Labour History*, 26 (1974), 1–10.

Markus, Andrew. *Fear and Hatred: Purifying Australia and California, 1850–1901* (Sydney: Hale & Iremonger, 1979).

Martin, Allan. 'Free trade and protectionist parties in New South Wales', *Historical Studies: Australia and New Zealand*, 6:23 (1954), 315–323.

May, Cathie. *Topsawyers: The Chinese in Cairns, 1970–1920* (Townsville: James Cook University Press, 1984).

McGowan, Barry. 'Reconsidering Race: The Chinese experience on the goldfields of southern New South Wales', *Australian Historical Studies*, 36:124 (2004), 312–331.

McGowan, Barry. 'The economics and organisation of Chinese mining in colonial Australia', *Australian Economic History Review*, 45:2 (2005), 119–138.

McGowan, Barry. 'Ringbarkers and Market Gardeners: A Comparison of the Rural Chinese of New South Wales and California', *Chinese America: History and Perspectives*, 19 (2006), 31–46.

McKeown, Adam. *Chinese Migrant Networks and Cultural Change: Peru, Chicago, Hawai'i, 1900–1936* (Chicago: Chicago University Press, 2001).

McKeown, Adam. *Melancholy Order: Asian Migration and the Globalization of Borders* (New York: Columbia University Press, 2012).

Merrett, David. 'Big Business and Foreign Firms', in Simon Ville and Glenn Withers, eds., *The Cambridge Economic History of Australia* (Melbourne: Cambridge University Press, 2015), 309–329.

Mungello, David. *The Great Encounter of China and the West, 1500–1800* (Plymouth: Rowman and Littlefield, 2013).

Bibliography

Murphy, William. *History of the Eight Hours' Movement* (Melbourne: Spectator, 1896).

Ng, Michael. 'Dirt of whitewashing: re-conceptualising debtors' obligations in Chinese business by transplanting bankruptcy law to early British Hong Kong', *Business History*, 57:8 (2015), 1219–1247.

Ngai, Mae M. *The Lucky Ones: One Family and the Extraordinary Invention of Chinese America* (Princeton: Princeton University Press, 2012).

Ngai, Mae M. 'The True Story of Ah Jake: Language, Labor, and Justice in Late-Nineteenth-Century Sierra County, California', in Daniel T. Rogers, Bhavani Raman and Helmut Reimitz, eds., *Cultures in Motion* (Princeton: Princeton University Press, 2014), 197–214.

Ngai, Mae M. 'Chinese Gold Miners and the "Chinese Question" in Nineteenth-Century California and Victoria', *Journal of American History*, 101:4 (2015), 1082–1105.

Oakman, Warwick. 'Influence of Anglo-Indian and Anglo-Chinese Furniture in Colonial Australia', in Greg Peters and Jim Kennedy, eds., *Proceedings of the Inaugural Australian Furniture History Symposium* (Canberra: Greg Peters and Jim Kennedy, 2008), 18–22.

Pan, Lynn. *Sons of the Yellow Emperor: A History of the Chinese Diaspora* (New York: Kodansha, 1994).

Pescod, Keith. *The Emerald Strand: The Irish-born Manufacturers of Nineteenth-century Victoria* (North Melbourne: Australian Scholarly Publishing, 2007).

Pong, David. 'Government Enterprises & Industrial Relations in Late Qing China', *Australian Journal of Politics and History*, 47:1 (2001), 4–23.

Price, Charles. *The Great White Walls Are Built: Restrictive Immigration to North America and Australasia, 1836–1888* (Canberra: Australian National University Press, 1974).

Rankin, Mary Theresa. *Arbitration and Conciliation in Australasia: The Legal Wage in Victoria and New Zealand* (London: Allen and Unwin, 1916).

Reeves, Keir. 'Sojourners or a new diaspora? Economic implications of the movement of Chinese miners to the south-west Pacific goldfields', *Australian Economic History Review*, 50:2 (2010), 178–192.

Reeves, Keir and Benjamin Mountford. 'Sojourning and Settling: Locating Chinese Australian History', *Australian Historical Studies*, 42:1 (2011), 111–125.

Reeves, William Pember. *State Experiments in Australia & New Zealand* (New York: E. P. Dutton & Co., 1903).

Rhook, Nadia. '"The Chief Chinese Interpreter" Charles Hodges: mapping the aurality of race and governance in colonial Melbourne', *Postcolonial Studies*, 18:1 (2015), 1–18.

Rolls, Eric. *Sojourners: The Epic Story of China's Centuries-Old Relationship with Australia* (St. Lucia: University of Queensland Press, 1992).
Rolls, Eric. *Citizens: Continuing the Epic Story of China's Centuries-Old Relationship with Australia* (St. Lucia: University of Queensland Press, 1996).
Ruitenbeek, Klaas. *Carpentry and Building in Late Imperial China: A Study of the Fifteenth-Century Carpenter's Manual Lu Ban Jing* (Leiden: Brill, 1993).
Saxton, Alexander. *The Indispensable Enemy: Labor and the Anti-Chinese Movement in California* (Berkeley: University of California Press, 1975).
Sandemeyer, Elmer. *The Anti-Chinese Movement in California* (Chicago: University of Illinois, 1939).
Scott, Peter. 'Mr Drage, Mr Everyman, and the creation of a mass market for domestic furniture in interwar Britain', *Economic History Review*, 62:4 (2009), 802–827.
Shann, Edward. *An Economic History of Australia* (Cambridge: Cambridge University Press, 1930).
Sheehan, Brett. *Industrial Eden: A Chinese Capitalist Vision* (Cambridge: Harvard University Press, 2015).
Sinn, Elizabeth. *Pacific Crossing: California Gold, Chinese Migration and the Making of Hong Kong* (Hong Kong: Hong Kong University Press, 2012).
Slocomb, Margaret. *Among Australia's Pioneers: Chinese Indentured Pastoral Workers on the Northern Frontier, 1848 to c. 1880* (Bloomington: Balboa Press, 2014).
Spence, William. *Australia's Awakening: Thirty Years in the Life of an Australian Agitator* (Sydney and Melbourne: Worker Trustees, 1909).
Tan, Thomas Tsu-wee. *Chinese Dialect Groups: Traits and Trades* (Singapore: Opinion Books, 1990).
Tavan, Gwenda. *The Long, Slow Death of White Australia* (Melbourne: Scribe, 2005).
Trocki, Carl. 'Boundaries and Transgressions: Chinese Enterprise in Eighteenth- and Nineteenth-Century Southeast Asia', in Hong Liu, ed., *The Chinese Overseas*, V3 (London: Routledge, 2006), 45–68.
Tsin, Michael T. W. *Nation, Governance, and Modernity in China: Canton, 1900–1927* (Stanford: Stanford University Press, 1999).
Tsu, Cecilia. *Garden of the World: Asian Immigrants and the Making of Agriculture in California's Santa Clara Valley* (New York: Oxford University Press, 2013).
van Dongen, Els. 'Entangled Loyalties: *Qiaopi*, Chinese community structures, and the state in Southeast Asia', in Gregor Benton, Hong Liu and Huimei Zhang, eds., *The* Qiaopi *Trade and Transnational Networks in the Chinese Diaspora* (London: Routledge, 2018), 5–32.

Bibliography

Van Dyke, Paul A. *The Canton Trade: Life and Enterprise on the China Coast, 1700–1845* (Hong Kong: Hong Kong University Press, 2005).

Van Dyke, Paul A. *Merchants of Canton and Macao: Success and Failure in Eighteenth-Century Chinese Trade* (Hong Kong: Hong Kong University Press, 2016).

Ville, Simon. 'Business Development in Colonial Australia', *Australian Economic History Review*, 38:1 (1998), 16–41.

Ville, Simon. 'Colonial Enterprise', in Simon Ville and Glenn Withers, eds., *The Cambridge Economic History of Australia* (Melbourne: Cambridge University Press, 2014), 202–221.

Ville, Simon and Glenn Withers, eds. *The Cambridge Economic History of Australia* (Melbourne: Cambridge University Press, 2014).

Ville, Simon and Claire Wright. 'Neither a Discipline nor a Colony: Renaissance and Re-imagination in Economic History', *Australian Historical Studies*, 48:2 (2017), 152–168.

Wang Gungwu. *Anglo-Chinese Encounters since 1800: War, Trade, Science and Governance* (Cambridge: Cambridge University Press, 2003).

Wang Shizhen (王世襄) and Yuan Wei (袁荃猷). *Mingshi jiaju yanjiu* [Ming-style furniture research] (Hong Kong: Joint Publishing, 2007).

Wang, Tai Peng. *The Origins of the Chinese Kongsi* (Selangor: Pelanduk Publications, 1994).

Wen Zhengde. 'Breaking Racial Barriers: Wo Kee Company', *Chinese America: History and Perspectives*, 19 (2006), 13–17.

Willard, Myra. *History of the White Australia Policy to 1920* (Melbourne: Melbourne University Press, 1923).

Williams, Michael. *Chinese Settlement in NSW: A Thematic History* (Sydney: Heritage Office of New South Wales, 1999).

Williams, Michael. *Returning Home with Glory: Chinese Villagers around the Pacific, 1849 to 1949* (Hong Kong: Hong Kong University Press, 2018).

Williams, Michael. '"Would This Not Help Your Federation?"', in Sophie Couchman, John Fitzgerald and Paul Macgregor, eds., *After the Rush: Regulation, Participation and Chinese Communities in Australia, 1860–1940* (Fitzroy: Otherland Literary Journal, 2004), 35–50.

Xiong Yuezhi. *Eastward Dissemination of Western Learning in the Late Qing Dynasty* (Singapore: Enrich Professional Publishing, 2013).

Xu Dixin and Wu Chengming. *Chinese Capitalism, 1522–1840* (London: Palgrave Macmillan, 2000).

Yarwood, Alexander. *Asian Migration to Australia* (Melbourne: Melbourne University Press, 1964).

Yen, Ching-hwang. *Ethnic Chinese Business in Asia: History, Culture and Business Enterprise* (Singapore: World Scientific, 2013).
Yong Ching Fatt. *The New Gold Mountain: The Chinese in Australia, 1901–21* (Richmond: Raphael Arts, 1977).
Yow Cheun Hoe. *Guangdong and Chinese Diaspora: The changing landscape of qiaoxiang* (London: Routledge, 2013).
Yu, Henry. 'Mountains of Gold: Canada, North America and the Cantonese Pacific', in Tan Chee-Beng, ed., *Routledge Handbook of the Chinese Diaspora* (London: Routledge, 2013), 108–121.
Yu, Henry. 'Unbound Space: Migration, Aspiration, and the Making of Time in the Cantonese Pacific', in Warwick Anderson, Miranda Johnson and Barbara Brookes, eds., *Pacific Futures: Past and Present* (Honolulu: University of Hawai'i Press, 2018), 178–204.
Yun, Lisa. *The Coolie Speaks: Chinese Indentured Laborers and African Slaves in Cuba* (Philadelphia: Temple University Press, 2008).
Yung, Judy, Gordon Chang and Him Mark Lai, eds. *Chinese American Voices: From the Gold Rush to the Present* (Berkeley: University of California Press, 2006).
Zhuang Guotu. 'China's Policies on Chinese Overseas: Past and Present', in Tan Chee-Beng, ed., *Routledge Handbook of the Chinese Diaspora* (London: Routledge, 2013), 31–41.
Zhu Jieqin (朱杰勤). *Dongnanya huaqiao shi* [A history of Chinese overseas in Southeast Asia] (Beijing: Zhonghua Book Company, 2008).
Zhu Yun (朱云), 'Guangdong chuantong jiaju de tese fenxi' [Analysis of the characteristics of Guangdong traditional furniture], *Baozhuang gongcheng* [Packaging engineering], 39:16 (2018), 236–242.
Zuo Xuchu (左旭初), 'Zhongguo shangbiao falv zhidu de lishi huigu' [Historical review of China's trademark legal system], *Zhonghua shangbiao* [China trademark], 11 (2012), 19–21.

Theses
Birrell, Ralph. 'The Development of Mining Technology in Australia 1801–1945' (PhD Thesis: University of Melbourne, 2005).
Boileau, Joanna. 'Chinese Market Gardening in Australia and New Zealand, 1860s–1960s: A Study in Technological Transfer' (PhD Thesis: University of New England, 2014).
Chen Ming (陈铭). '20 shiji Zhongguo jiaju jiagong jishu yu shebei fazhan yanjiu' [20th century Chinese furniture processing technology and equipment development research] (PhD Thesis: Nanjing Forestry University, 2011).

Bibliography

Darnell, Maxine. 'The Chinese Labour Trade to New South Wales, 1783–1853: An Exposition of Motives and Outcomes' (PhD Thesis: University of New England, 1997).

Jiang Wei (蒋茜), '1700–1840 nian Zhong Ying maoyi beijing xia de sheji jiaoliu yanjiu' [Design exchange research on the background of Sino-British trade, 1700–1840] (PhD Thesis: Nanjing Arts Institute, 2017).

Leckey, John. 'Low, Degraded Broots? Industry and Entrepreneurialism in Melbourne's Little Lon, 1860–1950' (PhD Thesis: University of Melbourne, 2003).

Loy-Wilson, Sophie. 'The Smiling Professions: Salesmanship and Promotional Culture in Australia and China, 1920–1939' (PhD Thesis: University of Sydney, 2012).

Rasmussen, Amanda. 'The Chinese in Nation and Community Bendigo 1870s–1920s' (PhD Thesis: La Trobe University, 2009).

Welch, Ian. 'Alien Son: The Life and Times of Cheok Hong Cheong, 1851–1928' (PhD Thesis: Australian National University, 2003).

Williams, Michael. 'Destination Qiaoxiang: Pearl River Delta Villages and Pacific Ports, 1849–1949' (PhD Thesis: University of Hong Kong, 2002).

Xue Yongjun (薛拥军). 'Guangshi mudiao yishu jiqi zai jianzhu he shinei zhuangshi zhong de yingyong yanjiu' [Cantonese-style woodcarving craft and its architecture centring on applied research in interior decoration] (PhD Thesis: Nanjing Forestry University, 2012).

Zhou Bei (周蓓). 'Ershi shiji Zhongguo jiaju fazhan licheng yanjiu' [Twentieth-century Chinese furniture development process research] (MA Thesis: Nanjing Forestry University, 2004).

Unpublished Discussion Papers

Andrew Seltzer and Jeff Borland, 'The Impact of the 1896 Factory and Shops Act on Victorian Labour Markets', IZA Discussion Paper, 10388 (2016), 1–43.

Conference Papers

Lech, Michael. '"European Labour Only": Stamping/marking of Chinese-Australian furniture, 1880–1930', paper presented to the Chinese Women's Association of Australia, Sydney Mechanics' School of Arts, 14 February 2015.

Wong, Wing-Fai. 'The significance of Lu Ban Jing, the carpenter's and builder's geomancy manual, in Chinese Australian heritage conservation', paper presented at Dragon Tails, the Fourth Australasian Conference on Overseas Chinese History and Heritage, Cairns Sheridan Hotel, 2–5 July 2015.

Online Sources
'110 years of trade marks', IP Australia, accessed 26 January 2018, https://www.ipaustralia.gov.au/about-us/news-and-community/news/110-years-trade-marks.
Bagnall, Kate. 'Man Sue Bach, 1790–1862: the "oldest Chinese colonist" in New South Wales', *The Tiger's Mouth: Thoughts on the History and Heritage of Chinese Australia*, 23 February 2013, accessed 1 July 2018, http://chineseaustralia.org/tag/john-shying/.
Darnell, Maxine. 'Indentured Chinese Labourers and Employers Identified, New South Wales, 1828–1856', *Chinese Heritage of Australian Federation Project*, accessed 1 July 2018, https://arrow.latrobe.edu.au/store/3/4/5/5/1/public/indentured.htm.
Lyons, Mark. 'Moore, Charles (1820–1895)', *Australian Dictionary of Biography*, accessed 1 June 2018, http://adb.anu.edu.au/biography/moore-charles-4228.
Mansfield, Bruce E. 'Melville, Ninian (1843–1897)', *Australian Dictionary of Biography*, accessed 21 September 2018, http://adb.anu.edu.au/biography/melville-ninian-4184/text6725.
Markey, Ray. 'Schreiber, Oscar Ferdinand Gordon (1887–1963)', *Australian Dictionary of Biography*, accessed 21 September 2018, http://adb.anu.edu.au/biography/schreiber-oscar-ferdinand-gordon-11635/text20783.
Maushart, Susan. 'Pine and Prejudice', *PocketDocs*, ABC Radio National, accessed 26 January 2018, http://www.abc.net.au/radionational/programs/pocketdocs/pine-and-prejudice/7275008.
Nairn, Bede. 'Holman, William Arthur (1871–1934)', *Australian Dictionary of Biography*, accessed 21 September 2018, http://adb.anu.edu.au/biography/holman-william-arthur-6713/text11589.
Nairn, Bede. 'Lang, John Thomas (Jack) (1876–1975)', *Australian Dictionary of Biography*, accessed 21 September 2018, http://adb.anu.edu.au/biography/lang-john-thomas-jack-7027/text12223.
Sahni, Neera. 'Mak Sai Ying Aka John Shying', *Research Services, City of Paramatta Council*, 27 January 2017, accessed 3 July 2018, http://arc.parracity.nsw.gov.au/blog/2017/01/27/mak-sai-ying-aka-john-shying/.
Yong Ching Fatt. 'Louis Ah Mouy', *Australian Dictionary of Biography*, accessed 1 July 2018, http://adb.anu.edu.au/biography/ah-mouy-louis-2872.

Other Sources
Wing Young and Co., Banana Wholesalers and Cabinet Makers, 1920s, Chinese Museum plaque, Melbourne.

Index

Ack Chow 2, 33
activism 135
Adelaide 12
advertising 100, 106, 117
agriculture 19
Ah Hing 2
Ah Toy 17, 26, 46, 69, 108, 145
Ah Wong xiii
Ah Yet 50, 102
Anthony Hordern and Sons 38, 102
anti-Chinese sentiment 132, 139, 172
apprenticeships 78
assembly of furniture components 14, 23, 78; *see also* imported furniture

bankruptcy xxiii, 30, 43, 57, 68, 84, 158
 records xxiii, 166
Beauchamp Brothers 110
Blanchfield, Ernest 35, 42
business practices 171

cabinetmakers *see* woodwork experts, Chinese
Cairns 19
California xiv, 15, 21, 26
carpenters 74, 96; *see also* woodwork experts, Chinese

Certificates Exempting from Dictation Test (CEDT) 54, 87
chairs 17, 101
charitable causes 121, 171
'cheap labour' 14, 68, 135, 140, 170
Chinese Australian Herald xxiii, 61, 94, 145, 148
Chinese furniture styles 6; *see also* furniture design
 European demand 6
Chinese migration 7, 25
 to India 7
 to Singapore 8
 to Australia 8
Chinese nationalism 93
chinoiserie *see* Chinese furniture styles
Chung Lee 45
Cohen Brothers and Co. 111, 113
competition, business xix, 112
Cutler, Edgar 144

David Jones and Co. 99
delivery 113
department stores *see* retailers
depression (1890s) 142
diplomatic assistance 140, 158
directories 120

Dongguan 17
dormitories *see* furniture factories: sleeping onsite
dressing table 104, 125

English language 116
European furniture firms 37

Factories and Shops Acts 144, 146, 148, 153–155, 157, 162
factory culture xxii
factory kitchens 46, 63, 80, 87
finances 37, 40, 64, 167
  trade credit 42, 168
Fitzgerald, Shirley xix
furniture design 103
furniture factories xiv, 20, 24, 30, 166
  buildings 44, 50, 109
  locations 50
  ownership 26, 30–37, 39, 91, 99, 167
  sleeping onsite 47, 67, 87, 144, 161
  size 138
  sole traders 30, 65
furniture industry 22, 139, 173
  Melbourne 94, 141
  Sydney 22, 94, 99, 162
furniture markets xxvi, 170
  demand 10, 16, 21, 28
furniture materials xxvi, 59
  components 56, 61, 112
furniture range 100

gambling 43
Gangton Brothers 106
Go Bo Brothers 36, 71
gold rushes 1
  Australia 14, 28
  carpentry work 17
  racism and violence 18

Golden Dragon Museum, Bendigo 52, 105
Gooey Choon 113
Guangdong 25, 96
Guangzhou 6, 12

Hang Jan and Co. 90
Hoe, John xxiv, 68
Holman, William 145
Hookam Chan 9
hours of work 88

Immigration Restriction Act xxiii, 71, 150, 165; *see also* White Australia policy
imported furniture 14, 16, 23, 110
indentured labourers 12
industrial action and labour 94, 129, 133, 142, 147, 152
industrial law xv, 130, 137, 147, 162

Kem Wah 20
kinship 93

Lambing Flat 18
Lasseter and Co. 99
Lay Jong 26, 51
Laycock, Son and Nettleton 99, 111
Lee Fee 2, 33
Lee Kum 2
legislation xxvii
  limiting Chinese migration 18, 25, 39, 136, 139
Liang Qichao 150
Liu, William 161
Loon Cheong and Co. 2, 20, 32
Loong, Sun Sing 26, 27, 52, 74, 76, 79, 87, 111, 125
Louey, Henry 40
Lu Ban 3, 7, 75, 167

Index

Lu Ban Jing 4, 17
Lucas, John 51
Lum, Charles 32

machinery and mechanisation 55, 57, 77; *see also* tools
makers' marks 55
Marcus Clark and Sons 103
market gardening xiv, 31, 79
Moore, Charles 110
Mouy, Louis Ah 17, 27, 134
Myer Emporium 103

Opium Wars 11, 15, 24

Pearl River Delta xiv, 15, 35, 71, 167
polishing 46, 169
profits and losses 124, 126

quality 23, 145
Qing Dynasty 148

racism xviii, xix, 134, 152, 166; *see also* White Australia policy
railway construction 20
remittances to China 44
retailers 102, 170
  Chinese retailers 106
Rising and Co. 123
Rolls, Eric xix, 47
Royal Commission into manufacturing (Victoria) 151
Royal Easter Show (Sydney) 123

sales 102, 111, 127
  auction houses 110, 124, 127
  direct to customer 108
  regional 105, 108
  travelling salesmen 114, 171
Sang Tim 12

shipbuilding 4
signs 121
Simpson's 119
Sing Lee 30
Solomon Brothers and Co. 69
stamps and stamping 62, 104, 129, 133, 137, 138, 140, 143, 144, 151, 160, 171
stationery 115
storage of materials 48
strikes *see* industrial action and labour
Sun Kwong Loong and Co. 34, 38, 43, 67, 103
Sun Tong War and Co. 33, 34, 41, 110
Sun War Hop 47

tables 101, 109
Tack Lee 26, 99
timber xiii, 20, 48, 59, 60, 65
tools 52, 53
trade exhibitions 123
trade unions 95, 131
transport costs 50, 64, 106, 114
Tung Wah News xxiii, 148
Tung Wah Times xxiii, xxv, 57, 85, 118–120, 158

United Furniture Trade Society 125, 138

wages 81–84, 96, 134, 156
  piece rates 83, 137, 144
War Hing 105
War Hing Tiy 109
War Sing and Co. 121
washstands 125
White Australia policy xv, xviii, 131, 150–152
Willard, Myra xvii
Wing Lee Brothers 104, 129

woodwork experts, Chinese xxv, 24, 27,
　　70, 169
　artisans 27
　in history 4
　in New South Wales 8
　in Western Australia 9
　workers' guild 92, 94, 97, 156
　workforce 69–74, 137, 163, 169
　　non-Chinese employees 73
　　returning to China 72, 165
　　size 69

skills 79, 91
W. W. Campbell and Co. 99

Xiamen 12

Yee Lee 26, 99, 124
Yee Wye 29, 37, 51, 79
Yon Brothers and Co. 35, 42, 103

Zhong Tongxing 58
Zick Zong 12

www.ingramcontent.com/pod-product-compliance
Lightning Source LLC
Chambersburg PA
CBHW071740150426
43191CB00010B/1646